ADOLESCENT MENTAL HEALTH

Adolescence is a period characterized by both increased susceptibility to risks and new-found strength to withstand them. Whilst most young people are well equipped to manage the changes associated with growing up, other maladjusted and marginalized adolescents already have, or are at risk of developing, mental health problems.

Adolescent Mental Health: Prevention and Intervention is a concise and accessible overview of our current knowledge on effective treatment and prevention programs for young people with mental health problems. Whilst addressing some of the most common mental health issues among young people, such as behavioral problems and drug-related difficulties, it also offers a fuller understanding of the evidence-based treatment and prevention programs that are built upon what we know about how these behavioral and emotional problems develop and are sustained.

The volume illustrates contemporary and empirically supported interventions and prevention efforts through a series of case studies. It has been fully updated in line with the latest NICE and DSM-V guidelines, and now includes an added chapter on implementation, and what factors facilitate implementation processes of intervention efforts.

Adolescent Mental Health: Prevention and Intervention will be essential reading for students and practitioners in the fields of child welfare and mental health services, and any professional working with adolescents at risk of developing mental health problems.

Terje Ogden, Ph.D., is Research Director at the Norwegian Center for Child Behavioral Development, Unirand and a Professor at the Institute of Psychology, University of Oslo, Norway.

Kristine Amlund Hagen, Ph.D., is Senior Researcher at the Norwegian Center for Child Behavioral Development. Her research has focused on social competence, antisocial behavior, implementation of intervention efforts, and risk and protective factors.

Adolescence and Society

Series Editor: John C. Coleman

Department of Education, University of Oxford

In the 20 years since it began, this series has published some of the key texts in the field of adolescent studies. The series has covered a very wide range of subjects, almost all of them being of central concern to students, researchers and practitioners. A mark of its success is that a number of books have gone to second and third editions, illustrating its popularity and reputation.

The primary aim of the series is to make accessible to the widest possible readership important and topical evidence relating to adolescent development. Much of this material is published in relatively inaccessible professional journals, and the objective of the books has been to summarize, review, and place in context current work in the field, so as to interest and engage both an undergraduate and a professional audience.

The intention of the authors is to raise the profile of adolescent studies among professionals and in institutions of higher education. By publishing relatively short, readable books on topics of current interest to do with youth and society, the series makes people more aware of the relevance of the subject of adolescence to a wide range of social concerns.

The books do not put forward any one theoretical viewpoint. The authors outline the most prominent theories in the field and include a balanced and critical assessment of each of these. Whilst some of the books may have a clinical or applied slant, the majority concentrate on normal development.

The readership rests primarily in two major areas: the undergraduate market, particularly in the fields of psychology, sociology and education; and the professional training market, with particular emphasis on social work, clinical and educational psychology, counselling, youth work, nursing and teacher training.

ADOLESCENT MENTAL HEALTH

Prevention and Intervention

Second Edition

Terje Ogden and Kristine Amlund Hagen

Routledge
Taylor & Francis Group

LONDON AND NEW YORK

Second edition published 2019
by Routledge
2 Park Square, Milton Park, Abingdon, Oxon, OX14 4RN

and by Routledge
711 Third Avenue, New York, NY 10017

Routledge is an imprint of the Taylor & Francis Group, an informa business

© 2019 Terje Ogden and Kristine Amlund Hagen

First edition published by Routledge 2013

British Library Cataloguing-in-Publication Data
A catalogue record for this book is available from the British Library

Library of Congress Cataloging-in-Publication Data
Names: Ogden, Terje, author. | Hagen, Kristine Amlund, author.
Title: Adolescent mental health : prevention and intervention /
Terje Ogden and Kristine Amlund Hagen.
Description: 2nd edition. | Milton Park, Abingdon, Oxon ;
New York, NY : Routledge, 2019. | Includes index.
Identifiers: LCCN 2018003723 (print) | LCCN 2018004025 (ebook) |
ISBN 9781315295350 (epub) | ISBN 9781315295367 (Web pdf) |
ISBN 9781315295343 (Mobi/Kindle) | ISBN 9781138239630 (hbk) |
ISBN 9781138239647 (pbk) | ISBN 9781315295374 (ebk)
Subjects: LCSH: Adolescent psychopathology. | Adolescent psychiatry. |
Teenagers–Mental health. | Child mental health services.
Classification: LCC RJ503 (ebook) | LCC RJ503 .O44 2019 (print) |
DDC 616.8900835–dc23
LC record available at https://lccn.loc.gov/2018003723

ISBN: 978-1-138-23963-0 (hbk)
ISBN: 978-1-138-23964-7 (pbk)
ISBN: 978-1-315-29537-4 (ebk)

Typeset in Bembo
by Out of House Publishing

CONTENTS

PREFACE

Adolescence is a period characterized by both increased susceptibility to risks and new-found strength to withstand them. How well an adolescent adjusts to the changes, challenges, and opportunities of this period oftentimes depends on the willingness and ability of the context to accommodate the young person's emerging needs and capacities.

Fortunately, most adolescents go through this period of life in a healthy way; they can master their schoolwork, make and keep friends, get along with their parents and teachers, stay out of trouble, and lead fulfilling lives. For some individuals however, and for a variety of reasons, the adolescence period also renders a significant number of maladjusted, unhappy, and marginalized adolescents. This volume brings together our current knowledge about how common mental health problems in adolescence develop, what the risk factors associated with these are, and presents well-established methods and programs designed to alleviate or prevent such problems.

We originally accepted the invitation to write this book, primarily because we found it to be missing from the shelves. This is not to say that the material we present in this volume is new; on the contrary, we rely heavily on prior research endeavors, theories, and wisdom of other experts and scientists in the field. What is new in this book are rather the synthesis of available and current scientific findings on effective intervention and prevention efforts as they are developed specifically for reducing common mental health issues in adolescence. We have taken on an ecological and transactional approach in our line of presenting the material, and our discussions of how problems can be understood are inspired by the field of developmental psychopathology.

What further motivated us to write this book was our strong belief that mental health problems in children and adolescents can be both alleviated and prevented. Every day, mental health professionals make a difference for youths who are on their way down an unhealthy and unhappy path. We are equally convinced that our efforts to help require of us to make use of the best and most up-to-date knowledge available; we owe it to the individuals and the families in whose lives we intervene. An important part of this knowledge comes from clinical research studies that build on solid designs and that supply dependable documentation. How else can we say with some confidence that something is effective? And how else can we replicate or disseminate a method, if effective, or alter it, if it is not?

Since the previous edition of this book was submitted from the authors, a large amount of relevant research has been published internationally. We have no intention of covering all of what has been published, but we have tried to update the book in a way that clearly reflects some of the main developmental lines. We have taken a particular interest in advances from European countries and incorporated several relevant references, including some of our own.

Among the developmental lines appearing in Europe we would like to mention the tendency to integrate specialized interventions into wider or trans-diagnostic or modularized approaches. Experiences from the child and adolescent therapies have shown that co-occurring problems or comorbidity are the rule rather than the exception. This is not to say that the specialized programs are redundant but that more inclusive versions should be developed alongside these well-established approaches. Modularized treatments cover a wider scope of problems than the specialized or "silo" interventions. A good example is the MATCH program, developed by John Weisz et al., which is currently tested in several child and adolescent mental health clinics in Norway. In addition to having broader intake criteria, it also incorporates core treatment ingredients identified from a range of research-based treatments.

A second developmental line highlights the importance of implementing research-based interventions with fidelity. If controlled evaluations of new interventions reveal no effects, the explanation may be that the intervention did not work, or that it was not implemented properly. Several studies have shown that high-quality implementation is essential for good outcomes. Consequently, we have dedicated a whole new chapter to this topic. We consider the quality of implementation to be of the utmost importance for making interventions work as intended by their developers, and for sustaining high-quality treatment delivery.

A third developmental line concerns the classification of interventions according to level of individualization and intensity. In order to match interventions to client characteristics and needs, they are often presented in a hierarchical manner with universal interventions at the bottom, selected interventions at the next level, and indicated interventions at the top. Whilst universal interventions target the whole population of children, selected interventions are adapted to groups of children at risk and who may have similar needs. Moreover, indicated interventions are both highly intensive and individualized and are implemented according to the child's "response to intervention."

A fourth developmental line is the search for "core components," "active ingredients," and "behavioral kernels." These are the vital parts of an intervention, without which the intervention is expected to have no effect. The identification of practice elements that work across interventions may reduce the number of programs clinicians have to learn, or reduce the amount of time and effort needed for treatments to succeed. At the same time, core components are to date mostly studied within the context of whole programs, and their effectiveness in new contexts is still under examination.

And last but not least, a developmental line worth mentioning is the increasing tendency to include clients or users in the planning, development, and evaluation of interventions. This is an important ingredient in the original definition of evidence-based practice, and participants' feedback and involvement are important at all stages to improve the accuracy and acceptability of the intervention and, consequently, its effectiveness.

The challenge of developing and refining new prevention and treatment approaches targeting child and adolescent problem behaviors has also to be considered in light of a social gradient. It is abundantly clear that children with low socioeconomic background have a greater probability of developing mental health or behavioral problems than those from more affluent backgrounds. These children often live in families that are less prone to seek or accept offers of help, and they more often terminate treatment prematurely. These families may be in need of help to increase their economic or social stability before or alongside benefiting from psychosocial counseling or treatment.

In some ways, adolescence appears to be a qualitatively different phase than other periods of life. The cognitive, social, sexual, and emotional advances emerging in adolescence separate the teenager from the adult, and these very developmental domains also clearly separate the teenager from the child. Indeed, the adolescent period affords the individual with a whole new set of tools, and we discuss these in Chapter 1. New capabilities, however, rarely develop in concert and there is sometimes a mismatch between the needs and skills of the adolescent on the one hand and the support and affordances of the environment on the other. Such mismatches can turn vulnerabilities into mental health problems.

And it is true; certain types of problem behaviors increase in adolescence, such as drug and alcohol use, school dropout, delinquency, and depression. The question of whether there is something unique about this period that may explain these increased rates has therefore been the focus of much research. We present many of these research findings throughout the book, both because they shed light on this developmental period in particular, but also because they have been important in the development of effective intervention and intervention programs.

In other ways, however, adolescence is part of a gradual progression on a continuum of human development. Even though teachers, peers, and parents will often attest to their belief that specific problems started as the child in question entered adolescence, the maladjusted teenager rarely suddenly emerges. As we discuss in the book, both the resources and abilities, vulnerabilities and problems that a youth brings to the table typically have early precursors. Or, said differently, mental health problems usually do not afflict individuals at random.

Prevention programs try to equip adolescents with resources and skills that enable them to sidestep unhealthy trajectories that often result from being exposed to multiple or severe risk (either individual or contextual or both). Such resources, or protective factors, act as safeguards against maladaptive paths. One such powerful protective factor is *social competence*. In this book, we have devoted a chapter to social competence and social skills, for two reasons. First, we want to highlight the significance of such interpersonal and life skills because they are important in their own right, and because the lack of these skills appears to be a salient forerunner of later problems. Social competence thus stands out as a primary set of skills that can protect individuals from unhealthy outcomes. Second, we wanted to balance an otherwise "problem-oriented" volume with a resource-focused chapter, underscoring the fact that bringing out and encouraging good and adaptive capacities in adolescents may be just as important as ridding them of difficulties. The bad news is that lack of social skills often accompanies a range of problem behaviors; the good news is that they can be taught!

Adolescents normally spend a great amount of time in school. Schools can act as a normalizing institution for some and as a place of achievement and mastery in academics as well as in social activities. But for some youngsters, schools are the equivalent to failure, marginalization, and terror. In some instances, schools exacerbate existing difficulties, placing already vulnerable youths at an even greater disadvantage.

Children and youth are a society's greatest resource, so ensuring their well-being and health ought to be prioritized. In this book, we give an account of what we should demand of initiatives put forth that try to alleviate or prevent common mental health problems in adolescence. We present the elements of effective programs, recognizing that not all service delivery systems (or single professionals) have the resources or staff available to adopt entire programs with the often demanding training, quality assurance, and implementation strategies characteristic of well-established programs. We present those preventive and intervening actions that have fulfilled the requirements of well-established design and documentation demands. It is not enough to *believe* that certain actions are effective, and it is not enough to rely on tradition, ideology, or authority. We need to be able to document the best way we can, with the best available methods, based on the best available knowledge and know-how, that something is worthy of deliverance to vulnerable youths and their families.

In reading this book, readers will gain a fuller understanding of how evidence-based treatment and prevention programs are linked to and designed out of what we currently know about how behavioral, emotional, and drug-use problems develop and are sustained, and what the risk and protective factors are for developing such problems. Whilst we take on an evidence-based approach to the presentation of intervention and prevention, we also discuss limitations and common objections to this approach. Evidence-based treatment and prevention is not the answer to everything, but the methodology does represent the best way we currently have to answer some fundamental questions, the most important of which are "does it work?" "for whom does it work?" and "why does it work?"

Over the years, we have conducted several studies on treatment and prevention programs for children and youths with mental health problems. These have primarily been conducted in existing service delivery agencies. It is a complicated line of work, indeed. In doing so, we have seen that good support systems, training, supervision, and a collective sense of mastery are pivotal for the successful implementation of programs. Equally important are clinicians' willingness to have their own activities evaluated and their openness to try out new and well-founded methods of delivering service. Based on our own and others' research endeavors, we discuss what factors facilitate implementation processes.

Finally, this book would not have been realized without the good suggestions and clinical knowledge from our valuable colleagues, here listed in alphabetical order: Elisabeth Askeland, Anett Apeland, Kasper Alexander Arnberg, Bernadette Christensen, Kyrre Lønnum, Tori Mauseth, Dagfinn Mørkrid Thøgersen, Nina Tollefsen, and Marianne Aalberg Villabø.

1

ADOLESCENT DEVELOPMENT

What is adolescence?

Adolescence has been described as a period of life that starts in biology and ends in society (Kagan, 1975). This portrayal indicates that the onset of adolescence is denoted by the hormonal changes of puberty, whereas becoming an integral part of one's social environment marks the conclusion of this period of life. For many youths, however, the description is unfitting: whilst virtually all youths go through the biological transformations of sexual maturity and increased cognitive capacity, a significant proportion of young people do not *end up in society*; rather, they become maladjusted and marginalized. Youths who become marginalized, that is, end up on the outskirts of society, are the very youths this book is about. They show maladaptive and dysfunctional behavior and they can teach us much about how to intervene and how to prevent such problems in future generations of adolescents. Adolescence is the period between childhood and adulthood and is often referred to as the teenage years. The period is divided into early (11–13 years), mid- (14–16 years), and late (17–19 years) adolescence. Historically, adolescence has expanded in length, probably due to teenagers' increased time spent in school and decreased time spent in the work force during this period. Adolescence has been described as a period of reconstruction, characterized by significant changes in biological, cognitive, social, and emotional systems. To some extent, adolescent development is fairly predictable in the sense that most young individuals experience similar changes in multiple systems and face many of the same developmental challenges. Yet, in other ways, development is utterly idiosyncratic. For example, the way adolescents cope with new demands, contexts, and expectations varies considerably, and how well they deal with these tasks is important for their well-being and mental health, both at the present and in the future (Garbarino, 1985).

The question of whether it is something unique about the adolescent period that places individuals at greater risk for difficulty as they pass through it has been posed (Eccles et al., 1993, p. 90). The question is timely, but the flip side of this inquiry is whether it is something unique about the adolescent period that equips individuals to tackle the developmental challenges of this period. The answer to either question is yes. As we will discuss next, the adolescent period is characterized by changes in both susceptibility to risks and new-found strength to withstand them. Oftentimes, the outcomes will depend on the willingness and ability of the context to accommodate these changes in a healthy way. The challenge for researchers and clinicians alike is to identify those who are vulnerable and in what contexts their vulnerability results in deviant or unhealthy development.

In order to understand normal and abnormal development in adolescence, we think it is important to shed light on some of the important features of this developmental period. Although it is not the aim of this book to give a full account of adolescent development, we want to emphasize several developmental characteristics that are of importance in the process of planning, developing, and testing preventive and treatment interventions.

Biological and physical development: maturation

The biological development of adolescence includes many physiological alterations, and the hormonal changes that trigger puberty are important in understanding adolescent development. Biological changes and psychosocial development, however, do not develop in a vacuum; they are dependent on and influenced by each other. Moreover, each of these developmental domains are systems within a greater system, that is, the youth him- or herself who, in turn, is part of even higher-order systems made up by the family, the social network, and the culture, each interconnected and exerting mutual influence on each other (Garbarino, 1985). Many changes of maturity are visible, such as growth in height, weight, secondary sex characteristics, fat, and muscles. Because youth of the same chronological age may look and act differently from each other, they are, as a result, often treated differently, creating variability in individual experiences. At a period of life when social comparison is at its most salient, the youth who perceives him- or herself to fall short of such comparisons may develop a lack of self-esteem or a poor self-concept.

There are great individual differences in both onset and tempo of pubertal development, though the sequence of puberty is fairly consistent across individuals. With regard to timing, the onset of sexual maturation has been identified as a potential risk factor for mental health problems. For example, the *maturational deviance hypothesis* proposes that any aberration from the norm is associated with vulnerability for both mood and behavioral problems. Because girls, on average, mature earlier than do boys, early-maturing girls and late-maturing boys will be at greatest risk for maladjustment because these girls and boys will be the most physically "deviant" in the peer group. It could be the case, however, that adolescents compare themselves more readily to peers of the same gender, in which case early- and late-maturing adolescents of both genders will be at heightened risk for developing adjustment problems. Alternatively, the *developmental readiness hypothesis* posits that increases in vulnerability to mental health problems during the transition to adolescence are due to an asynchrony between physical, cognitive, social, and emotional growth. Specifically, the less time an adolescent has had to adapt to these new biological changes, to assimilate stimuli, and to develop healthy coping skills, the worse the youth will fare. Hence, early-maturing adolescents, and early-maturing girls in particular, will have had less time to adapt to changes and new demands and are thus at greater risk for maladaptive outcomes. Late-maturing children, and late-maturing males especially, will be the least likely to develop mental health problems (Negriff & Susman, 2011).

Both of these assumptions find support in empirical work, and their accuracy depends in part on which outcome is in focus. Caspi and Moffitt (1991) reported that early-maturing girls were more prone to develop behavioral problems and adjustment difficulties than their "on-time" or late-developing female counterparts. Other studies have shown, however, that some of the negative effects of very early puberty may be transient. For example, by age 25, early-maturing girls of a Stockholm sample no longer differed from their age-mates when it came to rule-breaking behavior (Stattin & Magnusson, 1990). They did, however, evince lower educational qualifications due to early school dropout.

A third possibility has been introduced, namely, *the stressful change hypothesis* (Caspi & Moffitt, 1991). If true, it would repudiate a commonly held belief that great changes offer opportunities for discontinuity of "old" patterns in individuals. Research findings indicate that stressful transitions such as entrance to puberty actually accentuate preexisting individual characteristics. In other words, when individuals go through stressful transitions, such as puberty, individuals' dispositions emerge more clearly, leaving adolescents who were already at risk with an even greater vulnerability. As such, the manner in which new challenges are met and handled depends in large part on the assets and competencies that the individual brings to the table. If these are few and/or maladaptive, then the way new demands are handled will likely set the stage for further dysfunction.

Pubertal timing, however, is but one side of the story. The time it takes for an adolescent to progress through the different stages of puberty—that is, the tempo—also plays a role in determining how well the youth adapts. Mendle, Harden, Brooks-Gunn, and Graber (2010) reported that, for boys, the rate of pubertal development was more important in predicting depressive symptoms than was pubertal timing, and boys who matured both quickly and early reported the highest levels of depressive symptoms. For girls, the onset of puberty was a significant predictor of depressive symptoms, whereas pubertal tempo was not.

Belsky, Steinberg, and Draper (1991) introduced an evolutionary-based model of reproductive development that is appropriate to mention in this regard. The authors posited that early experiences of availability of resources and endurance of close relationships both affect individuals' reproductive strategies. Children who grow up with limited resources and with the expectation that emotional bonds are unstable or unsupportive tend to enter puberty sooner and to reproduce at an earlier age. Conversely, children reared in contexts of sufficient resources and that are characterized by warm, stable, and trustworthy caregiving are more likely to delay entrance to puberty and defer sexual activity. Ellis, Shirtcliff, Boyce, Deardorff, and Essex (2011) investigated this assumption empirically and took the line of reasoning one step further. The results from their study suggested that children who were brought up in high-quality parenting contexts entered puberty later and showed slower initial pubertal progression, *if* they demonstrated heightened sensitivity to environmental effects. For such highly susceptible children, the reverse outcome (early and hastened pubertal development) was more likely if their rearing environment was harsher and more negative. For the less environmentally sensitive children, the association between rearing environment and onset of puberty was non-significant.

Brain maturation and cognitive development

Modern brain imaging technology has shown that brains take longer to develop than previously assumed, and the brain maturation process continues as young people move through adolescence. Brains undergo a massive reorganization and remodeling between the 12th and 25th year, resembling a network and wiring upgrade (Dobbs, 2011). In her book about the teenage brain, Jensen (2015) draws on her personal experiences as well as on neuroscience when she describes the challenges and opportunities relating to bringing up adolescents:

> In order to truly understand why teenagers are moody, impulsive, and bored: why they act out, talk back, and don't pay attention; why drugs and alcohol are so dangerous for them; and why they make poor decisions about drinking, driving, sex – you name it – we have to look at their brain circuits for answers.
>
> *(p. 22)*

In adolescence, the biggest changes occur in the parts of the brain that process cognitive and emotional information: the frontal lobes. Executive functions, which represent the ability to plan, gain insight, make judgments, and generate abstractions are located in the frontal lobes. They are involved in decision-making and cognitive control, as well as other higher cognitive functions. They are also the source of self-awareness and the ability to assess danger and risk, so they use this area of the brain to choose their course of action.

The maturation of the brain lays the foundation of new cognitive skills in adolescence, such as increased capacity for abstract reasoning, as well as critical and creative thinking (Blakemore & Choudhury, 2006). The ability to think *creatively* is often demonstrated by an increase in divergent thinking, originality, and flexibility, and can be exemplified by engagement in popular youth activities such as writing, drawing, acting, and playing musical instruments. During this time, the majority of young people, though not all, develop formal operational abilities that allow them to analyze problems, generate solutions, consider consequences, make logical decisions, and form links from specific examples to general principles as well as from the general to the specific. A more complex level of information processing that is closely related to intelligence is enabled, including more advanced and differentiated *social information processing* skills (Crick & Dodge, 1994). The concept of "the social brain" is used to describe major social functions such as interaction synchrony (or turn-taking), empathy, social cognition, interaction skills, and concern for others (Goleman, 2007). Lieberman (2013), asserts that we are "wired to be social," that is, "we are driven by deep motivation to stay connected with friends and family" and that we are "naturally curious about what is going on in the minds of other people" (p. 1). In other words, adolescents are wired for reaching out and interacting with others and when they have nothing else to do, they think about themselves in the social world. The development of social–cognitive competence underlies school success, both socially and academically. Deficits in social information processing skills are actually one of the major problems of aggressive individuals (Fontaine & Dodge, 2009). For example, antisocial adolescents often have a tendency to attribute hostile intentions to others, when these intents are in fact positive or neutral. They often also have problems recognizing and decoding feelings of others. Moreover, they have difficulties generating solutions to social problems and assessing the potential consequences of alternative solutions and regulating emotional arousal (Crick & Dodge, 1994).

Adolescents have been described as *egocentric* or self-centered in their thinking. For example, teenagers are oftentimes perceived (most often by adults) to be self-conscious and focused on their own ideas and experiences. Paradoxically, teenagers are typically also hypersensitive to everyone else's evaluation of them. Furthermore, they have a tendency to become more idealistic and critical of other people, particularly parents and teachers. The cognitive development in the teenage years changes adolescents' relationships to their parents because they are better equipped to question rules and expectations, they are more ardent to be heard, they show greater appreciation for social reciprocity, they are better at social reasoning, and show greater mental flexibility (Holmbeck, Paikoff, & Brooks-Gunn, 1995).

Identity formation

The process of forming an *identity* is a central endeavor during the teenage years and, for the adolescent, it involves gaining a sense of who he or she is as an individual and as a member of various social groups. Developing a sense of identity starts in adolescence but is a lifelong and dynamic process (Beyers & Gossens, 2008). It is a daunting task, especially because of the multiple influences from family, school, peers, and from their greater social networks. It is somewhat of a paradox that the task of forming a personal identity (a highly individual endeavor), actually involves ongoing adjustment to transactions with other people. Thus, identity grows in response to both internal and external factors and is shaped by how they are perceived to be by important persons in their environment. During adolescence, the young person typically moves from dependency to independence and autonomy. Autonomy, however, does not mean the

absence of connectedness. Adolescents who rate themselves as being more positively attached to their parents also tend to be more advanced in their identity
development, be more interested in exploratory activities (such as going abroad),
be better able to differentiate themselves from their parents, and be less indecisive
of career choices (Quintana & Lapsley, 1990).

The process of forming an identity is also affected by an adolescent's self-theory.
A self-theory involves a person's tendency to view his or her own characteristics
and abilities as either stable and fixed or as malleable and subject to change
(Rosenberg, Burt, Forehand, & Paysnick, 2016). When faced with social or personal
challenges, this division in self-theory is especially salient. Adolescents who are fixed
in their beliefs about themselves and their abilities are less prone to seek out various
solutions to problems and are in turn also at greater risk of developing mental
health problems. In a study of adolescents (aged 14–17 years) and emerging adults
(aged 18–39 years), results indicated that having more flexible beliefs about oneself
was associated with more productive coping strategies and lower levels of internalizing and externalizing problems. Findings also indicated that this was true for
adolescents only; self-theory and coping strategies were not related to behavioral
problems for adults (Rosenberg et al., 2016).

Coping strategies and emotion regulation

The refinement of *coping strategies* is also a part of adolescent development as the
handling of adversities are related to the management of stress and negative life
events. When in a difficult or stressful situation, like everyone else, adolescents
cope. Coping strategies, however, may be effective or ineffective and consequently
result in more or less adaptive functioning. Positive coping skills such as seeking
the advice or support from others including family, friends, teachers, or health
professionals are related to better mental health among youths. Another adaptive
strategy is to reformulate or reframe a problem into a challenge to be overcome so
as to make it less threatening or difficult. Humor and optimism may also be helpful
in the process of reframing experiences. For some, finding alternative goals or activities may be a constructive coping strategy for handling failure, for instance when
failed academic ambitions are replaced by successes in sports. Adolescents may, however, actively devalue good grades and school achievement if they perceive these
goals as unattainable. Among the less adaptive and often ineffective coping skills are
denial, rumination (a repetitive focus on stressors, and on their possible causes and
consequences), and the tendency to blame oneself or others: "He asked for it," "I
always screw up," or "Everyone else does it!"

How well an adolescent copes with stressors or challenges is also affected by his
or her emotion regulation. Emotion regulation is part of emotional competence;
adolescents often experience swift and strong mood changes. They may evince
strong emotions such as anger, sadness, or frustration and react strongly to social
rejection, such as when they are deceived by a friend or not invited to a party. But
during the adolescent years, most boys and girls learn effective ways of controlling

or regulating emotions. Emotion regulation and effortful control show marked advances in the adolescent years.

The famous marshmallow experiment conducted by Walter Mischel (1958) removed attention from self-esteem to *self-control* as the latter predicted positive outcomes in several areas of development. The ability to delay gratification, in addition to parent supervision, seemed to promote the development of self-control. The relationship between parent supervision and self-control was demonstrated in Joan McCord's (1979) study which showed that lack of adult supervision in the teenage years turned out to be one of the strongest predictors of criminal behavior. In a recent study of 420 seventh-graders who were followed over a period of 30 months, the results showed that teachers' report of students' emotional regulation predicted whether the youth had been arrested. Adolescents whose teachers assessed them to have better emotion regulation skills were less likely to have been arrested. Interestingly, neither self-report nor parent report of emotion regulation skills were predictive of arrests.

Some decades later, Baumeister and Tierny (2011) summarized: "Adolescents have higher self-control to the extent that their parents generally know where their offspring are after school and at night, what they do with their free-time, who their friends are, and how they spend money" (p. 210).

Social development

Social development has several important aspects, one being the formation of the interrelated concepts of self-awareness, self-concept, and self-esteem, and the other the establishment of social relationships in family, at school, and among peers. Greater *self-awareness*, and greater awareness of others and their emotions and thoughts is characteristic of adolescence. As children, they defined themselves by physical traits whereas, as adolescents, they define themselves based on their values, thoughts, and opinions. Self-awareness is considered to be one of the core components of emotional intelligence and relies on accurate self-assessment and self-confidence. The idea of *self-concept* is known as the ability of a person to have opinions and beliefs that are defined confidently, are consistent, and stable. One's self-concept is a collection of beliefs about oneself. Generally, self-concept embodies the answer to "Who am I?" Self-concept differs from self-esteem: self-concept is a cognitive or descriptive component of oneself (e.g., "I am a fast runner"), whilst self-esteem is evaluative and opinionated (e.g., "I feel good about being a fast runner"). *Self-esteem* has, however, recently been challenged as a universal key to success (Baumeister & Tierny, 2011). Originally, research showed that children with high self-esteem had better grades, and it was assumed that high self-esteem was the causal factor. But in later studies, it became clear that the grades came first and self-esteem developed as a result. Other evidence showed that, across the country, students' self-esteem went up whilst their performance declined.

Social relations or social interaction is any relationship between two or more individuals. Social relations are to a great extent based on the learning and practice of social competence and social skills within the dynamics of parenting and schooling. *Social competence* is important for coping with the transition from youth to secondary education, for learning skills that are useful in higher education or in working life, for engaging in recreational activities, and developing close friendships with people of both sexes. The outcomes may be good parent–child and sibling relationships, good friendships, and good student–teacher relationships. *Social skills* are essential in the process of learning to interact with others and how to successfully reach personal social goals or meet social needs. Both verbal and non-verbal skills must be learned, for instance by observing others or practicing and receiving feedback on own actions. In the next section of this chapter, we take a closer look at transactions between adolescents and their proximal contexts represented by the school, the family, and peers.

Adolescents, learning, and school

Young brains are easily shaped by experience, and in neuroscience, the human brain's ability to mold itself is referred to as neuroplasticity. Learning produces plastic changes in the structure of the developing brain. The neural plasticity of the teen brain means that the adolescent may learn things faster and their memories are more robust. That means that the timing is great for remediation, and for getting special help with learning and emotional problems. But even if teenage brains are getting more powerful, they are also more vulnerable and inefficient when it comes to attention, self-discipline, task completion, and interfering emotions. They may also become uncritically committed to ideas and take on a gullible position toward people they look up to. The short-term memory constantly receives input from the senses and compares it with existing memories. Information that matches existing memories is discarded as redundant, but new information is transferred to the long-term memory. The transmission is occasionally interrupted and explains why memories are never perfect but have holes and discontinuities that may be filled in with false information. The brain is particularly receptive to the acquisition of new information, and that is when learning occurs. The more a piece of information is repeated or relearned, the stronger the brain connection becomes. "Frequency" and "recency" are therefore the key words. In other words, the more frequently and the more recently we learn something, and recall it or use it again, the more established the knowledge becomes (Jensen, 2015).

Virtually all adolescents go to school. Because they spend a considerable amount of time in school and are faced with both cognitive and social demands there, schools are an important arena for adolescent mental health. The school may be a place for mastery and inspiration for some, whereas for others it may be a place associated with discouragement and failure. When students move from primary to secondary or junior high school the rate of truancy and school dropout increases and, for many youths, school grades are likely to decline. These two are related concerns as declining grades are predictive of later school dropout and both may be symptoms of a number of other underlying difficulties.

According to Lieberman (2013), seventh- and eighth-graders are at particular risk for educational misfortune. There is a drop on several key educational indicators during those years, and there are numerous reasons why academic performance and interest drop during junior high school. Emotionality peaks around eighth grade, but the capacity for emotion regulation doesn't reach its full maturity until students leave their teenage years. One of the main risk factors may be that the basic need of social bonding is not being met. According to Lieberman, then, the big question is whether creating a sense of belonging in students can improve learning and educational outcomes. On the one hand, there is no bigger threat to an adolescent's sense of acceptance than being bullied whilst others stand by doing nothing; bullying has also proven to lead to dramatic reductions in test performance. On the other, it has been difficult for researchers to establish that enhanced feelings of belonging increase academic performance. But there are exceptions. After examining the latest research on the social brain, Lieberman concludes, rhetorically, that "schools typically take the position that our social urges ought to be left at the door, outside the classroom" and "Please turn off your social brain when you enter the classroom; we have learning to do!" (p. 283).

Talking, passing notes, or texting one's classmates during class are punishable offenses. Adolescents are distracted by the social world and the solution could be to engage the social brain as part of the learning process, to learn social skills and make more efficient use of the traditional learning system (i.e., working memory regions plus the medial temporal lobe). Effective social skills are as important to most careers as other facts and skills currently being taught in school. But since adolescents have to figure out the social world by themselves, they are susceptible to a wide variety of social–cognitive and self-processing errors and biases, such as fundamental attribution errors, false consensus effects, affective forecasting errors, favoritism in groups, and overconfidence. Teaching students about these processes and why they occur won't eliminate them all but may likely diminish some of them. Lieberman argues that schools should teach students about their social motivations and take advantage of lines of research that have focused on working memory training, how to better read the minds of others and to be more able to overcome impulses, and how to train self-control (see also Chapter 6 in this book).

Eccles et al. (1993) sought to explain these adverse trends and, drawing on the *person–environment fit* theory, write: "Individuals are not likely to do well, or to be motivated, if they are in social environments that do not meet their psychological needs" (p. 91). They go on to demonstrate that for most children entering puberty and at the same time typically entering middle school or junior high, there is a mismatch between the needs of the young adolescent and the opportunities, support, and adaptations offered by the school system. First, whilst emerging adolescents have an increasing desire for greater self-determination and decision-making, middle and junior high school classrooms often place greater emphasis on discipline and control than do elementary school classrooms. Second, evidence shows that teacher–student relationships become less positive and supportive after elementary school, at a developmental period when young adolescents are in particular need of supportive interpersonal relations with extra-familial adults. Third, at a time when social comparison is intensified, middle school instruction is delivered—more so than in elementary school—as whole-class teaching or between-class ability grouping, with normative grading criteria and more public forms of evaluation. Fourth, it has also been shown that middle or junior high school teachers feel less confident about their teaching effectiveness, especially in mathematics and particularly for low-ability students, even though, as compared to elementary school teachers, middle school math teachers are more likely to be specialists. Fifth, there is some empirical work suggesting that the cognitive demands put on students actually decline as they transition from primary to secondary school and this at a time in development when intellectual growth is marked. Finally, secondary school teachers also appear to be stricter in their judging of students' competence and in their grading of students' performance than are primary school teachers. Many adolescents achieve lower grades when they leave elementary school and enter middle school, but this decline does not correspond with similar declines on standardized achievement tests (Eccles et al., 1993). In addition, if there is no better predictor of students' self-perception and sense of efficacy than the grades they achieve, then it comes as no surprise that for many youths scholastic motivation, self-image, and engagement in school drop as they enter middle school. The message from research is that schools should strive toward a "stage–environment fit" in which the social and academic environment matches the psychological needs of adolescents. Moreover, the learning environment should be flexible enough to accommodate individual differences in students' abilities and needs.

Adolescents and families

In many ways, entering adolescence signals an asynchronous phase of family life in which the number of parent–child conflicts tends to increase. When children enter adolescence, both the youth him- or herself and parents must renegotiate their respective roles within the family. Much centers around the issues of control and autonomy, and heated discussions or even confrontations may occur. The biological changes that take place in puberty create a reproductively mature individual and some parents may on the one hand expect more adult-like behavior from their teenager, but they may on the other hand want to more closely monitor and control their child's activities, particularly in situations with members of the opposite sex (Holmbeck et al., 1995). Even if the parents have the best intentions and want to protect their children, the tightening of supervision may represent the very opposite of what the adolescent feels he or she is entitled to in terms of freedom of choice and autonomy. Thus, a poor person–environment fit may be the result as the adolescent becomes more critical of the legitimacy of their parents' rules; they expect more symmetrical relations with their parents and expect to be heard, respected, and trusted.

Fortunately, most adolescents regard their parents as the most important sources of support, values, and belongingness, and as socializing agents. Even if they want more autonomy and freedom, few demand total freedom or want to be emotionally detached from their parents. Parents' anticipatory beliefs about adolescence likely affect the way they parent their adolescents. As is the case with most developmental milestones, the manner in which parents and adolescents resolve these challenges depends in large part on the quality of their relationship prior to the child entering puberty. Youths and their parents influence each other in a bidirectional and trans-actional manner. For example, research has suggested that not only does a high-quality home environment produce more competent children, but also that more competent children also elicit better parenting (Nihira, Mink, & Meyers, 1985). Such a transactional sequence likely cuts both ways; dysfunctional home contexts likely produce less competent adolescents, but difficult and maladapted adolescents may also to a certain extent evoke poor parenting practices. Unfortunately, it is the very adolescents who are in greatest need of high-quality home contexts who are the least likely to have it.

The most studied family dynamic is the coercion process. In relationships characterized by coercive interactions, family members become increasingly hostile toward one another and, as a consequence, adolescents' pro-social behavior often goes unnoticed and unrewarded (Ogden & Amlund Hagen, 2008). Coercion processes have gained much research attention mainly because of their impact on children and adolescents' problem behavior (Dishion & Stormshak, 2007; Patterson, 1982). In the coercion process, the adolescent "[…] learns how to turn off parental demands by engaging in aversive and avoidant behaviors" (Dishion & Stormshak, p. 34). In response to a parent's requests or demands, the youth counterattacks by whining or screaming. In efforts to set reasonable limits, the parent eventually gives in to an openly uncooperative or confrontational adolescent, thus reinforcing such behavior. Several structured, well-articulated, and evaluated approaches to parent training are recommended for intervening in the family coercion cycle by improving family relationships, increasing incentives for positive behavior, monitoring the whereabouts of the offspring, and using small and effective consequences for negative behavior. Some of these parenting programs are presented in the next chapters. The family is influential in most adolescents' lives, although the importance of peers and other important individuals in their social network increases.

Adolescents and peers

When teenagers' tendency to seek excitement, novelty, and risk is particularly strong in the company of peers, it is partly because they respond strongly to social rewards (Dobbs, 2011): "Teens prefer the company of those their age more than ever before or after" (p. 55). The reason why peers become the main show rather than a side-show is that they usually offer far more novelty than the family does. But even if adolescents want to learn primarily from friends, they also turn to their parents for support and advice. If youths experience too little autonomy in their relationships with adults, they may turn to peers for contact and support. However, those who deviate too much from the norms and values of age-mates are likely to be rejected by peers too. Among those most at risk for being socially excluded are aggressive and uncooperative adolescents who lack self-control and withdrawn adolescents who lack a positive self-image and who do not know how to be assertive.

In the teenage years, peers become more important than they were in the childhood years, both as confidantes and as socializing agents. Adolescents spend more time with friends, share their feelings and thoughts with them, engage in activities together, and friends use each other mutually as sparring partners; peer relationships in adolescence take on an increasingly central role. During adolescence, to a much greater extent than in childhood, friends select each other and youths oftentimes pick friends that are similar to themselves. The term "birds of a feather flock together" can be applied to adolescent friendship (Hamm, 2000). Moreover, friends tend to become more similar to one another over time. For example, the extent to which the peers of an adolescent are involved in anti-social behavior is among the best predictors of the adolescent's own problematic or delinquent behavior (Latendresse et al., 2011). That does not necessarily mean that friends and peers pressure the adolescent to commit crime or act antisocially, although that is likely to happen too. Rather, it suggests that friends are usually similar to one another or try to be. There seem to be two processes going on at the same time: one involved in the selection of friends, and one demonstrated by the maintenance and reciprocal nature of behavioral patterns between friends once friendships are established. The dynamics that may explain negative peer influences on social and emotional development were conceptualized as *deviancy training* by Dishion and the essential influence pattern seemed to be positive reinforcement (Dishion & Stormshak, 2007). Peers seem to influence development in two ways: by agreeing to be a friend (selection and association), and by selectively attending to and reinforcing deviant talk and ignoring pro-social talk.

The transactional and ecological models, as well as the principles of developmental psychopathology, have found much support in research. In line with the approach of this book, Dishion and Stormshak (2007) conceive individual adjustment as being embedded within social relations, and therefore interventions to improve mental health must assess and motivate change in social interactions to improve problem behavior (externalizing) and emotional adjustment (internalizing). Throughout this book, we use these principles when discussing externalizing and internalizing problems, as well as substance use, social competence, and the role that schools play in the lives of adolescents.

Concluding comments

The adolescent period is both a sensitive period and an age of fortitude. Both positive and negative influences are often amplified as children make the transition to adolescence. Due in part to the media's rather caricatured portrayal of the teenager as an individual with raging hormones, rebellious behavior, an insatiable thirst for risky activities and experimentation, and in a constant search for their own identity, the negative aspects of adolescent development are often overemphasized.

There are several likely reasons for this. First, statistics presented in the media or in health officials' pamphlets with statements such as "one in five adolescents suffers from depression" or "three in ten teenagers have a significant problem with alcohol or drugs" can give an inaccurate picture. Such repeated figures may suggest that, taken together, more than 100 percent of today's youths are struggling with a serious problem in one area or another, thereby ignoring the fact that many of the adolescents who show up in one statistic are the same adolescents who are counted in another (Garbarino, 2005a, b). Second, some claims about the increase of difficulties in adolescence are in fact substantiated. For example, certain types of both internalizing problems, such as depression, and externalizing behavior, such as delinquency, escalate during the teenage years. It is also during the adolescent period that initial experimentation with alcohol and other illegal substances most often takes place. And for those at risk, the upsurge of many of these difficulties is either a contributing factor to, or is a result of, school dropout—a major societal problem and one that is itself associated with a host of other problems later on. Third, stories in the media that tell of adolescents' reckless driving, drug use, or suicide give rise to both worry and outrage, but they may also strengthen the popular, though biased, view of the typical teenager as an extreme risk-taker. Risk-taking behaviors do increase during the teenage years (Dobbs, 2011, Jensen, 2015), but serious problem behaviors are not typical of most adolescents. To sum up, the picture of the typical teenager is more nuanced than that often depicted and whilst there is an increase in some types of problems during the teenage years, most adolescents go through this period without excessive storm and stress.

Overview of the book

Chapter 1 starts with a description of adolescence with emphasis on some of the characteristics we think are important for the main topics of this book; the promotion of mental health and the prevention and treatment of mental health problems. We elaborate on the ecological perspective by examining more closely the important settings that make up the meso-system of adolescents: the school, the family, and peers. In Chapter 2, we introduce the concepts of evidence-based prevention and intervention and how they relate to each other. In Chapter 3, we deal with externalizing problem behavior; how it develops and how such problems may be prevented, reduced, or stopped. The chapter describes how the combined effect of individual and environmental risk factors contribute to the development of antisocial behavior or conduct problems, and how these are targeted in prevention and treatment efforts. Examples of evidence-based prevention and intervention programs are presented, with emphasis on early interventions such as parent management training and systemic treatment models in adolescence. Chapter 4 addresses internalizing problems with a particular focus on anxiety and depression. Knowledge about underlying psychological and social processes has been implemented in evidence-based prevention and treatment programs, and several of these have been subject to extensive evaluation research.

Chapter 5 reviews theories and research that contribute to our understanding of and intervention in alcohol and drug use. Starting with a description of characteristics of substance use, we briefly review the risk factors, many of which overlap with those driving externalizing problems. Based on the multi-theoretical foundation of substance use, we emphasize the promising main effects of selected evidence-based interventions and supplement these findings with relevant knowledge about variables that seem to moderate or predict clinical outcomes. In Chapter 6, we turn to a resource-oriented perspective and emphasize the importance of social skills and social competence for the development of mental health and the change strategies for preventing and reducing both externalizing and internalizing problem behavior. The idea of promoting health and competence in youth seems to be appealing to parents and teachers and may help explain why the promotion of competence and health has become equally important as the risk-focused approach. In Chapter 7, we elaborate on the relationship between schooling and mental health. Adolescents spend a considerable amount of their time in schools, and the school is an important arena for academic, social, and personal growth. Several models for the delivery of mental health services in schools have been developed and tested in regular practice with encouraging results, particularly integrated models that adapt interventions to the students' risk level with a broad perspective on the school, family, and peer meso-system. The last chapter is entirely new to this book, and here we introduce and elaborate on the concept of implementation. The goal of implementation is to change practice, and implementation activities are needed to make decisions, plans, or interventions work.

2

EVIDENCE-BASED INTERVENTION AND PREVENTION

This chapter starts with concept definitions and descriptions of different types of interventions and prevention efforts. Evidence-based practice (EBP) in medicine, psychological practice, and social work is covered next, followed by a more detailed discussion of evidence-based treatments (EBTs) and empirically supported programs (ESPs). Next, we discuss the importance of examining mechanisms of change (mediators) and the conditions under which and for whom treatment may work well or poorly (moderators). Throughout this book we review the strengths, limitations, and challenges of EBP, and how it compares to other ways of delivering services to young people. We take the position that prevention and intervention addressing adolescent problem behaviors ought to have a good theoretical and empirical foundation and, if at all possible, be evaluated in controlled evaluation studies, preferably prior to full-scale implementation. In other words, our belief is that practice should be evidence based rather than authority based, consensus based, or ideology based. It should not be taken to mean, however, that we disregard other types of research or practice-based knowledge, but rather that we give priority to prevention efforts and treatment programs that have a sound theoretical and empirical basis.

Prevention and intervention described

Prevention, as the name implies, is an initiative put forth to avert the occurrence or development of illness, symptoms, problems, or maladjustment. Intervention, on the other hand, is treatment or other actions undertaken after an illness, symptoms, problems, or maladjustment have developed and therefore aims to alleviate or reduce these. The crossing from prevention to intervention is not always clear-cut, and sometimes the "ingredients" of an effective intervention will share many of those in successful prevention programs. Typically, it is the characteristics of the targeted population that demarcates whether a youth program is preventive or intervening.

Prevention

In 1957, the Commission on Chronic Illness presented a classification system differentiating between three different types of prevention in terms of the goals they sought to achieve:

- *Primary prevention:* reducing the likelihood of new cases with a disorder or illness within a population. That is, reducing the *incidence* of a given disorder.
- *Secondary prevention:* reducing the rate of established cases presenting disorder or illness, that is, lowering the *prevalence* of a given disorder.
- *Tertiary prevention:* decreasing the amount of disability or maladjustment associated with a particular disorder.

This classification scheme gave rise to considerable disagreement and in 1987, Gordon devised a new system of classification using a risk–benefit perspective (Kutash, Duchnowski, & Lynn, 2006). Gordon (1987) differentiated between:

- *Universal prevention:* this level of prevention is thought to be beneficial for the entire population in question (e.g., adolescents in general, the local community, schools) and seeks to prevent or delay the occurrence of a disorder or problem. All individuals, without screening, are provided with information and/or skills needed to prevent the problem;
- *Selective prevention:* this level of prevention is aimed at groups of individuals whose risk of developing a disorder or symptoms is above average. These subgroups of the population may be identified by exhibiting characteristics such as exposure to known contextual risk factors, family history, economic status (e.g., adolescents of parents with mental health problems); and
- *Indicated prevention:* this level of prevention involves a screening process, and targets individuals who exhibit early signs of a particular disorder or syndromes. Identifiers are often known risk factors for the illness in question exhibited by a teenager. For example, behaviorally inhibited youths are at risk of developing anxiety disorders. Likewise, falling grades and truancy are risk factors for juvenile delinquency.

Prevention as risk reduction

Increased understanding of the complex causal processes underlying mental health may be used in the process of developing more effective methods of intervention. Risk and protective factors may be related to the family, the school, the peer group, and the individual, and may be targeted in preventive interventions at the universal level. They may also be used as selection criteria to identify adolescents at risk in order to offer more comprehensive and intensive interventions at the indicated or selected level. It is quite customary for prevention programs and strategies to target risk factors for the development of mental health problems. In fact, this is probably the most common preventive strategy that includes efforts to identify and target malleable social, cognitive, emotional, and contextual risk variables. One example is the Fast Track Program in which the preventive intervention design targets primary risk factors for antisocial behavior, including poor parenting practices, deficient problem-solving and ineffective coping skills, poor peer relations, weak academic skills, disruptive classroom environments, and poor home–school relations (CPPRG, Conduct Problems Prevention Research Group, 2010b). The importance of addressing multiple rather than single risk factors and identifying risk factors that are malleable is often underlined in the research literature (e.g., Frick & Viding, 2009; Rutter, Giller, & Hagell, 1998).

Health promotion

Health promotion is sometimes considered a preventive strategy and sometimes not. Bloom and Gullotta (2003) in their inclusive perspective describe primary prevention as: (1) preventing predictable and interrelated problems, (2) protecting existing states of health and healthy functioning, and (3) promoting psychosocial wellness for identified populations of people (p. 13). Others are more restrictive and argue that health promotion, rather than having a focus on illness, emphasizes the enhancement of well-being. In the view of Mrazek and Haggerty (1994), health promotion is more concerned with raising competence, self-esteem, or well-being rather than preventing psychological or social problems or mental disorders (p. 27). The APA Presidential Task Force on Prevention: Promoting Strength, Resilience and Health in Young People on the other hand, supports the broader perspective of Bloom and Gullotta and claims that primary prevention for young people involves the dual goals of reducing the incidence of psychological and physical health problems and of enhancing social competence and health (Weissberg & Greenberg, 1998; Weissberg, Kumpfer, & Seligman, 2003).

Resilience- and competence-focused prevention

The epidemiological findings that many children who are exposed to serious risk or adversity "beat the odds" have prompted an increase in the search for processes and variables that foster desistance from problem behavior over time. Miller, Brehm, and Whitehouse (1998) argue in favor of combining risk- and resilience-focused prevention strategies in order to prevent psychopathology. Although they are focusing on antisocial behavior, this change in strategy may also apply to the prevention of other mental health problems discussed in this book. At the same time, there has been an increase in the number of studies of competence and resilience in which competence is explained as patterns of effective pro-social adaptation and resilience as the manifestation of competence in the face of hardship (Masten & Coatsworth, 1998). Competence may be considered as compensatory resources, and resilience as protective resources. Such compensatory and protective resources increase the probability of social adjustment because it indirectly moderates the effects of risk factors. The combination of risk- and resilience-focused prevention seems to hold great promise because the risk level is lowered at the same time as the fostering of competencies is taking place. Three types of school-based programs for the prevention of antisocial behavior are presented by Miller, Brehm, and Whitehouse (1998) as an illustration of how compensatory and protective resources can be combined. The first program includes *individual* efforts to enhance academic, social–cognitive, and self-regulation skills, with clear behavioral expectations and proactive, positive behavior management systems. The second program includes *family* efforts to strengthen positive parenting practices, enhance family relationships, and increase family support and home–school connectedness and bonding. The third program targets the *school organization* to promote pro-social behavioral expectations, bonding with pro-social peers and adults, and effective instructional practices to increase the academic competence of the students. Masten and Coatsworth (1998) also support the position that prevention should include both an effort to foster competence and to prevent problems. Interventions can thus be conceptualized as a protective process by which one deliberately attempts to steer development in a more favorable direction.

Interventions as change strategies

Interventions may take the form of strategies, models, programs, methods, or guidelines. They are action strategies that are used in service domains such as mental health, child welfare, and education. A definition of interventions is offered by Fraser, Richman, Galinsky, and Day (2009) as "intentional change strategies" and further described as purposeful actions that may operate at the individual, family, organizational, local, regional, or national level. They may include several actions like assessment, prevention, education, treatment, and aftercare or any combination of these. Some intervening actions are as simple and straightforward as the use of praise and encouragement for positive youth behavior, and others are more complex like the intervention program Multisystemic Therapy (MST; see Chapter 4).

This research also shows that it is a formidable challenge to implement successful models or programs on a large scale so that they become effective in normal practice, nationally or regionally. However, it is concluded that this can be handled, at least in part, by establishing and routinely monitoring quality standards for the services. Among well-established programs, none have proven to be superior, but some factors appear to be important for children's positive development in the first 5 years of life. These active ingredients or "efficacy factors" include, inter alia: (1) basic medical follow-up of pregnant mothers and their children; (2) early and intensive support from competent home-seekers in vulnerable families who are expecting their first child; (3) early high-quality intervention programs in kindergartens to strengthen cognitive and social development, especially for children from low-income families; (4) programs that simultaneously support multiple families and children in high-quality kindergartens; (5) good cognitive skills in children and young people who perform well at school and who look to the future; and (6) individually adapted intensive interventions that promote positive development in children who experience repeated abuse, family violence, and maternal failure, who have parents with severe depression or substance abuse.

Matching interventions to risk level and context

The principle of matching intervention to risk level signals that "one approach" does not fit all, and accordingly, intervention plans should be tailored to the individual needs of young people. The principle also takes into consideration that interventions should be contextually appropriate and adapted to the ecological characteristics of the home, school, or community environment in which the adolescents live. One consequence of this principle is the widely accepted three-tiered model of assessment and intervention that matches the previously mentioned universal, selected, and indicated prevention levels (Algozzine, Duanic, & Smith 2010). Interventions at the first tier are considered to be universally preventive or supportive of adolescents at low risk. For instance, most students in school are well behaved but still profit from a reasonable amount of praise, encouragement, and rewards for complying with school rules, norms, and expectations. At the second level, adolescents at moderate risk may have difficulties in coping with expectations from parents, teachers, and peers and may be in need of selected interventions like social support, social skills training, counseling, or additional academic support. Approximately 15–20 percent of an age cohort may be in need of additional help and support, which may be organized as small group interventions in schools or mental health services. Interventions at the indicated level target the 5–10 percent of adolescents at high risk and are individually tailored to their needs and level of functioning. At this third tier, functional behavior assessments may be carried out and used as the basis for the formulation of individual plans of action that are comprehensive and intensive (Algozzine et al., 2010; Ogden, Sørlie, Arnesen, & Meek-Hansen, 2012b).

Evidence-based practice

Evidence-based practice (EBP) started in medicine (Sackett, Richardson, Rosenberg, & Haynes, 1997), but has since been adapted by several other professional domains like psychology (APA, 2006), social work (Fraser et al., 2009), and education (Marzano, Marzano, & Pickering, 2003). The essence of EBP is the promotion of relevant research in patient or client care. For instance, in social work, the aim of evidence-based interventions is usually to prevent or reduce social or health problems. In psychology, EBP is defined as "the integration of the best available research with clinical expertise in the context of patient characteristics, culture and preferences" (APA, 2006). The definition of evidence-based psychological practice (EBPP) is thus threefold, taking into account a broader range of clinical activities, such as assessment, case description, and the therapeutic relationship along with the recognition of individual characteristics.

A distinction is made between EBT and EBP. EBT consists of practices that have repeatedly proved to be effective with a particular population in several controlled evaluation trials. EBP on the other hand is "[...] an explicit process for making practice related decisions based on the best currently available evidence" (Fraser et al., 2009, p. 135). In this chapter, we discuss EBTs in more detail but first present the role of the three "branches" in EBPP: best available research, clinical expertise, and patient characteristics.

Patient characteristics, culture, and preferences refer to individual differences such as age, gender, ethnic background, personality traits, values, and worldviews. Such client-related variables may not only affect treatment outcomes but may also influence a person's proclivity to seek and receive help, the way he or she describes and presents problems or symptoms, and his or her expectations about treatment outcomes. Intervening with adolescents is usually more complex than with adults because young people rarely refer themselves to treatment and it is sometimes difficult to get them involved in interventions they may consider to be unnecessary, unimportant, or irrelevant. Moreover, treating the adolescent may be but one part of the intervention; efforts to alter the social context and the behaviors of others with whom the adolescent interacts could be of equal importance (Kazdin & Weisz, 1998). Indeed, features of the social context of the adolescent, including his or her social support, family resources, stressors, and relationships with extra-familial people such as teachers and friends are also part of what makes each adolescent unique. These characteristics need to be considered when making clinical decisions (McNeish, Newman, & Roberts, 2002).

Nevertheless, many presenting symptoms or problems such as delinquency, depression, drug use, or school failure are similar across adolescent groups, and well-designed interventions aimed to alleviate specific problems typically focus on these empirically derived common features. It is rarely the case, however, that adolescents present a clear-cut, single, or discrete disorder; the presence of co-occurring conditions or comorbidity may also have an impact on treatment outcomes. In making well-informed clinical decisions about treatment of individual adolescents, one important, but challenging, task therefore should be to consider the characteristics of the youth in question in comparison with the characteristics of adolescents in samples examined in relevant studies. To meet this challenge, intervention research has for some time now been concerned with identifying which characteristics of both the adolescent (e.g., comorbidity) and the social context (e.g., parental divorce) either facilitate or obstruct therapeutic gains. These are referred to as moderators of intervention efforts and we discuss these later in the chapter.

Clinical expertise refers broadly to the "competence attained by psychologists [or other helping professions] through education, training, and experience that result in effective practice" (APA, 2006, p. 275). Included is a wide range of competencies, such as the ability to make accurate assessments and case formulations, identify relevant patient characteristics and values, plan a theoretically coherent and communicable treatment strategy, and monitor patient progress. Because psychological treatment typically takes place in an interpersonal setting, clinical expertise also encompasses social skills on the part of the therapist. This includes the ability to self-reflect on one's own experiences, emotional reactions, limitations, and biases, all of which may impact the therapeutic relationship and, consequently, treatment outcomes. Clinical expertise also involves the use of relevant and up-to-date research evidence, the acquisition of a scientific approach toward clinical work, and a commitment to seek additional resources if required and available. For clinicians and practitioners who are not familiar with evaluating and drawing on research data, this may constitute a barrier to EBP.

The third and last "branch" in EBPP, namely, the *best available research*, refers to a wide range of psychological research, including clinical observations studies, qualitative research, epidemiological research, process-outcome studies, efficacy and effectiveness trials, and meta-analyses. All of these different research approaches contribute to the cumulative knowledge base upon which both new treatments are developed and well-informed clinical decisions can be made. The strength of the evidence supporting an intervention is measured by the strength of the research design used in the evaluation studies and is ranked in the *hierarchy of evidence* for assessing the effectiveness of interventions. The highest levels of evidence are meta-analyses and systematic reviews of multiple randomized controlled trials (RCTs). The next levels consist of RCTs followed by cohort studies, case control studies, case series studies, cross-sectional studies and case reports and, at the lowest level, expert opinions, including those of practitioners, clients, and users. When the best available research is represented by EBTs, it is typically assumed that they have repeatedly demonstrated both their effectiveness with a particular population and usefulness in local settings (APA, 2006; Fraser et al., 2009). We now go on to discuss EBTs in more detail.

Evidence-based treatments

Consider the parents of a teenager who has started skipping school, who gets in fights, and uses drugs. They decide to seek professional help for their teenager's problem behavior. Likely, the single most important goal for these parents as they refer their child to treatment is that the services they receive are helpful and effective, that their youngster starts going to school, refrains from fighting, and ceases his drug use. Is it possible to enable this family to make informed decisions about what treatment they could request?

Consider a teenager who feels helpless at making friends, constantly fears she will be ridiculed and embarrassed in social situations and feels physically ill when called up in class: Can this young girl be taught adaptive social skills and be assisted in developing a positive self-concept, and is it likely that this would be helpful?

Consider a therapist who is presented with a young patient who has attempted suicide several times. He starts treating the youth and hopes that what he offers will prevent the youngster from trying to commit suicide again. Is the treatment he gives perceived to be helpful? Does he provide the youth and her family with the necessary tools for getting the young girl's life back on track? Would it be helpful for this therapist to have effective therapeutic techniques at his disposal?

Consider a government official in the department of public health. Every day, she makes decisions about resource allocation to various mental health initiatives. Is it possible for her to make well-informed decisions about which prevention program should receive financial support? Would her decision be easier if the effectiveness of the programs had been tested and documented?

What is meant by evidence-based treatments and "model programs"?

The answer to the questions in the previous paragraph is yes. Regardless of whether it is the parent, the adolescent, the therapist, or the policymaker, making decisions about preventive efforts and treatment is easier if we know what is likely to be effective and for whom (Roth & Fonagy, 2005). Simply put, evidence-based treatment (EBT) refers to programs, techniques, or methods that have produced therapeutic change in controlled trials (Kazdin, 2008). The act of demonstrating "therapeutic change in controlled trials" is not a simple endeavor and carries with it its own set of criteria. When the randomization procedure has been successful, it has ruled out the effects of confounders as these are thought to be distributed equally by chance across groups (e.g., the intervention and control groups) and, thus, any difference between groups can be attributed to the one factor on which they differ: the group assignment. Insofar as a program or a treatment stands the test of empirical investigation in controlled designs and with good results, it is typically referred to as an empirically supported treatment (EST). When ESTs have been found to be effective and have been replicated in new settings and with new samples, they are referred to as EBTs. Thus, the criteria for EBTs are more stringent than those of ESTs by having to demonstrate greater generalizability. Ideally, EBTs should also stand the test of high-quality meta-analyses, especially if the treatment is to be disseminated to regular services. Proper reporting of randomized trials is described in what is called the CONSORT statement (Consolidated Standards of Reporting Trials, www.consort-statement.org/consort-statement/).

Model programs are well structured and predefined, and they have well-developed systems for training and supervision of practitioners. Examples are Multidimensional Treatment Foster Care (MTFC; Chamberlain, 1998) and MST (Henggeler, Schoenwald, Borduin, Rowland, & Cunningham, 2009) for the treatment of anti-social behavior, and Coping Cat (Kendall & Hedtke, 2006) for the treatment of anxiety. Some of these programs also have routines for pre-evaluation of treatment sites, including guidelines for local implementation, standardized routines for the measurement of treatment adherence and for monitoring treatment outcomes as well as regular site evaluation of program operation, and routines for monitoring and quality assurance. Most importantly, they have also been shown to be effective in controlled clinical trials. A number of model programs have been developed and tested in the United States (US) and later implemented in several European countries. In the US, the Blueprints for Violence Prevention is the most extensive effort to date to disseminate EBPs widely and effectively (Elliott, 1997). It also assists applicant communities in implementing its programs. As yet, more than 600 programs have been examined, but only 11 programs have met stringent quality criteria (Biglan & Ogden, 2008). Later, we will present programs that meet certain criteria of scientific quality and relevance, either by being labeled a model program in the Blueprints report, by showing high-quality research design with good outcomes in the Substance Abuse and Mental Health Services Administration's (SAMHSA) National Registry of Evidence-Based Programs and Practices, or by being particularly pertinent to European and adolescent samples (successful transfer programs to, or developed and tested on, European adolescents).

The evidence debate

In a very real sense, EBTs in general and ESPs in particular have been controversial, subject to critique, and debated among supporters and opponents. Even if many programs have been developed and tested, particularly in the US, it has also been pointed out that transfer from knowledge to practice has remained slow. Many clinicians have shown little enthusiasm for ESPs (APA, 2006). In summing up the critique from researchers and practitioners, Chambless and Ollendick (2001) quoted some examples in which EBT was described as a "foolproof, stepwise instruction to paraprofessionals," as "promoting a cookbook mentality," or was being compared to "painting by numbers." Why is this the case?

Despite the fact that researchers and clinicians share a common goal, namely, to be able to provide the best possible care to clients, there has been a long-standing divide between scientists on the one side and practitioners on the other. Kazdin (2008) lists several reasons for why this may be the case and makes suggestions on how to bridge the gap between clinical research and practice in an effort to expand the knowledge base and improve services. One of the concerns about EBT often voiced among practitioners is that the characteristics and conditions of treatment research do not correspond to the practice context. The control of the recruitment process, the measures, and the therapy sought in the randomized trial are difficult to achieve in "real-life" clinics and, thus, results from these trials are considered less relevant by practitioners. It is true that RCTs require a high degree of control and involve scientific manipulation; thus, not all empirical questions may be answered in randomized designs. Still, there are no other designs that are better suited for inferences about causality.

Therapist experience

Another criticism of EBTs is that they ignore therapist experience. EBTs are, however, fundamentally based on experience, but perhaps in a different manner than what is normally meant by therapist's experience. When used to describe psychological treatment, it refers to systematizing this experience. The word *evidence* in evidence-based treatment means that evidence or knowledge has been derived empirically. The process of systematizing empirical evidence bears with it a stringent set of methodological standards that are meant to protect the knowledge we attain from bias, subjective interpretations, and erroneously drawn conclusions about the study participants.

Individual adaptations

A common conception among practitioners is that EBTs are inflexible (Borntrager, Chorpita, Higa-McMillan, & Weisz, 2009) or follow a one-size-fits-all principle. However, most EBTs start out with a tailoring of the youth or family's specific situation to a treatment plan. Typically, EBTs have a core set of components or treatment principles that are applied in the therapeutic process, since most psychological or social problems share certain features. But it is also the case that no EBT to date has ever earned the description of a "wonder cure for all." The ideal to strive for is to develop a treatment that is better than what we can offer thus far, and to constantly refine the treatments to offer better help and to help more. Many intervention researchers are trying to find out why some participants do not respond to a generally effective treatment. Clearly defined treatment principles, for example in the form of a manual, are a requirement for both controlled trials (we need to know what the independent variable is) and for replication purposes (new trials of a given treatment must know what to test).

Treatment integrity versus therapist autonomy

Several opponents perceive EBT as a threat to clinical freedom or therapist autonomy. Within the field of psychology, EBT has been accused of trying to establish a competitive alternative to pharmacologic treatment by offering short-term treatments of well-defined problems. Within the domain of social work, EBT has been described as an attempt to create a cognitive and behavioral hegemony, because these approaches are easier to adapt to the framework of predefined short-term therapy (Gibbs & Gambrill, 2002). Integrity describes the extent to which the core treatment or program components are delivered as intended and is referred to as program integrity or treatment integrity. It may describe how much of the program was delivered to the users or how much time was spent on certain treatment components. A high degree of treatment integrity is also referred to as fidelity or adherence. The intervention should be carried out according to the aims, guidelines, and underlying theory described by the developer. A high level of integrity is dependent on the combined characteristics of the practitioner (therapist), the user (the client), and the program. High fidelity or adherence is used to describe how well a trained therapist masters the protocol and the tools, and may be measured by observer, therapist, or client reports. The quality of the treatment or the competence of the therapist describes practitioner skills and attitudes that promote program goals. The competent therapist may add treatment components that are compatible, but not necessarily parts of the program. The level of treatment integrity is influenced by the number and length of sessions the client has been exposed to, and is also determined by how responsive, engaged, or involved the client is during sessions. A high degree of exposure is associated with increased likelihood of high fidelity and positive treatment gains for the client. Research findings are not entirely consistent on this issue, and may indicate that both too high and too low levels of treatment integrity may be detrimental to the outcomes if the treatment delivered is too rigid or too diluted (Huey, Henggeler, Brondino, & Pickrel, 2000; Mihalic, Fagan, Irwin, Ballard, & Elliott, 2004; Perepletchikova & Kazdin, 2005).

Therapeutic alliance

EBTs have been faulted for discounting therapists' skills, such as the ability to show warmth, respect, and to establish trust. Regardless of therapeutic approach, however, building a working alliance with an adolescent or a family is likely to enhance treatment outcomes. Building a good rapport with the youth or his or her family is often referred to as therapeutic alliance. Therapeutic alliance, defined as the mutual feeling of respect, empathy, and reciprocity between practitioner and client, is assumed to play a part in the therapeutic process, although how is not fully understood. Some studies find alliance to correlate positively with treatment response and others do not (Liber et al., 2010; Amlund Hagen & Ogden, manuscript in preparation). Kazdin and Whitley (2006) investigated therapeutic alliance in a series of studies and reported that, for parents of children with oppositional and antisocial behavior, the positive correlation between therapeutic alliance and improvement in parenting was partially explained by the pretreatment social relations of the parents. It seems likely that the rapport that the therapist tries to establish with the youth or family is at least partially dependent upon the characteristics of the client that existed prior to the therapeutic relationship. A friendly and respectful therapist with an effective treatment method is probably better than a friendly and respectful therapist with no method or a poorly defined method.

Common factors and program factors

In the field of psychotherapy, much of the debate has focused on specific program factors versus therapeutic common factors. Common factors do not belong to any particular theoretical approach or treatment model as compared to specific factors that are considered to be unique for a certain program, model, or approach. Radical proponents of the common factor approach have claimed that program factors are unimportant, and that common factors are responsible for most of the clinical change during therapy. According to this view, the quality of the therapeutic alliance or working relationship is considered more important for the outcome of therapy than the therapeutic methods and manuals applied (Norcross, Beutler, & Levant, 2006). A similar approach was taken by Wampold et al. (1997) when they claimed that therapist qualities were the best predictors of successful treatments. The critique was taken to the next level by Duncan and Miller (2005), who claimed that therapists who went by the book developed a better relationship with the manual than with the client. They emphasized that the client was the real hero in psychotherapy because treatment only worked if it activated the natural healing potential of the client. The often cited "Dodo bird verdict," taken to mean that no treatment models or programs are any better than others (Luborsky, Singer, & Luborsky, 1975; Wampold, 2001), has gradually been moderated (Fluckiger, Del Re, Wampold, Symonds, & Horvath, 2012; Wampold & Budge, 2012). Among those who supported the "Dodo bird verdict," Sprenkle and Blow (2004) admitted that the phrase was ill chosen, because if no therapy is better than any other, it will be difficult to distinguish between ESTs and Ouija boards. At present, it has become more customary to claim that similar outcome effects can be expected when trained therapists offer empirically well-established treatments to clients with some of the most common and well-defined mental health problems. In support of empirically supported practice, Weisz, Weersing, and Henggeler (2005) claim that treatment protocols neither minimize the client's active participation in the treatment process nor prevent the therapist from making sound clinical judgments. According to their view, treatment manuals usually describe the intervention in a logical sequence, such as when assessment and alliance building comes before the interventions. Treatment principles and guidelines are usually presented as recommended techniques rather than injunctions. Manuals may also communicate that certain procedures may be counterproductive or ineffective, like group treatment of acting-out adolescents. However, within the framework of the logical and empirical guidelines of the manual, the practitioners have ample room for flexibility and may use their creativity and resources to promote behavioral change (Weisz, Weersing, & Henggeler, 2005). So, whilst the critics are most concerned with the restrictions that manuals put on creativity and judgment in clinical practice, the supporters focus on the opportunities that practitioners have to individualize the treatment, and also the possibilities of clients to influence the treatment process within the defined framework of the protocol. Furthermore, Weisz, Jensen, and McLeod (2005) admit that competent practicing of evidence-based therapy includes more than mastering manual-defined treatment procedures. Variations in treatment effects may be due to differences in the therapists' professional clinical competence or general therapeutic skills. Therefore, the manuals must be supplemented with program-specific treatment and supervision of the therapists. On the positive side, it should also be noted that manuals have a positive function by having a standardizing effect and promote the program-specific competence of the therapists. When therapists undergo standardized training and receive systematic supervision in a specific model, it also strengthens the treatment integrity.

As mentioned previously in this chapter, several authors have commented on the fact that many effective EBTs are not available in practice (Fixsen, Naoom, Blase,

Friedman, & Wallace, 2005; Glasgow, Lichtenstein, & Marcus, 2003). The process of moving EBT programs to practice has proven to be difficult and has led to an increased focus on topics like diffusion and dissemination of programs and adaptation to different cultural and local contexts (Rogers, 1995). Recently, there has been much focus on the concept of *implementation* and the sustainability of program effectiveness when they are moved into routine practice. When programs have shown to be effective, preferably across many studies, the next challenges are first to implement them into real-world practice whilst maintaining program integrity and treatment adherence, and then to examine change mechanisms that operate within programs and potential moderators of treatment effects (Weersing & Weisz, 2002).

What works for whom, when, and how?

The question of what works for whom and how is highly important in the process of program adaptation and refinement. Several individual and contextual factors may moderate the impact of interventions and, to identify what makes interventions work, it is vital to analyze change processes. Mechanisms of therapeutic change refer to those processes that lead to and cause therapeutic change (the "active ingredient" of a program). That is, mechanisms refer to the processes through which change occurs. Moderators, on the other hand, refer to those characteristics (of the youth, family, context, or therapy) that influence whether change occurs or the extent to which change occurs. The study of how therapy works might have implications for how to intervene to change social, emotional, and behavioral characteristics (Kazdin & Nock, 2003; Weersing & Weisz, 2002).

There seems to be a common misconception that EBTs disregard the therapeutic process or the mechanisms at play during treatment. Many researchers in the evidence-based tradition, however, are active pursuers of trying to describe and explain therapeutic processes, with the aims of both improving the chances of good outcomes and understanding therapeutic development. But before identifying "the active ingredient," the mechanisms at work or process variables, the method in question ought to document effectiveness. In recent years, the field of EBTs has moved to trying to answer not only "what works?" but also the questions "what works for whom?" and "how?" Many researchers are now publishing studies examining mediation and moderation effects of treatment in addition to findings regarding the therapeutic relationship, alliance, and treatment fidelity.

Moderators. Intervention research has been concerned with the moderating effects of variables such as age, gender, social background, or co-occurring conditions on outcomes. Identifying moderators includes the identification of subgroups or conditions under which the intervention works well and, likewise, under which circumstances and for whom the treatment in question works less well. For instance, treatment is more likely to be effective when it is responsive to the client's specific problems, strengths, personality, sociocultural context, and preferences (Levant, 2008). Many of these characteristics can be tested scientifically and the goal of such interaction analyses is to identify adolescents who do not respond to the treatment and why. The identification of such factors not only helps signal when treatment is likely to produce favorable results, but also under what conditions and for whom modifications of treatments, different treatments, or multiple-treatment combinations should be applied (Kazdin, 1995).

An important part of testing model programs in clinical trials has been the monitoring and formal measurement of intervention adherence (or treatment fidelity). In efficacy trials, this moderating variable is usually under the control of the investigator who recruits, trains, supervises, and monitors the therapists, usually based on a written treatment manual or protocol. In regular practice, the question of treatment integrity is more complex and depends both on the training and supervision of clinicians, their allegiance to the program, and the quality of routines for monitoring fidelity. The successful transfer of ESPs or interventions to regular practice may be hindered by negative attitudes and central values in service settings that often place high value on clinical freedom, autonomy, and eclecticism (Mitchell, 2011).

Change mechanisms or mediators. The importance of searching for "active ingredients" or treatment mechanisms has been increasingly acknowledged in the literature, and the search for evidence-based model programs has been supplemented by the search for evidence-based principles underlying these programs. Examining not just whether, and for whom, but *how* changes in outcomes are produced is essential to advancing theory and improving services delivered (La Greca, Silverman, & Lochman, 2009). Mediators of therapeutic change are becoming a focus in studies of EBT, though perhaps somewhat late, considering the great emergence of EBTs for children and youths (Eyberg, Nelson, & Boggs, 2008). For example, Weersing and Weisz (2002) only found six studies that included mediation analyses in their review of 67 clinical trials with children and youths. Follow-up studies, whilst important in their own right, are well suited for examining mediators' mechanisms because mediation models necessitate a temporal order of the phenomena involved; as the mediator occurs before the outcome. For many treatment programs for delinquent youths (e.g., MST and MTFC), improved family cohesion, increased parental monitoring, and reductions in deviant peer contact are hypothesized mechanisms through which behavioral change occurs, whereas changes in maladaptive thinking patterns are likely to play a part in how youths with depressive symptoms or disorder may benefit from cognitive behavioral therapy (CBT) (Weisz, Southam-Gerow, Gordis, & Connor-Smith, 2003).

The transatlantic relevance of evidence-based programs

Ferrer-Wreder, Stattin, Lorente, Tubman, and Adamson (2004) reviewed several interventions that had been developed in the US and transferred to Europe. These authors examined the transatlantic relevance of the intervention programs following their implementation in Europe. They concluded that the scientifically evaluated interventions from North America seemed to work equally well in European countries. For most of these treatment methods, the core intervention components were kept intact and surface changes were considered necessary to adapt the programs to European contexts. Thus, even if important cultural differences exist, the countries involved still shared what seemed to be some fundamental features, for instance how families and parent–child relations or teacher–student relations work. Among the critical factors for successful transference of new interventions to Norway and other European countries, Ferrer-Wreder et al. (2004) mention sufficient resources, strong collaborative relations between the program purveyors and implementers, popular support, availability, and enthusiasm for EBP. Successful transatlantic collaboration takes time, money, and energy, and time constraints and lack of financial support or personal energy were identified as barriers. According to the panel interviewed, the interventions should appeal to practitioners and be able to match or be adapted to different settings and cultures. A close and careful examination of the fit between an intervention and cultural values and traditions of the host country should therefore be made up front. The intervention should be robust enough to adapt to contextual variations, and cultural appropriateness should be addressed within the interventions: "flexibility, openness, as well as attention to culture and context, in many cases, were central facets of the interventions themselves" (Ferrer-Wreder et al., 2004, p. 205). The implementation of complex ecological models is challenging and is often dependent on the contributions of purveyor organizations and specialized implementation teams. The dependence on training and supervision by specialized purveyor organizations or implementation teams limits the access to such models. Students cannot learn these models as long as they are not taught in universities and colleges. It is also difficult to integrate ecological programs or models in private practice. And if non-supervised interventionists are claiming that they are practicing ESPs or models, how can that be validated?

Even if many of the programs developed and tested in North America have been successfully transferred to Europe (Van Yperen & Boendemaker, 2008), the generalizability of US findings has been questioned. This has been due to differences between the US and European countries in social, political, cultural, and economic contexts, and in the organization and availability of mental health and welfare services (Asscher, Deković, van der Laan, Prins, & Arum, 2007). Differences may also exist in the type and amount of risk factors to which young delinquents are exposed, such as differences in poverty, violence, and crime rates and the availability of drugs and guns. Scandinavian countries like Norway and Sweden have no juvenile justice system and the age of criminal responsibility is higher than in the US. In the Scandinavian countries, services targeting children who commit crimes and abuse drugs are more treatment oriented than punitive and most youths are kept out of the justice system and taken into the care of child welfare services. When comparing Europe to the US, Bullock (1992) states that continental Europe traditionally applies a philosophical and logical rather than empirical approach to youth problems. Britain, on the other hand, has a long history of linking empirical findings and policy. In the US, demonstration projects and outcome studies that sell programs fit in well with its enterprise culture. This may explain why most evidence-based programs are developed and tested in efficacy studies in the US before they are transferred to other countries such as Norway or the Netherlands. There are also some indications suggesting that RCTs are more accepted and less controversial among practitioners and researchers in the US than in European countries. The obstacles and resistance toward RCTs reported from the Netherlands (Asscher et al., 2007) are also experienced in other European countries (Nutley, Walter, & Davies, 2007; Ogden, Christensen, Sheidow, & Holth, 2008), which might make this kind of research sparse and appear less attractive. Generally, it seems that it is far more difficult to carry out the operations of implementing and evaluating new model programs than to succeed in the actual treatment of adolescents and families. At the same time, structural forces seem to be at work across both continents; indeed, juvenile crime and delinquency are a major challenge on both sides of the Atlantic. To some extent, this also indicates that the risk and protective factors targeted in several of the EBT programs operate similarly in most Western countries. With reference to education, Kelly (2012) writes that the demand for evidence-based intervention and practice is less explicit at the policy level in the UK, but is expected of educational, psychological, and other practitioners. In the UK, the aims and ideals of education seem not to rest on research and there is little emphasis on demonstrating and measuring effectiveness.

Concluding comments

In this chapter, we have presented evidence-based approaches and strategies for the prevention and treatment of mental health problems. In the domain of prevention, we side with scholars who recommend a combination of risk reduction and the promotion of health, competence, and resilience. Preventive interventions for adolescents include those who target problems in childhood, but also preventive efforts that are universally available to all adolescents. Treatment interventions operate at the selected and indicated level by offering services to youth at risk. Small group interventions to groups of adolescents who share the same risk status may be offered in schools, in child welfare, or the mental health services. Treatment interventions may also be individually tailored to prevent further escalation or continuation of mental health problems. We have a particular focus on EBP in which the best available research-based evidence is adapted to clinical expertise and client characteristics and preferences. Moving on to EBT, we discussed ESPs for the treatment of defined problems in defined populations. We also summarized the evidence debate which showed that the evidence-based paradigm has been controversial and fiercely debated among practitioners as well as among researchers. We refer and comment on some of the most common critical arguments but argue in favor of the application of the core elements of EBTs. Some of the counterarguments seem to be misconceptions, but others are based on real differences in theoretical and empirical positions in which the individual researcher and practitioner simply must take a stand. We would, however, like to repeat our position, stated in the opening of this chapter, that practice should be evidence based rather than based on authority, ideology, or consensus, whenever possible. Still, we do not disregard other types of research or practice-based knowledge, but rather give priority to evidence-based prevention and treatments.

The developing and testing of empirically supported interventions make high demands on competence, leadership, and funding. First, evidence-based interventions may be costlier if they are established and carried out alongside traditional ways of delivering services. Intervention research is complex and expensive, and dependent on the funding of both interventionists and researchers. Additional funding may be needed unless resources are reallocated from regular services. Second, high-quality program implementation and intervention adherence put high demands on the competence and leadership of the purveyor as well as on the host organization. Procedures and guidelines for the recruitment, training, supervision, and evaluation of practitioners have to be established. In addition, procedures for sustained monitoring of the intervention adherence and quality control of services have to be in place (Fixsen et al., 2005). The costs and complexity of high-quality implementation may actually restrict the system-wide dissemination of empirically supported interventions and decision-makers, and organization leaders may look for simpler and cheaper ways of establishing services and interventions that match their needs. The ultimate benefits of interventions and preventive efforts are reductions in prevalence and incidence, respectively, of problems in the targeted population (Biglan & Ogden, 2008). Therefore, the evolution of EBPs must include surveillance systems to monitor the well-being of populations over time and to register the rate of occurrences of new cases. In any human system, one can expect drift in practice and changing conditions which may result in a deterioration of implementation fidelity or loss of effectiveness due to changes in the environment or in the target population.

3

EXTERNALIZING PROBLEMS

This chapter starts with an overview and description of the characteristics, prevalence rates, and subgroups of externalizing problems, including gender differences and different ages of onset. We then present research on the risk and protective factors associated with the development of aggression, delinquency, and deviant behavior and how these are manifested and, in some cases, exacerbated in adolescence. The development of problem behavior is considered from the ecological–transactional perspective. The remaining part of the chapter is a presentation of evidence-based prevention and treatment programs for externalizing behavior problems.

Externalizing behavior problems: definitions and descriptions

Externalizing behaviors are outward-directed and characterize youths who are negatively acting on the external environment. We have chosen to use the term *externalizing behavior* as an overarching construct for behaviors that reflect under-controlled regulation of emotion and behavioral problems and that include similar, albeit distinct, clusters of behavior such as aggression, delinquency, hyperactivity, and opposition. Common to these behaviors is that they are experienced as aversive and troublesome to other people and that they transgress social boundaries. Often, such behavior, particularly aggressive behavior, also involves a victim. Whilst the externalizing construct also includes hyperactivity, we are not discussing attention deficits or hyperactivity specifically in this book.

Distinctions are often made between overt versus covert aggression on the one hand and destructive versus non-destructive behavior on the other (Frick, 1998; Olson et al., 2013). Overt and non-destructive behavior (e.g., oppositional defiant behavior) includes temper tantrums, stubbornness, and defiance and is more common in the preschool and early school-age years. Overt and destructive behavior or open aggression is characterized by cruelty to animals, fighting, and bullying. Covert and destructive conduct encompasses behaviors such as stealing, relational aggression, and fire-setting. Finally, the covert and non-destructive profile (e.g., status offenses) includes running away, substance use, and truancy. These distinctions may be more a matter of age or developmental period and less a matter of individual differences. For example, temper tantrums, stubbornness, and defiance are behaviors more often seen in children rather than in adolescents, whereas substance use and truancy are typical teenage problems. Covert, or hidden, antisocial behavior increases in adolescence, seeks to avoid adult detection, and often implicates peers (Dishion & Patterson, 2006).

Aggression is behavior of individuals who intentionally inflict physical or psychological damage on others and is often understood as a subtopic of the broader term of externalizing behavior (Eisner & Malti, 2015). Within the dimension of *aggressive behavior* (overt forms of problem behavior), a further distinction is often also made between *proactive* and *reactive* aggression. Proactive aggression is instrumental (or cold-hearted, predatory), that is, behavior lacking in emotion and with a goal of obtaining something desired or gaining dominance. A teenager who pushes a classmate out of the way to advance his own place in line is an example of proactive aggression. Reactive (or hot-headed, defensive) aggression refers to a pattern of uncontrolled and emotionally charged behavioral responses that are inappropriately hostile in relation to the perceived cause. An example of reactive aggression is the youth who starts fighting a peer because she tumbles and falls over a foot that she thinks was deliberately positioned to trip her. Relational aggression, exemplified as antisocial behavior in the form of social exclusion, slandering, or manipulating relationships is not easily placed within the classification scheme of either the *Diagnostic and Statistical Manual of Mental Disorders* (4th ed.) (DSM-IV; American Psychiatric Association, 1994) or the International Classification of Diseases diagnostic system. Relational aggression is nevertheless a serious problem that causes hurt and detriment to the victim and reflects social and behavioral dysfunction.

Antisocial behavior

Antisocial behavior and externalizing problems are similar constructs and the terms are oftentimes used interchangeably. Nevertheless, antisocial behavior usually marks more serious problem behaviors than externalizing behaviors, behaviors of adolescents and adults (rather than of children), and is sometimes discussed in relation to adult antisocial personality disorder. A general definition of antisocial behavior is: "[…] a recurrent and persistent conflict with socially prescribed patterns of behavior" (Simcha-Fagan, Langner, Gersten, & Eisenberg, 1975, p. 7). Antisocial behavior is fairly stable and predictable and is largely unaffected by social consequences in different settings (Walker, Ramsey, & Gresham, 2004). Antisocial youths lie, bully, steal, fight, vandalize, manipulate, and sabotage. What are typically seen as "new" problems emerging in adolescence are patterns such as truancy, sexual promiscuity, and substance use. Such victimless actions of youths are strong predictors of problems in adulthood and are a major cause of conflict in families

(Dishion & Patterson, 2006). Among co-occurring problems in adolescence is the tendency to show feelings of misery and to have difficulties in reading (Rutter, Giller, & Hagell, 1998).

Age and gender differences

The manifestation of the various forms of antisocial behavior is often related to the age and gender of the youth. For example, certain types of physical aggression (e.g., hitting, biting, and pushing) peak in frequency at about 20–22 months followed by a decline toward 26 months (Nærde, Ogden, Janson, & Zachrisson, 2014) and further decreases across the preschool and early school-age years (NICHD, 2004). But even if children's physical aggression tends to decrease in frequency between 2 and 9 years of age, some children add new problems to those they already have when they enter school (Miner & Clarke-Stewart, 2008). Some children have problems controlling their aggression; they throw temper tantrums and show oppositional behavior. Such problems are highly predictive of continued problems in adolescence and early adulthood (Moffitt, Caspi, Harrington, & Milne, 2002) including peer rejection, delinquency, school dropout, criminal offenses, and interpersonal violence (Patterson & Yoerger, 1997). For most types of law-breaking behavior, the prevalence rates peak at around the age of 17, and boys are more likely to be involved in such activities than girls (McCart, Ogden, & Henggeler, 2014). More covert types of antisocial behavior, such as truancy and vandalism, are characterized by a period of almost no occurrences in the early school years, followed by an upward slope from early to late adolescence (Patterson & Yoerger, 1997).

The age of onset of conduct problems appears to be important in distinguishing between different trajectories of problem behavior in children and youths. A certain level of adolescent delinquency is to be expected and is near normative. It is, however, when norm- and law-breaking behavior becomes frequent, pervasive, has roots in childhood, and persists into adulthood that such conduct is indicative of pathological development. Moffitt (1993) distinguished between what she labeled the life course persistence (LCP) and adolescence-limited (AL) types. These two trajectories have also been referred to, respectively, as early and late onset of antisocial behavior (Patterson, Debaryshe, & Ramsey, 1990).

The Life Course Persistence type (or early onset; LCP) is rare. It begins early in life, is pervasive across multiple systems such as the home, school, and neighborhood, and is characterized by aggressive personality traits. It is also much more frequent in boys. Two groups of childhood antisocial behavior are described by Frick and Viding (2009). The first group of antisocial children has issues relating to cognitive failure and ineffective socialization that lead to problems in the normal development of behavioral and emotional regulation. Those who debut early on show aggressive behavior both in childhood and adolescence and are more likely to continue antisocial behavior when they grow up. Childhood problems are more closely related to neuropsychological (e.g., executive functions deficits) and cognitive (e.g., low intelligence) problems. Risk factors related to temperament and personality are characteristic of these children, including impulsivity, attention deficit, and emotional regulation problems. They typically come from unstable homes and families with coercive and dysfunctional parenting strategies.

The second group is characterized by Callous Unemotional (CU) traits that seem to be related to the way these children and youths process emotional stimuli and respond to punishment. Children with CU traits seem to have preferences for dangerous and new stimuli, evince a reward-oriented response style, and lack appropriate reactivity to emotional stimuli that signal discomfort or distress in others. These characteristics seem to make it more difficult for these children to develop guilt, empathy, and other dimensions of conscience (Frick & Viding, 2009). Moreover, they are much more challenging to help and treat (Bjørnebekk & Kjøbli, 2017; Kjøbli, Zachrisson & Bjørnebekk, 2017).

The Adolescent Limited type (or late onset; AL) occurs in boys and girls at almost similar rates, emerges with the onset of puberty, and is thought to have a strong contextual basis (Moffitt, 2006). Whilst AL may be almost indistinguishable from the LCP in adolescence, the AL type is nevertheless considered a less severe condition, less difficult to treat, and to have a better prognosis, at least for boys. This group seems to demonstrate an excessive amount of normative youth rebellion as a misunderstood way of experiencing maturity and adulthood and is often encouraged by antisocial friends (Frick & Viding, 2009). CU traits also seem to predict serious, stable, and aggressive behavioral patterns in antisocial adolescents. Frick and White (2008) summarized the characteristics of youth with CU traits. Those who score high on the CU trait seem to have difficulties in processing negative emotional stimuli, and indications of fear and turmoil in others. CU adolescents are also less sensitive to punitive signals, especially when they are in a reward-oriented mode. They have more positive experiences in aggressive encounters with peers, and more often have verbal shortcomings compared with other antisocial groups. And last but not least, youths with CU traits have unique personality characteristics, such as being more fearless and showing more excitatory behavior.

Gender differences. There is clear evidence of gender differences in both type and incidence of antisocial behavior. As a group, boys show significantly higher rates of conduct problems than do girls and this gender disparity appears to hold across cultures, contexts, and reporting agent (Delligatti, Akin-Little, & Little, 2003). Boys are over-represented in psychiatric diagnoses and referrals to child mental health services regarding conduct problems (Delligatti et al., 2003; Moffitt & Caspi, 2001). In their longitudinal study, Moffitt and Caspi (2001) found that males were ten times more likely to develop childhood-onset delinquency than were females. These tendencies were replicated in a study of 117 Norwegian adolescents who had received MST (Ogden & Amlund Hagen, 2009) in which results suggested that more than half of the parents of boys reported that their sons' problem behavior started before the age of ten, whereas less than one fifth of the parents of girls reported the same. The discrepancy decreases in adolescence, though, with a reported 1.5:1 male–female ratio for adolescence-onset delinquency (Moffitt, Caspi, Rutter, & Silva, 2001).

Generally, boys' problem behavior is typically more overt and non-directive whereas girls' antisociality is more often covert and relationship focused. Conflicting findings regarding gender differences in the manifestation of antisocial behavior seem to be the rule in studies with adolescent samples. However, the notion that the rate of aggressive behavior in girls and boys becomes more similar in adolescence than at any other time during the life course is a fairly consistent finding (Bongers, Koot, van der Ende, & Verhulst, 2004; Moffit & Caspi, 2001). Moffitt (1993) argued that girls' opportunities for going down an antisocial path are greater in adolescence than in childhood. Girls seem to be better protected against constitutional risk factors (temperament, neurological risk) than are boys, however the risk factors associated with adolescent delinquency likely affect girls and boys more similarly.

The prevalence of externalizing problems

Externalizing problems are one of the most common psychiatric problems in children and adolescents. In the US, it is estimated that 50–75 percent of all referrals to mental health services are related to behavioral problems (Kazdin, 1993). The high referral rate does not necessarily mean that the majority of children and adolescents who have mental health problems are conduct disordered, aggressive, or delinquent; to some degree, this rate reflects the fact that adolescents with antisocial behavior are *more likely to be referred* than youths with other types of problems (e.g., anxious or depressed adolescents). Most international population-based studies estimate the prevalence of serious behavior problems to be between 5 and 10 percent for the age group 8–16 years (Moffitt & Scott, 2009). A Norwegian report summarized that there are large variations in the estimated range of conduct disorders (Skogen & Torvik, 2013). In Norway, it was estimated that approximately 1.8 percent of children and young people met the diagnostic criteria for Oppositional Defiant Disorder, whilst about 1.7 percent of children and young people met the criteria for conduct disorder—a total of 3.5 percent. This number is close to the "best estimate" of 3 percent for the prevalence of behavioral disorder in children aged 5–17 years in Europe (Wittchen et al., 2011). Conduct problems were found to be more common among older children than among younger children and more common among boys than among girls (Skogen & Torvik, 2013).

Thus far, we have described the behavioral manifestations of externalizing types of behavior, and the prevalence rates of such problems. But these problems do not develop in a vacuum, nor do they appear suddenly (Hill, 2002). We now turn to theories of how externalizing problems develop and discuss the factors that place youth at risk of developing such problems.

Theoretical frameworks

No single theory is sufficient to explain the development, desistance, prevention, and treatment of externalizing problem behaviors. Several theories have influenced research as well as the development of treatment approaches. Among the influential theories are social learning and social interaction theory, both integrated in Patterson's coercion model and the social ecology of Bronfenbrenner (1979), but also social control theory (Hirschi, 1969), and the overarching transactional perspective of developmental psychopathology (Sameroff, 2009).

Social interaction and learning theory

One of the most influential theories about the development and treatment of anti-social behavior originates from Gerald Patterson and his colleagues at the Oregon Social Learning Center (Patterson, 1982, 2002). The social interaction learning (SIL) model draws on ecological and transactional principles (Reid, Patterson, & Snyder, 2002) and has been highly influential in most parenting programs. The SIL model holds that children's behavior is directly affected by parenting and that, over time, children and parents enter into transactional patterns that for some families can become coercive and overlearned. In relationships characterized by coercive interactions, family members are inadvertently shaped to become increasingly hostile. Parental expression of warmth and encouragement may be in short supply, and the youths are seldom reinforced for developing positive skills. Thus, one of the things parents of antisocial children and adolescents are encouraged to do is to "catch them being good," so that pro-social behaviors are reinforced by praise and acknowledgment.

The ecological and systemic perspective

The theoretical foundation underlying treatment approaches targeting adolescents is partly based on Patterson's SIL model (as in Treatment Foster Care Oregon [TFCO]; Chamberlain, 1998) and partly based on the social ecological framework of Bronfenbrenner (1979). In addition to ecological principles, MST is based on causal models of delinquency and drug use. The empirical causal model demonstrates how influences from the family (e.g., a high conflict level and the lack of monitoring and care), the school (e.g., school failure and lack of social bonding to school) and deviant peers, in combination, drive deviant behavior such as delinquency and drug use (Elliott, Huizinga, & Ageton, 1985). The treatment rationale further builds on the notion that adolescent problem behavior is multi-determined by risk factors of the youth him- or herself, of the family, and the broader environment in which the youth is embedded. Thus, in MST, the locus of change is the *ecology* surrounding the youth (Amlund Hagen & Christensen, 2010). At the therapeutic level, the treatment is guided by family systems theories, as in strategic (Haley, 1976) and structural family therapy (Minuchin, 1974), and by theoretical principles guiding cognitive and social learning interventions.

A transactional example

As with many psychological and behavioral difficulties, externalizing problems too often start out less serious but may quickly worsen to become more pervasive. It is well established in both research and theory that the family environment in general and parenting practices in particular are contributing factors to the growth and maintenance of externalizing problems. Early in life, parental factors of low warmth and harsh discipline are clear risk factors as they may lead some children to lag in their development of social–cognitive competence. When a child with such deficiencies comes to school, her peers are more likely to reject her and she might frequently get involved in hostile conflicts with other people. In turn, these conflicts make it difficult for a teacher or parent to express warmth and offer supportive parenting, and as a result these adults often withdraw supervision and monitoring during early adolescence when it is needed most.

Individual and contextual risk factors

The search for causal explanations has gradually been replaced by research on risk factors; that is, influences that increase the probability of the development and sustainability of serious behavior problems. These risk factors may be targeted in prevention and intervention, and risk-oriented approaches have proven quite promising. From an ecological and transactional perspective, the effects of risk are often more meaningfully understood when studied jointly and with regard to multiple risks, because it is the build-up of risk over time that has consistently been shown to predict children's psychosocial functioning (Lengua, 2002). Both risk factors for and protective factors against the development and maintenance of externalizing problems in youth can be categorized into three levels or systems: (1) neurobiological features in youths' executive functioning, genetic liability, and other constitutional characteristics; (2) family interactions; and (3) peer group and environmental or contextual influences (Weersing & Weisz, 2002) and the interaction between the systems. These categories parallel the three of the systems of the ecological model: the ontogenic system, the micro-system, and the meso-system, respectively.

Individual risk: genetic influences

At the ontogenetic level, there is evidence for a genetic vulnerability to the development of externalizing behavioral problems. For example, adopted children seem to be more likely to show externalizing problems if their biological parents were violent and/or criminal than adopted children with law-abiding biological parents (Mason & Frick, 1994; Rhee & Waldman, 2002). An alternative or additional explanation in such adoption studies may be that the effects of parental violence and crime can exert themselves both prenatally and in the early experiential environment of the child prior to adoption. Regardless of their cause, research has shown rather consistently that difficult temperament, emotion dysregulation, impulsivity, social information processing problems, and aggression have a fairly strong biological basis.

Family risk factors

Proximal family risk factors are environmental influences of the immediate family that jeopardize the child or youth's optimal development. For example, parents' own problems related to drug use, criminality, mental illness, and low IQ can negatively affect the upbringing environment. Also included are family stress, conflicts and violence, too lax or too harsh parenting, and attachment problems in the parent–child relationship. Relatively harmless misconduct or non-compliance on the part of the child or youth may escalate through a series of dysfunctional transactions with others and eventually develop into coercive patterns in some parenting contexts (Dishion & Patterson, 2006; Patterson, 1982). The way these early, more benign manifestations of problem behavior are responded to and acted upon by people in the child's immediate environment contribute to whether the behavior is likely to be repeated, cease, or worsen. A coercive cycle of family interaction is initiated when adolescents are reinforced for their disruptive behavior. Reinforcement can be both positive (rewards) or negative (avoidance of a negative condition), and common to both is that they increase the likelihood of a behavior being repeated. Reprimand or punishment (in the learning theory sense), decreases the likelihood of a behavior being repeated and is only effective if it, in fact, is experienced as a negative and if it outweighs the expected positive outcomes. Many parents may not be aware of the fact that their responses or lack thereof actually contribute to a worsening of a youth's problem behavior. For example, defiance becomes negatively reinforced and therefore likely to reoccur if it leads to withdrawal of parental commands. In other words, parents may contribute to deviant behavior in their adolescents by backing off when their request is met with angry outbursts of the youth (known as escape conditioning). As an illustration, consider a 14-year-old boy who says to his father that he wants to go to a party. The father, having suspicions about alcohol being served at the party, does not give his son permission to go. As a response, the young teenager throws a fit, starts yelling, and accuses his parents of bringing him up in a prison-like home. Experiencing his son's reactions as aversive and damaging to their relationship, the father gives in to his son's demands and lets him go to the party. There are at least three detrimental outcomes from such a scenario. First, the teenage boy will learn fairly quickly that opposition and aggression pay off. Second, the father's role as an authority figure is weakened. And third, the boy may be exposed to risk when he goes to the party (e.g., alcohol initiation, older adolescents). Additionally, parents may over time choose to stay clear of aggressive reactions by immediately giving in to their teenager's demands (Dishion & Patterson, 2006) and, with that, further expanding the youth's unhealthy reign.

Risk factors in school

Schools too play an important role in shaping adolescent behavior (Mayberry, Espelage, & Koenig, 2009). The climate and organization of the school affect its students. The elements that contribute to the school environment include teacher–student relations, rules, respect, care, and the importance placed on education. If, for example, the school takes on a lenient role regarding bullying, it simultaneously pushes the limit of what is considered acceptable behavior of its students. And expelling a disruptive student from the classroom for half an hour will likely not result in the desired behavior on the part of the youth if the student actually enjoys being outside and if the student is not taught alternative behaviors. Angry students might be particularly sensitive toward what they conceive as negative intentions and provocations from others, and this may create difficulties in contact and interactions with others. Anger and frustration hamper learning or practicing of skills and impact schoolwork in a negative way (Harden et al., 2001).

The interplay between the youth and the environment is bidirectional and transactional: positive school experiences on the part of the adolescent contribute to his or her healthy development, but positive school experiences are more likely to befall students who exhibit good behaviors in the first place. Moreover, schools often draw student populations from similar backgrounds, such that adolescents who live in disadvantaged communities frequently congregate in the same schools; as noted earlier, adolescents in disadvantaged neighborhoods often exhibit more behavioral and emotional problems. It is more demanding to establish a positive school environment in schools with a large proportion of students with many risks and problems. An unfavorable school environment is likely to have more detrimental effects on students who exhibit behavioral problems, and the disheartening circumstance is that these are the very students with the greatest need of positive environments. We discuss further the role of the school system as an arena for the development of youth mental health in Chapter 7.

Peer group transactions

A robust finding in the literature on the development of antisocial behavior in adolescence is that youths who affiliate with deviant peers are themselves much more likely to engage in antisocial or delinquent behavior. The phenomenon of peer similarity is due to both *selection* and *socialization*. Selection refers to youths' tendency to pick friends who are similar to themselves, and socialization reflects susceptibility to peer influence over time. Susceptibility to peer influence with regard to engagement in and tolerance of antisocial acts peaks at around age 14, followed by a steady decline as the youth reaches young adulthood (Monahan, Steinberg, & Cauffman, 2009). Both risk-taking and law-breaking behavior are more likely to take place in groups than when the teenager is by him- or herself. The decrease in peer influence is likely due to gains in behavioral autonomy and more advanced identity development in older adolescents and young adults (Collins & Steinberg, 2006).

Environmental risk factors

Environmental risk factors include poverty, family instability, multiple transitions, crime, and exposure to violence. These risk factors operate to a greater extent in meso- and macro-systems, but they nonetheless affect micro-system processes and the youth him- or herself. Adolescents who live in disorganized and dangerous communities tend to show more problems with emotion-based regulatory behaviors in part because the context may compel them to be more insecure, vigilant, and worried. If these contexts also include exposure to violence, youths may also be distrustful and develop an aggressive and confrontational stance. Adolescents living in danger may become fearful and, as Shields and Cicchetti (1998) write: "they may experience an exaggerated need to defend themselves" (p. 382). Some youths even find it risky to stop and think before acting in certain situations and acting on impulse may seem to them as a self-protecting strategy. But again, the negative effects of a youth's environment (such as neighborhood characteristics) can be mitigated. Many youths who live in violent and crime-ridden communities grow up in a healthy way. Supportive and structured parenting is likely a powerful buffer against mental health problems in these contexts.

From risk factors to causes

Even if risk-oriented approaches have proved to be promising, there are challenges to this approach. The list of potential risk factors is long, and it may be difficult to determine the relative risk of each factor. The causal relationships between risk factors and antisocial behavior were therefore the topic of an article by Jaffee, Strait, and Odgers (2012) in which they evaluated which risk factors had repeatedly been identified and likely to be related to antisocial behavior. First, research indicated that there were reciprocal influences between harsh parenting with excessive and hard limit setting and antisocial behavior in children. Second, research suggests that abuse is a cause of antisocial behavior, even if a limitation of the studies considered is that none involved documented cases of child abuse. Third, an abundance of literature shows that children of divorced parents have an increased incidence of antisocial behavior, and a number of research designs converge in demonstrating that divorce or family breakup cause an increased risk of antisocial behavior. Fourth, even if children clearly inherit a genetic vulnerability to depression, maternal depression is also an environmentally mediated causal factor for children's behavioral problems. Fifth, there are strong indications of a high degree of heredity for all behaviors within the externalizing spectrum, and parents' antisocial behavior and drug use tend to follow families. Most research indicates that the transmission of problem behavior is both genetic and environmentally mediated. Sixth, some studies show that adolescents who join gangs are more antisocial than those who do not and that problem behavior increases after joining the gang. Both social selection and social influencing seem to operate in the context of gang membership and antisocial behavior. And last but not least, social background risk factors have been shown to predict antisocial behavior regardless of individual and family factors. Included among these are neighborhoods characterized by poverty, and low levels of collective efficacy. A challenge to drawing causal conclusions is unobserved heterogeneity: poor families and non-poor families may differ in ways that not only explain their situation, but also their children's antisocial behavior (Jaffee, Strait, & Odgers, 2012). There are challenges to observational studies of risk factors for antisocial behavior. First, the connection between a risk factor and antisocial behavior may be influenced by a third variable or set of variables. Mothers who smoke during pregnancy may be distinguished from non-smokers in several ways, such as having an antisocial history, less education, lower income, and all of these factors can explain the child's antisocial behavior (Wakschlag et al., 2003). Second, there may be a reversed causal link. Spanking a child can make him or her aggressive and disobedient, but children who are already difficult to raise can also trigger physical punishment from their parents. Third, children tend to choose environments that are congruent with their abilities and behaviors: sensation-seeking children tend to choose friends who also seek excitement. Fourth, a risk factor can come from a variable which is correlated to, but not caused by, the risk factor leading to incorrect inference about causation. Smoking during pregnancy often occurs with alcohol use and poor diet, both of which can be a cause of antisocial behavior.

Prevention of externalizing problem behavior

Adolescent problem behavior may be prevented by interventions in childhood and the preteen years. A systematic review indicated that early family/parent training was an effective intervention for reducing behavior problems among young children and supported the continued use of such training to prevent antisocial behavior and delinquency (Piquero, Farrington, Welsh, Tremblay, & Jennings, 2008; see also Barnes, 2010). Among the early intervention programs are The Incredible Years (Webster-Stratton, 1992; Webster-Stratton & Reid, 2017), Triple P. (Sanders, 2008; Sanders, Markie-Dadds, Tully, & Bor, 2000), and the Nurse Home Visiting program (Miller, 2015). For children aged 4–12 years, the Oregon model of Parent Management Training is among the empirically supported and well-established programs (Eyberg, Nelson, & Boggs, 2008; McCart & Sheidow, 2016). School-based prevention and intervention programs have also produced promising outcomes from middle childhood and may be categorized into three broad groups: (1) programs to enhance social competence and social problem-solving; (2) programs that target the reduction of aggressive behavior or promote self-control and anger management (e.g., The Good Behavior Game), Lochman's anger-coping program (Lochman & Wells, 2004), and Aggression Replacement Training (ART; Goldstein, 1999); and (3) programs to reduce bullying (Olweus & Limber, 1999). Moreover, universal prevention strategies in adolescence may include media campaigns that reduce youth engagement in problem behavior or other efforts to modify the community environment through laws and regulations that reduce opportunities to engage in problem behaviors (Biglan, Brennan, Foster, & Holder, 2004).

Treatment approaches

We start the treatment section by describing parent management training which comes in several forms and programs (Barth & Liggett-Creel, 2014; Scott, 2008). Although parenting programs primarily target children who are 12 years old or younger, it is highly relevant to describe interventions into the coercive family process in adolescent families as well. One example is the Oregon model of Parent Management Training (PMTO®) that was tested with promising outcomes for chronically offending delinquents and their caregivers (Bank, Marlowe, Reid, Patterson, & Weinrott, 1991). The parenting principles of the PMTO® are also central to the widely disseminated programs Family Check-Up (Dishion & Stormshak, 2007) and TFCO (Chamberlain, 1994; see also Gardner, Burton, & Klimes, 2006 and Gardner, Hutchings, Bywater, & Whitaker, 2010).

Parent Management Training: the Oregon model

The Oregon Parent Management Training (PMTO®) was developed by Gerald Patterson, Marion Forgatch, and their colleagues at the Oregon Social Learning Center (OSLC) to train parents to change their preadolescent child's antisocial behavior in the home (Forgatch, 1994; Forgatch, Patterson, & Gewirtz, 2013; Patterson, 1982; Patterson, Reid, & Dishion, 1992). Reviews of evidence-based psychosocial intervention programs have documented that Parent Management Training, which delivers treatment directly to the parents, is one of the most promising approaches for children with conduct problems (e.g., Kazdin, 1997).

During PMTO® treatment, parents learn to change dysfunctional strategies that are non-contingent or contingent for the wrong behaviors through: (1) increased use of positive teaching strategies for pro-social behavior (e.g., compliance and cooperation); and (2) contingent use of mild negative consequences for deviant behavior, usually in the form of removal of privileges (response cost) or with the use of "time-out." The aim of PMTO® is to enhance five central parenting skills: limit setting/discipline; monitoring/supervision; problem-solving; positive involvement; and skill encouragement.

- Effective *discipline and limit setting* discourage deviant behavior through the appropriate and contingent use of mild sanctions (Patterson, 1986) and they provide the child with clear boundaries for acceptable behavior.
- *Monitoring* protects youngsters from involvement in risky activities and it reflects parental tracking of children's whereabouts (Patterson & Forgatch, 2005).
- *Problem-solving* helps family members negotiate disagreements, establish house rules, and specify consequences for following or violating rules (Patterson & Forgatch, 2005).
- *Positive involvement* reflects how parents demonstrate interest in, attention to, and care for their child (Forgatch & DeGarmo, 1999).
- *Skill encouragement* promotes competence through positive contingencies (Forgatch & DeGarmo, 1999).

Whilst all parenting dimensions are central to improving child functioning, discipline and monitoring seem to be particularly important in preventing behavioral problems in children with externalizing problems (Amlund Hagen & Ogden, 2016; Patterson, Reid, & Dishion, 1992).

A CASE DESCRIPTION OF PARENT MANAGEMENT TRAINING: THE OREGON MODEL

Lars is an 11-year-old boy. He is a bright boy and good at sports. Still, many adults find his behavior rather challenging. He has a quick temper, can be restless, inattentive, and aggressive. He often disturbs other pupils, gets into fights during breaks, and can be verbally aggressive toward the teacher when corrected or confronted with his rule violations. He seeks contact with older boys and has been involved in some minor vandalism of the school property. Lars lives with his mother, Karen, an older sister, and a younger brother. The father left the family 2 years ago. Karen developed depression after her husband moved out. The family receives welfare. Karen feels rather isolated but has some support from her sister. At home, Lars often argues and comes into conflict with his mother and older sister. Mostly he is verbally aggressive, but there have been incidents where he has hit his mother. Afterwards, he withdraws and seems sad, and Karen thinks he is longing for his dad. Another problem is that Lars does not come home when the school day ends. Karen worries a lot and is afraid that Lars can get into serious trouble because he is so impulsive.

Referral

The school has, in cooperation with Karen, contacted the Child Welfare Services. In conclusion, they offered Karen PMTO®, based on her difficulty in disciplining and monitoring Lars' behavior. As part of the treatment planning, Karen and Lars were observed in a structured family task to identify resources and challenges in their interaction. In the initial interview, the mother completed some standardized forms and the therapist collected background information. The therapist also inquired about Karen's hopes for the treatment.

Treatment structure

During the PMTO® treatment, Karen met weekly for approximately 1-hour sessions, in which she was introduced to specific topics in a structured sequence. She met with her therapist for approximately 20 sessions. The sessions followed a structured agenda with introduction of a topic, followed by skill training through modeling, practicing, and receiving feedback and reflections to match the parental skills to the needs of her family. Each session ended with a practical home assignment with written material to support Karen's practicing at home. In addition, the therapist gave her midweek calls to follow up on any challenges related to the assignment. In the following session, the therapist and Karen would troubleshoot the home assignment and evaluate if any further adaptations were necessary. The amount of time used on each topic was matched to the needs of the family. Lars participated in sessions when the mother or the therapist saw the need for it.

Therapeutic process

Karen struggled with depression and low self-esteem as a parent. To motivate for change, the therapist created a working alliance by focusing on strengths, and by being supportive and empathetic. In role-plays the therapist modeled different solutions and involved Karen in brief step-by-step exercises. In debriefs after the exercises, the feedback was focused on strengths, Karen's reflections, and on further instructions.

Training content

The core parent components in PMTO® are *positive involvement* through communication, mutual activities and praise, systematic use of *encouragement* for pro-social behavior, *mild negative sanctions* for rule violation and aggression, *monitoring*, and *problem-solving*.

Treatment sequence

The first topic introduced was giving good directions. The therapist connected the information that Lars often disobeyed rules and was verbally aggressive when corrected with the relevance of working with compliance. Through role-play, the therapist demonstrated how to communicate in a clear and respectful way to facilitate Lars' motivation to comply. Karen was then encouraged to exercise the skill in the sessions. The session ended with a home assignment in which Karen was going to practice the skill with Lars, and to track and evaluate both her own directions and Lars' response.

The next topic was to strengthen positive involvement by using praise for pro-social behavior and identifying activities that Karen and Lars could do together. For a kid with these kinds of problems, at this age, praise is seldom enough to change behavior, so Karen's next home assignment was to find daily rewards that could be used in an incentive chart. The rewards could be material or parent–child activities that strengthened positive involvement with Lars, for example preparing a meal together. The third topic in this case was to make an incentive chart for walking straight home from school and bringing home the necessary materials for doing homework. Such an incentive chart had several gains, such as teaching Lars to comply with an agreement, be better prepared for the next day at school, and to keep him off the street and away from negative peers.

When Karen was able to give Lars more positive feedback and rewards for complying with family rules, the therapist introduced the topic of negative sanctions. Karen learned how to use mild, predictable consequences such as time-out and time-restricted privilege removal when Lars disobeyed or was aggressive, and how to use work chores for rule violation. For physical aggression, there was no tolerance and would result in Lars receiving small fines. Karen also learned how to regulate negative emotions to prevent coercive interaction in conflict situations with Lars. Lars learned that he could choose between complying or receiving a mild negative sanction. The home assignment was to find a safe place for time-out, suitable privileges that could be removed and to explain the negative sanctions to Lars, and then to start using the different procedures. The therapist also addressed how Karen could improve collaboration with the teacher. The therapist also advised the teacher in how to use more structured incentive systems and monitoring during the school day.

Outcomes

During treatment, Karen gradually improved her self-esteem and experienced that she was able to influence the family situation. Lars was less aggressive and sad at home, and the teacher reported that he was adapting better at school.

Implementation of PMTO® in Norway

PMTO® was, for several decades, only applied for research purposes, and there were few training opportunities for practitioners to learn the intervention (Kazdin, 1997). The first regular practitioner training program of PMTO® was therefore developed in Norway as a collaborative enterprise between the program developers Forgatch and Patterson and a national implementation team (Ogden, Forgatch, Askeland, Patterson, & Bullock, 2005). The training program included the PMTO® handbook, based on Patterson's social interaction and coercion model, and protocols from previous OSLC clinical trials (Forgatch, 1994). Forgatch and her colleagues at the OSLC provided an extensive 18-month training program for Norwegian trainees, resulting in the certification of 30 candidates from all health regions of Norway. This first generation of certified PMTO® therapists was central in the process of training, coaching, and supervising the next generations of therapists. By 2017, approximately 500 PMTO® therapists have been trained and certified in Norway, of whom 320 are still active. According to the national registry (www.pmto.no), 1,400 interventions were initiated or were completed in 2016. Even if this may seem to be an impressive number of cases in a small country with five million inhabitants, it is only a small fraction of all counseling interventions offered to children and families. Most children and families are not offered structured and knowledge-based interventions by the child welfare and child mental health services.

Currently, the Norwegian implementation team provides training, regular supervision, training protocols, and additional materials and technical support (Ogden & Amlund Hagen, 2012).

Empirical support

When PMTO® was first transferred to Norway, an RCT was conducted with 112 children aged 3–12 years and their parents. The participants were recruited through regular child welfare and child mental health services (Ogden & Amlund Hagen, 2008). Parents who received PMTO®, over a mean number of 26 sessions, reported fewer externalizing behavior problems in their children, and the children's teachers reported a higher level of social competence at post-assessment compared to the children who had received regular services. Parents in the PMTO® group were also more competent in limit setting for their children according to coded observations of video recordings performed by trained coders. PMTO® was particularly effective in the treatment of problem behavior in children aged 8 years or younger. Results also suggested that treatment condition (being in the PMTO® group) predicted compliance, fewer negative interactions initiated by the children, and less externalizing problem behavior via the effects of competent limit setting by parents. The evaluation of the families' satisfaction with the treatment showed that 77 percent of the parents in the PMTO® group would recommend the treatment to others who might need it, compared to 38 percent of the comparison families. In the follow-up study, 1 year after termination of treatment, findings indicated that two-parent families in PMTO® showed greater reduction in aversive behavior compared to their regular services counterparts (Amlund Hagen, Ogden, & Bjørnebekk, 2011). At follow-up, PMTO® children were also rated by their teachers as having fewer problem behaviors and greater social competence relative to the children in the comparison group. Moreover, PMTO® parents reported increases in family cohesion compared to parents in the comparison group. When parents managed to avoid coercive cycles and responded with contingent consequences for acting-out behavior, children learned that their aggression and defiance did not pay off. Moreover, when parents were able to prevent unwanted behavior, they were also in a better position to encourage their children's competencies. The discipline model supported such a chain of effects. The results implicated effective discipline as a potent parenting dimension and replicated results from other studies that have also demonstrated the importance of effective discipline (Patterson, 2005). Even if the overall effectiveness of PMTO® a year after treatment termination was modest, the results nevertheless indicated that helping parents use effective disciplinary skills and supporting families in developing a sense of connectedness and cohesion may be particularly important in the therapeutic setting (Amlund Hagen, Ogden, & Bjørnebekk, 2011).

Adapted version of PMTO®: Early Interventions for Children at Risk

The Early Interventions for Children at Risk program was designed to help parents in coercive families as early as possible, but who could manage with shorter interventions than full-scale PMTO® (Solholm, Kjøbli, & Christiansen, 2013). It has now been implemented in a variety of primary care settings in Norway. The intervention has a low threshold for intake, fewer sessions with lower intensity, and shorter duration than full-scale PMTO®. By 2015, 1,117 trained practitioners were active in 100 municipalities (out of 430) that implemented one or more of the modules. The adapted programs significantly outperformed usual care, although effect sizes were modest at post-treatment assessment with a mean of .15 for PMTO® (Weisz et al., 2013).

The new generation of adapted interventions demonstrated larger effect sizes than the clinical trials of PMTO®. The Brief Parent Training study demonstrated a mean effect size (ES) of 0.37 (Kjøbli & Ogden, 2012) and 0.31 at follow-up (Kjøbli & Bjørnebekk, 2013). The PMTO® parent group training had a mean ES of 0.37 at post-assessment and 0.39 at 6 months' follow-up (Kjøbli, Hukkelberg, & Ogden, 2013).

Overall, PMTO® principles and components were successfully transferred from the US to real-world health and welfare services in Norway with positive outcomes and maintenance of competent adherence. PMTO® and Early Interventions for Children at Risk have been tested with positive outcomes in both individual and group treatment settings and in high and low dosages of treatment (e.g., Brief Parent Training). Moreover, gender differences, differences between ethnic minority and majority groups (Bjørknes & Manger, 2013), and children with and without ADHD diagnoses were compared (Bjørnebekk, Kjøbli, & Ogden, 2015). Across all these studies, parent-rated improvements in children's behavior were reported, but the lack of improvement in child problem behaviors reported by teachers in most of the studies remains a challenge (Ogden, Askeland, Christensen, Christiansen, & Kjøbli, 2017).

Adolescent treatment

For youths whose delinquent behavior starts in puberty, family- and community-based treatments that also involve the youth him- or herself seem to be the most beneficial. Interventions typically fall into one of two categories: (1) a parent- and system-focused intervention, including parent training and MST; and (2) youth-focused interventions such as cognitive behavioral therapy. In the remaining part of this chapter, we present empirically supported family, school, and community interventions targeting adolescents, such as Functional Family Therapy (FFT; Alexander & Parsons, 1982), MST (Henggeler et al., 2009), and MTFC (Chamberlain, 1994). These are all programs we, as clinical researchers, have been involved in.

Multisystemic Therapy

Multisystemic Therapy (MST) is a family- and community-based program for adolescents aged 12–18 years with serious behavioral problems and their families (Henggeler et al., 2009). MST focuses on strengthening parenting practices and helping parents to interact with their teenagers in a predictable and explicit manner. The main aim of MST is to prevent further criminal activity and other antisocial acts, and to prevent placements out of home. The program has explicit intake criteria that give priority to adolescents with serious behavior problems such as criminality and drug use. The assessment as well as the treatment focus on both risk factors *and* resources at the individual, family, peer, school, and community level. MST intervenes by using the family as a starting point and delivers treatment in a highly individualized and comprehensive manner by addressing identified predictors of the adolescent's antisocial behavior, sources of conflict within their family, and their functioning in school (Elliott, 1998; Huey et al., 2000). The treatment requires that at least one central caregiver is willing to participate in the treatment, but successful treatment is also dependent on a well-functioning collaboration with the school or local services, including child welfare and/or mental health services. The theoretical foundation of MST is summed up in nine treatment principles (www.mstservices.com):

1. Finding the fit: understanding the "fit" between the youth's problems and how they interact with and are maintained by the context.
2. Focusing on positives and strengths: efforts are made to identify and build on the strengths in the youth's life, emphasizing protective factors and giving hope.
3. Increasing responsibility: the treatment seeks to promote responsible behavior in the family.
4. MST is focused on the here and now, it is action-oriented and well-defined: MST deals with what is happening in the adolescent's life now, targets specific and well-defined problems rather than focusing on past events and problems.
5. Targeting sequences: during treatment, sequenced interactions that contribute to the problem behavior are identified and targeted.
6. Developmentally appropriate: MST is age and development sensitive, seeking to find a fit between the maturity level of the youth and the environment and learning skills necessary to eventually make the transition to adulthood.
7. Continuous effort: treatment requires ongoing effort by the youth and his or her family members and it is intensive and multifaceted so as to ensure rapid problem resolution, earlier identification of when interventions need fine-tuning, and continuous evaluation of outcomes.
8. Evaluation and accountability: therapeutic gains are continuously evaluated and the MST team members are held accountable for securing good outcomes.
9. Generalization: a goal in MST is to empower families to be able to address the family needs after the treatment period is over.

The treatment model

The therapy aims to increase the empowerment of the caregivers and their capacity for problem-solving. The overarching therapeutic goals are to increase cohesion and care in the family, reduce the youth's contact with antisocial peers, increase pro-social contacts, improve attendance and achievements in school or at work, and to increase participation in pro-social leisure activities. Parents are encouraged to monitor their adolescent's activities, to establish clear rules and expectations in the home, and to implement consistent consequences for behavioral transgressions. First, the treatment takes place in the adolescent's home environment, in the family, at school, and in the local community. Second, it is a short-term treatment, which typically lasts from three to 6 months per family. Third, the therapeutic work is carried out by teams of three to four therapists, each being responsible for three to six families. Fourth, the therapist is available for the family 24 hours a day, 7 days a week and is in contact with the family on a daily basis, face to face, or by telephone. Depending on the age of the youth, great efforts are made to have the youth attend school or work on a regular basis. Outside of the family, the school is the most important arena for learning social skills and developing social competence. When possible, the adolescent should attend a regular class in a regular school where he or she can observe and interact with peers who are pro-social role models. The parents are responsible for communicating with the school, but with the support of the MST therapist who establishes an initial contact with the school staff. However, it is the caregivers rather than the MST therapists who are responsible for collaboration with the school and who should monitor, encourage, and support the young person's school achievement and homework. Parents are advised to show engagement in schooling by frequent and constructive communication with the teachers.

Measures are taken to motivate and engage the youth in the therapy, and positive behavioral changes are central to the assessment of treatment progress. The therapy is terminated when the treatment goals are achieved, and it is expected that the family and their social network have been empowered to solve additional problems on their own. There is no regular aftercare in MST, but the adolescents and their families are monitored on a regular basis by the team after 6, 12, and 18 months to check whether treatment outcomes are sustained.

From 2015, the Contingency Manual was implemented in Norway as an integral part of MST for adolescents with drug problems. Contingency Management (CM) is a family- and community-based drug treatment built on behavioral and cognitive behavioral therapeutic principles. As with other MST interventions, close collaboration with the family and others in the youth's natural environment is required to produce positive outcomes and enduring changes. CM consists of the following key elements:

- comprehensive and intensive assessment of drug abuse,
- drug testing by parents and a functional analysis of drug abuse,
- identification of triggers for drug use,
- development and continuous evaluation of plan for coping with drug problems,
- a points system for reward for substance abstinence, and
- generalization plans and plans for what to do in case of relapse.

A CASE DESCRIPTION OF MULTISYSTEMIC THERAPY

Peter was 15 years old when he was referred to MST because of criminal acts, drug abuse, verbal and physical aggression, particularly toward his stepfather, being out at nights, and truancy. The police had caught Peter four times for possession of hash, car thefts, and driving under the influence of drugs, and some of these incidents occurred when Peter was out all night. The Child Welfare Services had previously received a message of concern from the school about excessive absence and repeated expulsions from school because of fighting and violence toward peer students. He risked being thrown out of school and, because he had abused drugs, he risked being placed at an institution for adolescents with drug problems. He used to live with his biological father, who is now in prison, but for the last 3 years he has been living with his mother and stepfather. His mother and stepfather are concerned about his future, but they are now on the brink of giving up. Having tried everything, they are considering accepting placement in an institution. They are willing, however, to give MST a chance.

The assessment phase and overarching goals

In the first two to three weeks of the treatment, the MST therapist met frequently with the family and other key persons from the extended family and the school to gain an overview and adequate understanding of the case. Included in the assessment is a detailed baseline description of the frequency, intensity, and range of Peter's conduct problems. Key persons are contacted in the process of systematically assessing risk and protective factors in the ecology of the youth and to identify strengths that may be used in the treatment process. In addition to Peter, other informants were his mother, stepfather, grandmother, uncle, and the headmaster and a teacher at his local school. The assessment phase was concluded by the joint formulation of overarching goals for the treatment formulated by the therapist and the family. These goals were: (1) Peter will be drug-free, evidenced by clean drug tests for 10 weeks, and positive reports from parents, school, and police; (2) Peter will abide by the law, evidenced by reports from mother, stepfather, and the police; (3) Peter will stop using physical violence at home and at school, evidenced by reports from parents and the school; (4) he will get home on time, as agreed by his parents, and as evidenced by reports from mother and stepfather; and (5) Peter will attend school every day, participate in lessons, and do the tasks as required, as evidenced by reports from parents and the school.

Engagement and treatment alliance

Central to the first treatment phase was the process of creating engagement and establishing a good treatment alliance with the family and other key persons. The treatment sessions would typically take place in in the family home, and the therapist met with parents who were tired and about to give up. In order to increase responsiveness and establish a good working alliance, the therapist had flexible working hours and was able to meet with the family at convenient times. Moreover, the therapist and the MST team were available for the family 24 hours a day, 7 days a week to accommodate the family's needs and create stable conditions for treatment. Moreover, the formulation of overarching goals also contributed to engagement and alliance by taking the family input seriously and signaling hope for change.

Security

There were reports of high levels of family conflict and occasional physical attacks, particularly between Peter and his stepfather. As a standard procedure, a safety plan was established that contained information about how each family member should act and who they should contact in situations involving a danger of escalation of conflicts and violent behavior. In this case, support from the uncle was important to ensure safety in the process of changing family interactions.

The analytic process

The persons involved in the treatment analyzed the problems in ways that matched the complexity of the case, and to make the situation manageable. Since all key stakeholders were worried about Peter's drug use, this problem was prioritized early in the treatment. To determine the severity of drug use and the need for treatment, a thorough assessment of the type of drugs, amount, and frequency of use was carried out in addition to assessing the consequences of the drug use before adding the CM protocol to the MST. In order to illustrate this process, the information in Peter's case is included in a "fit-circle" that shows potential multifactorial drivers behind the problem behavior. In addition, sequencing analyses of incidences of drug abuse were made to identify important triggers and patterns that lead to drug use. The fit-circle may be used to analyze and develop interventions pertaining to the identified problem behavior.

The fact that Peter, who was 15 years old, ran away from home, stayed out at nights without supervision, and committed criminal acts represented a great risk for his further development. Lack of monitoring and supervision from the parents were characteristic of most of Peter's behavior patterns and therefore became central to the treatment, and also an important prerequisite for sufficient involvement and motivation for CM. Based on the fit-circle drawn by the therapist and the parents, as shown in Figure 3.1 below, this is where treatment started.

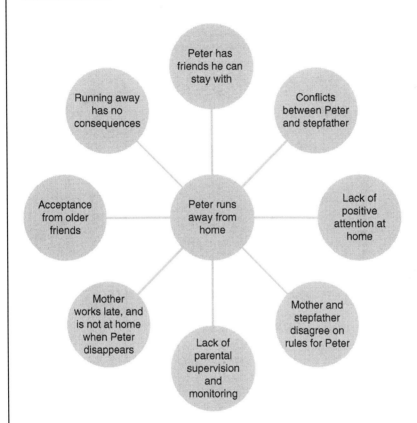

FIGURE 3.1 A fit-circle of multifactorial drivers behind problem behavior.

Intermediate goals and intervention plans

All risk factors that were identified in the fit-circle were important to understand the problem, but some factors were more malleable than others in the short term. The next step in the treatment was a family decision on which factors to prioritize. In this case, it was decided to focus on those the parents could modify, and that had the potential for reducing criminal acts, substance abuse, antisocial contacts, and conflicts at home. Central to this case were: conflicts between Peter and stepfather; little positive attention at home; parental disagreement on rules; lack of monitoring; and lack of consequences for running away—each of these were addressed in the treatment plan. Each of the factors required additional analyses (second-order analyses) to develop interventions that reflected the nine MST treatment principles (Henggeler et al., 2009). Relevant intermediate goals were that:

1. The parents collect information on where Peter stays and who he is spending time with when he runs away and stays out at night.
2. The parents agree on what time Peter should be in at night, and make a plan for what they will do if he does not comply.
3. The parents focus on positive things that Peter does and make plans for a pleasant activity next week.

This was an important prerequisite before initiating drug treatment (CM) and, since drug abuse was an important driver in other analyses, the hypothesis was that positive results could cause important ripple effects in relation to other problem behaviors. A further specification of what should be done, by whom, when, and how is also part of the family treatment plan. Another important prerequisite for success with CM were ideas about how to engage and include Peter in the treatment.

The CM manual contains many elements that may help create a good working alliance with the youth. Among these is openness about substance abuse, focusing on the youth's coping, assessment of his interests, wishes, dreams, and potential rewards on the road to abstinence. The "here-and-now" focus and well-planned strategies to avoid drug abuse (in cooperation with the youth) increase the likelihood of motivation for change. Involvement of parents and other key people is also very important in order to support behavioral changes. Objective measures for substance abuse and immediate consequences on clean/unclean tests are also key elements in CM. Therefore, parents are taught how to take drug tests and interpret the results so that positive or negative consequences could be given immediately after the test results were clear. Negative consequences of unclean tests included the loss of benefits (response cost) and that points in the reward system could not be earned before the next clean test was delivered. An important part of Peter's reward system was earning money for a moped and taking driving lessons with his stepfather. The analytic process is an ongoing part of the treatment, and the therapist must continually assess the outcomes of the interventions, including potential barriers and facilitators of change. As is evident from the fit-circle illustration, several potential risk factors may be targeted in the treatment. All factors may be addressed by interventions targeting Peter, the family system, and the school. According to the complexity of the situation, interventions will probably have to address several factors simultaneously in order to have an impact. The analytic process contributed to increasing the family's problem-solving skills and, hence, the likelihood of maintenance and generalization of positive treatment outcomes. Interventions to improve the emotional climate of the family, school attendance and work-efforts at school, clear agreements about when to come home at nights, and the change of friends all contributed to the improvement of Peter's situation and to long-term positive outcomes.

Research on Multisystemic Therapy

Numerous trials of Multisystemic Therapy (MST) have been conducted in the US with various samples of adolescents including aggressive youths, drug-using adolescents, delinquent youths, and violent offending juveniles (Curtis, Ronan, & Borduin, 2004). MST has been shown to produce favorable outcomes in many of these trials, including improving adjustment problems post-treatment and preventing future criminal behavior in a 4-year follow-up (Borduin et al., 1995), reducing engagement in aggressive criminal activity, and higher rates of marijuana abstinence (Henggeler, Pickrel, & Brondino, 1999). In a 14-year follow-up of MST, Schaeffer and Borduin (2005) reported that MST was more effective in lowering recidivism rates, arrest rates, and days in confinement in adult detention than was individual therapy. Recent outcome studies have been conducted in England (Butler, Baruch, Hickley, & Fonagy, 2011) and New Zealand (Curtis, Ronan, Heiblum, & Crellin, 2009). MST was also tested in Sweden but, there, the program was not found to outperform regular services (Sundell et al., 2008). A recent RCT study of MST in the UK (N = 108) compared MST to an equally comprehensive management protocol (Butler et al., 2011). Adolescents in both the MST and the comparison group showed reduced offending, but the MST youth also demonstrated a reduced likelihood of nonviolent offending during an 18-month follow-up period. Parent and youth reports further showed significantly greater reductions of aggressive and delinquent behaviors in the MST group. The study also demonstrated some delayed impact on offending. A recent multi-level meta-analysis of 22 MST studies with 4,066 participating adolescents was conducted to examine the effectiveness of MST (Van der Stouwe, Asscher, Stams, Deković, & van der Laan, 2014). Small but significant treatment effects were found on delinquency (primary outcome) and psychopathology, substance use, family factors, out-of-home placement, and peer factors. No significant treatment effect was found for skills and cognitions. MST seems most effective with adolescents under the age of 15, with severe behavior problems at intake. Furthermore, the effectiveness of MST for older juveniles may be improved when treatment is focused more on peer relationships and risks and protective factors in the school domain (van der Stouwe et al., 2014).

Implementation of Multisystemic Therapy

MST has been implemented throughout the US and in 14 other countries including Canada and Australia. Norway was the first country in Europe to implement

MST (Ogden & Amlund Hagen, 2012), and Sweden, Denmark, the Netherlands, Switzerland, Belgium, Iceland, Scotland, and England followed. In 2012, more than 500 teams have been established worldwide and more than 23,000 adolescents are treated annually (www.mstservices.com). MST has been endorsed by Blueprints for Violence Prevention, Office of the Surgeon General, the Coalition for Evidence-Based Policy, and SAMHSA's National Registry of Evidence-Based Programs and Practices. In Norway, MST was first introduced in 1999 and implemented nation-wide with 25 teams in child welfare services across the country (Ogden et al., 2008). The implementation of the therapy protocol and the treatment outcomes of the youths and their families have been continually documented by a vigorous research program. A pre post-effectiveness trial was first conducted, in which adolescents aged 12–17 years with serious behavior problems were randomly assigned to MST or regular child welfare services (RS; Ogden & Halliday-Boykins, 2004). Results showed that MST was more effective than usual treatment at preventing out-of-home placement, reducing youth behavior problems, and increasing youth social competence. MST families were also more satisfied with treatment than their RS counterparts. A follow-up study of the participants demonstrated that MST was capable of maintaining favorable effects on behavior problems in adolescents at three of the four sites, 2 years after intake (Ogden & Amlund Hagen, 2006). Compared to youths receiving regular interventions from the Child Welfare Services, MST participants scored significantly lower on multi-informant assessments of external-izing and internalizing behaviors and of delinquency at follow-up. Moreover, MST families were able to keep their adolescents at home to a greater extent than were families who received regular services. Next, an examination of program sustain-ability in its second year of operation was conducted (Ogden, Amlund Hagen, & Andersen, 2007). The goal of the study was to examine whether the favorable effects seen in MST youths during the program's initial phase were matched in later cohorts of adolescents receiving MST. The MST clinical outcomes in the second year of program operation matched and, for key indices of antisocial behavior, surpassed those outcomes achieved during the first year. Together, these results demonstrated sustained effectiveness of the program and indicated program maturation effects. MST youths treated in the second year were significantly younger than those referred to treatment in the first year, but age had no moderating effect on the outcomes.

Ogden and Amlund Hagen (2009) also examined gender differences in intake characteristics and treatment outcomes of MST. Because MST was originally developed to alleviate problem behaviors in boys, the goal of the study was to observe whether girls with behavioral problems benefited equally well from the MST program. Results suggested that girls were more likely to be referred to MST because of statutory offenses and drug use, whereas boys were more likely to be referred because of criminal offenses and domestic violence. There were no gender differences, however, in the rate of co-occurring problems (e.g., scoring high on both externalizing, internalizing, and attention problems), but the results suggested that co-occurring problems were the rule rather than the exception. Girls were rated by their parents as presenting fewer externalizing problems than boys at post-treatment, after controlling for their pretreatment scores, but girls rated themselves as having significantly more internalizing problems than did boys at post-assessment. Boys, however, scored significantly higher on the self-report delinquency scale than did girls. There were no gender differences in teacher-rated problems, though decreases were observed in both groups from pre- to post-treatment assessments. Also, there were no gender differences in family cohesion as rated by the youth him- or herself and a parent, though both groups reported slight increases from pre- to post-treatment assessment (Ogden & Amlund Hagen, 2009). Finally, Ogden et al. (2012a) compared implementation profiles of MST and PMTO® based on therapist, supervisor, and leadership reports 10 years after the nationwide dissemination in Norway and concluded that:

> The present study indicates that the strong focus on implementation in MST and PMTO has paid off 10 years after the programs were introduced in Norway by revealing a strong and ongoing presence within agencies, and a relatively long median lifespan of program practitioners. Several incentives for program sustainability, therapist engagement, and treatment fidelity were acknowledged by the respondents in their evaluations of the implementation components.
>
> *(p. 10)*

A somewhat related approach to the treatment of adolescent antisocial behavior is FFT. Chronologically, FFT is the oldest structured treatment program targeting externalizing behavior problems in teenagers, introduced in 1973. There are several similarities between MST and FFT, but also some important differences that make the programs complementary, rather than overlapping or competing.

Functional Family Therapy

Functional Family Therapy (FFT) was developed as a prevention program for families with adolescents aged 10–18 years at risk of delinquency and antisocial behavior (Alexander & Parsons, 1973, 1982). FFT is a short-term treatment with an average of 12 sessions conducted over three to four months. Services are conducted in both clinic and home settings and can also be delivered in schools, outpatient clinics, child welfare, and mental health facilities. FFT is a strength-based and relationally focused model with a focus on and assessment of those risk and protective factors that affect the adolescent and his or her environment. The program uses a multistep approach and relationships within the family are the main focus of FFT. The therapy aims to help family members shift their attention from focusing solely on the problem behavior of the youth and toward a mutual understanding of family processes and constructive problem-solving within the family. This will constitute a change in behavioral patterns for each family member—not only the youth. A core component of FFT is that the skills introduced in the family shall be tailored to the relational dynamics (degree of relational closeness and hierarchy) of each relationship dyad.

The five treatment phases of FFT following the pretreatment period are: (1) engagement, (2) motivation, (3) relational assessment, (4) behavior change, and (5) generalization. During the *engagement phase*, the focus is to ensure treatment participation from all family members. The therapist seeks to do this through establishing him- or herself as a credible helper, maintain a positive climate between the parents and the youth, and build alliance through identifying strengths within the family and seeing the family as an entity. During the *motivation phase*, emphasis is placed on giving parents and adolescents hope and assurance that change is possible. The therapist builds on the strengths and protective factors already present in the family and also helps family members to reinterpret the behavior and intentions of the other family members, assisting them to avoid placing blame. When all members of the family are "on board" with a relational understanding of their situation and each has expressed hopefulness and willingness to make changes, the goals of the engagement/motivation phases have been reached (Mørkrid & Christensen, 2007). During the motivation phase of FFT, the therapist is simultaneously engaging in the *relational assessment phase* of FFT. Whilst working on creating motivation and hope, the therapist is gathering information about the family's risk and protective factors and skill deficiencies that lead to the reoccurrence of problematic interactions. Together with an assessment of the relational dynamics/functions in the family dyads, this information is used by the therapist to develop a plan for the next treatment phase. In the *behavior change phase*, families are assisted in engaging in measures that will help them sidestep coercive interactions that have worked to maintain and reinforce negativity and hostile exchanges. Dysfunctional interactions, poor communication, and inappropriate parenting practices are identified and efforts are made to change these. When the family is able to make use of new communication, conflict management, problem-solving and parenting skills in the home, and when there is a significant reduction in the interactions characterized by fighting and/or disapproval, the second goal of the therapy is considered to have been reached. During the last part of the therapy, the *generalization phase*, the focus is on how families can maintain their skills and problem-solving abilities on their own and in new situations and settings outside the home. The last goal of the therapy has been reached when families have acquired new and positive ways of interacting with each other, have the ability to identify and mobilize support systems within and external to the family, and are able to make use of constructive problem-solving skills in general. To reach this objective, it is important that the family demonstrates the ability to overcome problems and disagreements (about school, curfew, truancy, friends, etc.) when they arise and that the family has the skills to interact in a constructive and consistent manner so that they reach an agreement together.

FFT is listed in the Blueprint for Violence Prevention and is one of four programs named by the US Surgeon General as a model program for seriously delinquent youth. It has been implemented throughout the US, in Canada, England, Norway, New Zealand, Denmark, Ireland, Scotland, the Netherlands, Sweden, Singapore, and most recently Australia.

A CASE DESCRIPTION OF FUNCTIONAL FAMILY THERAPY

Simon is a 14-year-old boy who was referred to Functional Family Therapy (FFT) for truancy, shoplifting, breaking curfew, and repeated conflicts with his parents. His parents had tried to set rules like Simon's curfew and bedtime, and morning rituals. This only increased the conflicts in the family and so they sought help.

The engagement phase

The FFT therapist, working in a team and getting weekly case supervision from the team supervisor, started his work with the first goals of FFT: getting all the family members *engaged in treatment*. After reviewing the referral and attempting to understand the family as a relational system, the FFT therapist made a phone call to Simon, his mom and his dad to introduce himself and find a possible time to meet with them. The parents were busy at work, but the therapist presented alternatives and suggestions that were acceptable to them. Simon was very clear on the phone that he saw no point in meeting with his parents to "do therapy." The FFT therapist acknowledged Simon's position and agreed that "if all hope is out, then why try." The FFT therapist then also suggested that Simon probably had important things he would like to say to his parents; that his parents most likely would show up even if he didn't, and that the therapist thought it was a bad idea if he only talked to Simon's parents. Simon eventually agreed to come to the first session. With them all showing up for the first session, the goals of the engagement phase were met.

The motivation phase

In the first minutes of the first session, the FFT therapist focused on *establishing a good relationship* with the family. The therapist then focused on what was currently going on in their relationships. The family talked formally and hesitantly at the start but, after a while, they showed more intense negativity toward each other and started blaming each other for the state of affairs in the family. The FFT therapist then used *change focus techniques* to lower the level of negativity and blame in the session and shifted the focus from an individual-problem focus to a relational and more optimistic focus on the family's situation. During the first three sessions of FFT, which took place within 10–14 days, the therapist started using a range of *change meaning techniques* (e.g., reframing) to increase the family members' hope for change and helped them see the relational nature of their problem. In the case of Simon's family, the mother's constant nagging was acknowledged as being annoying for Simon but at the same time the therapist reframed this as an expression of "mom's concern and care for her son." Similarly, Simon's refusal to talk about school was acknowledged as frustrating for the parents, but at the same time reframed as his attempt not to further disappoint his parents by agreeing to plans he was unable to carry out. Through the motivation phase of FFT treatment, the therapist made no attempts at changing the family members' behaviors but focused on changing their perceptions of the current situation and their relationships. The FFT therapist tried to establish motivation for change before introducing any behavior change intervention. In this case, the phase goals of motivation were met after the third session.

The relational assessment phase

During the first part of treatment, the FFT therapist gathered information about the family from the referral documents, from what the family shared in sessions, and also from observing the family in session. The FFT therapist did need to ask some sequencing questions to the family to obtain more detailed information about their interactions and possible risk and protective factors in the family. The FFT therapist focused on making the family assessment in such a way that it did not lead to increasing blame, negativity, and hopelessness, thereby working against the goals of the motivation phase. The FFT therapist assessed the problem behavior patterns in the family and also what skills the family could use to diminish the likelihood of the youth's problem behavior. It became clear that Simon and his parents were constantly quarreling about issues related to school and curfew; the parents presented ultimatums to threaten Simon into getting his act together and attend school. The therapist identified relevant skills to help the family deal with these situations in a better way.

The behavior change phase

To counter the heated arguments around school, the therapist introduced the family to a *conflict management* approach in which they agreed on a time-out strategy to avoid conflicts escalating. The therapist also introduced a five-step *problem-solving* technique to help them collaborate better in understanding and solving the issues of getting to school on time in the morning and getting home in time in the evenings. The FFT therapist made these skill-based interventions specifically *matched to the family's relational dynamics* (hierarchy and relational closeness). The time-out strategy helped Simon feel more in control and not so controlled by his parents, something he had previously rebelled against. Having a say in when he could take a break from an argument and then return at an agreed-upon time made it easier for him to discuss difficult topics. In the domain of relational closeness, Simon was quite autonomous in relation to his mother, but the mother was seeking more contact. Therefore, they were instructed to solve any problem that came up within a time frame of 10 minutes. If they did not agree on a solution by then, they would continue the problem-solving the next day. The mother was instructed to prepare herself for problem-solving (giving her a feeling of connection) and she would then take time to prepare and write something down if they continued the talk the next day. After five sessions over some weeks, Simon's family was successfully applying the skills practiced in sessions at home to reach agreements they all could rely on. There was a significant reduction in the problematic interactional patterns that also led to Simon being more willing to talk in more detail about going to school. With this goal achievement, the behavior change phase was completed and the therapist then focused on the last phase of treatment.

The generalization phase

To preserve the changes, the FFT therapist helped Simon and his parents continue to use the skills of problem-solving and conflict management as they faced new challenges. They also set up a *relapse prevention plan* where they identified triggers for new conflicts and how they would address them by using time-outs and focused problem-solving. As an example, the therapist helped the family find a solution to how Simon should improve his grades in certain subjects. They all agreed to meet with Simon's teacher to present their plan and to ask for his support in making resources available to Simon at school. They also discussed the issue of staying out with friends and agreed on how to negotiate curfew exceptions that avoided serious conflicts.

Research on Functional Family Therapy

Clinical trials have demonstrated that FFT is capable of (Barnoski, 2002):

- effectively treating adolescents with conduct disorder (CD), ODD, Disruptive Behavior Disorder, alcohol, and other drug abuse disorders, and who are delinquent and/or violent;
- interrupting the matriculation of these adolescents into more restrictive, higher-cost services;
- reducing the access and penetration of other social services by these adolescents;
- generating positive outcomes with the entire spectrum of intervention personnel;
- preventing further incidence of the presenting problem;
- preventing younger children in the family from penetrating the system of care;

- preventing adolescents from penetrating the adult criminal system; and
- effectively transferring treatment effects across treatment systems.

One of the earliest studies contributing to the empirical base supporting FFT was conducted by Alexander and Parsons (1973). In an RCT with 20 juvenile delinquent youths and their families, results showed that families in the intervention group improved more than comparison families on four of six measures of family interaction. A study of the long-term effects of FFT was reported by Gordon, Graves, and Arbuthnot (1995) in which recidivism rates in 27 adolescents who had received FFT were compared to a comparison group of 27 youths who received probation services only. Results suggested that participants who had received FFT showed a recidivism rate of 9 percent compared to a recidivism rate of 41 percent for the participants in the probation services group.

A recent investigation conducted by Sexton and Turner (2011) examined the effectiveness of FFT compared to probation services 12 months post-treatment. The findings showed that reductions in youth problem behavior were greater in the FFT group only when the therapists showed high levels of adherence to the treatment model. In cases with high adherence to the therapeutic model, FFT had a statistically significant effect on reduction of rates of felony (35 percent) and violent crime (30 percent) compared to the control condition. The results were opposite for the low-adherent therapists, in which FFT was associated with significantly higher recidivism rates than the control group. An interaction effect also emerged with regard to the level of youth risk and therapist adherence, in which the highest risk families had a greater likelihood of successful outcomes when their therapist was more adherent to the therapeutic model.

A meta-analysis of FFT reported that among seven non-randomized studies, FFT did no better than no treatment or treatment as usual (TAU), but outperformed alternative treatments (Hartnett, Carr, Hamilton, & O'Reilly, 2017). Among five published RCT studies, FFT did better than the comparison groups in all studies, but three of the five studies were conducted by the program developers and none of them were conducted outside of the US. An independent RCT was conducted in the UK comparing FFT and TAU with 111 participants aged 10–17 years (FFT + TAU: n = 65) (TAU: n = 46) (Humayun et al., 2017). Among the participants, 80 percent (n = 89) were followed up at 6 and 18 months after termination of treatment. In both groups, there were large reductions in all measures of offending and antisocial behavior, but no significant changes in parenting behavior or parent–child relationships. The authors concluded that FFT + TAU did not lead to greater reductions in adolescent antisocial behavior and offending, compared to TAU alone. Neither baseline severity of self-reported delinquency nor variations in therapist skills or treatment fidelity moderated outcomes. The outcomes may have differed from those in previous studies because this trial was more rigorous, using official records rather than parent report, longer follow-up, and it was conducted independently of the program developers. The authors discuss if TAU in the UK may be more effective than in the US, and also whether adolescents are less influenced by their parents than younger children. The authors argued that interventions targeting the individual adolescent may have a greater chance of success than those that are family based but offer no data in support of this conclusion. However, they recommend that further research on more intensively delivered FFT and individual-level interventions for young offenders be conducted (Humayun et al., 2017).

The last program to be presented among the empirically supported therapeutic programs for adolescents with serious behavior problems is MTFC, developed by Patricia Chamberlain (1994). Although it overlaps with MST and FFT as regards the target group and on its view on change mechanisms and outcomes, it is nevertheless organized differently and uses a somewhat different treatment structure.

Treatment Foster Care Oregon

Treatment Foster Care Oregon (TFCO) is a community-based intervention that targets adolescents aged 13–18 years with severe and chronic delinquency and their families (Chamberlain, 1994). The intervention is an alternative to group home treatment or correctional facilities for adolescents who have been removed from their home because of serious conduct problems, substance use, and/or delinquency. Youths are typically referred to TFCO after previous family preservation efforts or other out-of-home placements have failed. Referrals primarily come from juvenile courts and probation, mental health and child welfare agencies. Many of the adolescents have been exposed to violence or maltreatment, particularly female juvenile offenders. For these youths, TFCO represents an alternative to residential care by being placed with trained foster families who receive ongoing support through weekly group meetings and daily check-ins via phone or internet. TFCO is based on social learning theory and, like PMTO®, the treatment principles were developed through a number of clinical studies at the OSLC that identified specific family processes or interaction patterns as precursors of antisocial behavior (Reid, Patterson, & Snyder, 2002). The aim of TFCO is to help the adolescent and his or her biological parents to reunite and to prepare the youth to live successfully in their communities. Foster parents with whom the youths live are highly trained, supervised, and provided with intensive support and treatment in a setting that closely mirrors normal life. TFCO treatment usually lasts six to nine months and relies on coordinated efforts in the TFCO foster home together with the youth's biological or aftercare family. The essential treatment components include child individual therapy, parent training, and family therapy. TFCO treatment goals are achieved by providing the youth with:

- close supervision,
- a supportive relationship with at least one mentoring adult,
- fair and consistent limits,
- predictable consequences for rule breaking, and
- reduced exposure to peers with similar problems.

The intervention components include:

- behavioral parent training and support for TFCO foster parents,
- family therapy for biological parents (or other aftercare resources),
- individual therapy and skills training for the youth,
- school-based behavioral interventions and academic support, and
- psychiatric consultation and medication, when needed.

One of the key elements in the TFCO treatment program is the exceptional degree of teamwork. All members of the team are considered equally important and it is essential that they collaborate very closely, checking in with each other several times a day. This is to ensure that the youth is feeling safe, understood, and is progressing with both his or her goals, as well as the family's goals.

A CASE DESCRIPTION OF TREATMENT FOSTER CARE OREGON

Mary is 15 years old and was referred to Treatment Foster Care Oregon (TFCO) because her parents, the police, the school, and the child welfare services had been concerned about her behavior for a long time. Her parents tell a story of persistent conflicts at home, and that Mary's difficult temperament has led to numerous quarrels in the family. Mary's parents describe her as a willful child who always had a temper. Throughout her childhood, Mary's parents reached out to her teachers, and after persistent effort in describing their difficulties with their daughter they managed to get Mary into different treatment programs. She was thought to have both emotional regulation problems, attention deficit disorder, and was perceived as also having manipulative behavior.

On several occasions when her parents tried to set limits for her, Mary responded with physical attacks. In the last 6 months, her parents have more or less given in, and Mary has gotten her own way. The parents describe a vicious circle of interaction where they end up in conflict and disagreement with their daughter. This interaction leaves them with an even greater feeling of failure toward their daughter.

She runs away from home and may be gone for several days. When she disappears, her parents assume she is staying with an older drug-abusing boyfriend, but as she does not answer her telephone they are unsure what she is doing and with whom she is staying. The police have reported that her boyfriend is under suspicion of selling drugs. In the last few weeks, Mary has gradually lost contact with her pro-social friends and has joined a group of antisocial peers who are truant, commit crimes, and use drugs. Mary has also been observed heavily intoxicated and has been in emergency placement two times following drug incidents. She has only shown up at school occasionally in the last 6 months, and when she is present she is disobedient and inconsistent in her work and cooperation with the teachers. The teachers say they do not recognize her behavior as, in earlier years, she was considered an intelligent and well-adapted girl who was eager to learn.

Intake to TFCO

After having been contacted by the child welfare case worker, the TFCO case manager meticulously goes through the criteria for intake in TFCO. The TFCO team, consisting of the case manager, the family therapist, the youth therapist, and the skills coach, go through the information they have received and begin the pre-intake meetings. The youth therapist has meetings with Mary, the family therapist meets the parents, and the case manager collects information from school, mental health institutions, and from other significant parties. Mary has several meetings with her youth therapist and the case manager to ensure she is informed and understands the treatment program. This has also the beneficial effect of preventing both running away and physical aggression, due to the youth therapist talking through potential difficult situations and making individual plans for such occurrences.

After the assessment is finished and the team has decided that Mary most probably will benefit from the TFCO treatment program, she moves into one of the treatment foster homes.

The first few weeks of treatment

In the first weeks of the program, the main focus for both the foster parents and the team was to establish a good relationship with Mary. The qualities of this working relationship, i.e., how safe, understood, and meaningful Mary feels in the company of her foster parents, greatly impacts how much TFCO can help Mary with her problems.

The foster parents were supervised by the *case manager* in the process of creating a warm and supportive home environment for her. Mary was also supported by her individual therapist in her efforts to adapt and to cope with the transition to the foster family and their local community. The treatment structure consisted of a points system in which Mary earned points every day for positive behavior, such as getting up on time, getting ready in the morning, going to school, showing positive attitudes, and behaving in a developmentally appropriate way. The points she earned could be used to buy privileges of her own choice. The points system helped Mary come to terms with the expectations in TFCO, and also made the foster parents more aware and supportive of Mary's efforts and achievements. The points system also has the added benefit of creating a very safe and predictive everyday life; Mary knows what is expected of her and she feels more in control over what she can and cannot do.

A few days after the initiation of treatment, Mary started individual therapy and skills training. Both interventions aim at creating a good treatment alliance. Her therapist talked with her about settling into the foster home and the school and discussed solutions to the challenges she encountered. She also helped her negotiate with the case manager which privileges she could trade for the points she earned. Mary's individual therapist was also her "advocate" and voice in the treatment team, and her task was to make sure that Mary's viewpoints and perspectives were adequately considered during treatment.

In the first weeks of the treatment, she was closely monitored. In order to prevent negative interaction with the foster parents, the case manager made all decisions and set all limits that Mary could perceive as negative. She was not allowed to visit her home or to have unsupervised contact with her friends. The case manager also coordinated the treatment through weekly staff meetings and kept in contact with external agencies.

As Mary moved into the foster home, the family therapist had weekly meetings with her parents alone. As soon as Mary progressed (usually after two to three weeks) to the next level of the treatment, Mary and her parents participated together in family therapy. The central goal of the family therapy was to improve the relations, increase warmth, care and positive involvement, and improve the communication patterns within the family. An important task in the early phase of the treatment was to assess the interaction patterns in the family in order to clarify what the parents could do to make improvements. Efforts were made to help the parents be more involved, engage in positive activities, and to help them give more praise in order to reduce their negative interactions and increase their positive interactions with Mary. The parents were actively practicing these skills in role-plays with the therapist and were given homework between sessions. The family therapist also kept the parents up to date on Mary's behavior and her situation in the foster home. During the first weeks of TFCO, Mary settled into the program well, and met with the youths at school and behaved in a more pro-social way in the local community of the foster home.

After 2 to 3 weeks of treatment

After the initial three weeks of treatment, Mary had achieved enough points in the points system to move on to the next stage where she was monitored less and given more responsibilities. At this stage, she was allowed to meet with acceptable pre-approved friends, and to participate in positive activities without any adults present. She also started spending time with her family.

Due to more exposure to risk factors in her social environment, her behavior turned out to vary more; for example, when she was met with restrictions or demands, she often became angry, verbally abused the case manager, her parents or her foster mother, and threatened to run away. On several occasions during the last month, she ran away from the foster home in search of her boyfriend and her old network. In such situations, the treatment team put plans into operation that were developed for runaway incidents, and in a collaborative effort with the foster parents, parents, child welfare services, and the police, they were able to bring Mary back to the foster home. The local police also assisted by stressing the criminal drug environment that Mary sought out by searching flats, confiscating drugs, and reporting legally competent persons. Gradually, Mary was excluded from the antisocial environment.

In individual treatment, the therapist and Mary worked on several issues, like how she interacted with ordinary adolescents, which changes she would like to see at home, and her way of responding when demands were put on her. They developed communication and problem-solving strategies that she might use to better cope with challenging situations. The skills trainer practiced with Mary in order to apply the strategies in real life. The case manager included "coping with demands" in the points system in the foster home so that the foster parents noticed and reinforced Mary when she used the strategies she had learned.

The amount of time Mary spent with her family was gradually expanded in accordance with the advances made in the treatment. The family therapist met with Mary and her family to plan home visits and facilitate positive coping experiences for all. The individual therapist also took part in the family therapy to support Mary and help her address topics that were important to her. In the beginning, it was emphasized that the family should do pleasant things together to improve family relations and increase the parents' involvement and support. Parent training in monitoring skills was also central. Focus was put on how Mary might cope with demands at home, how her parents might support her, and also on how the family might improve their communication, both in general and in "demand situations." The family therapist spent much time in treatment discussing and role-playing alternative strategies in difficult situations at home.

After 3 to 4 months of treatment

After 3 to 4 months, Mary entered the last stage of the treatment. She started spending even more time at home with her family and, after a while, she lived at home the majority of the time with only brief visits to the foster home. The focus of the treatment shifted to how the changes achieved by Mary and her family during treatment could be sustained, and how the family might cope with setbacks and new problems that appeared. The family therapist helped find caring people in the social network who could support the family. Mary's grandmother and grandfather were getting more involved and a long-term neighbor offered to help find Mary if she ran away from the family.

Responsibility and decisions were gradually transferred from the case manager to Mary and her parents to empower the family. A close home–school collaboration was established and the cooperation between the parents and other agencies was improved. Nine months after treatment initiation, Mary and her family successfully terminated treatment. There were still occasional conflicts at home, but these were less frequent and less intense than before. Additionally, conflicts were usually successfully solved and without Mary running away. She started school in her old local community, participated in a handball club, and she had only occasional and brief contacts with former antisocial friends.

Implementation of, and research on, TFCO

The first TFCO program was established in 1983 in Eugene, Oregon. By 2009, approximately 115 sites had implemented TFCO, of which many were in operation or in the preparation phase. Most of the evidence base for TFCO comes from trials with US samples, although the program itself has been adopted by several countries. TFCO has been implemented in Denmark, Ireland, New Zealand, the Netherlands, Sweden, the UK, and Norway. In an RCT in the US with male adolescents who had histories of chronic and serious juvenile delinquency, Chamberlain and Reid (1998) compared the effectiveness of group care versus TFCO on criminal offending and incarceration rates. Boys who participated in TFCO had significantly fewer criminal referrals and returned to live with relatives more often than boys in the comparison group. Eddy and Chamberlain (2000) demonstrated that the *quality of adult care* of the adolescent and *reduction in contacts with antisocial peers* were the change mechanisms that helped reduce antisocial behavior among youths who received TFCO. In a recent follow-up study with delinquent girls who were assessed 2 years after they had been enrolled in TFCO, Chamberlain, Leve, and DeGarmo (2007) reported that effects of TFCO were maintained in terms of preventing delinquency, as measured by days in locked settings, number of criminal referrals, and self-reported delinquency. In a commentary, Biglan et al. (2004) point out that the program may be difficult to implement with integrity because it requires intensive training of dedicated foster parents. The program also puts high demands on the supervision and staff support requirements; committed well-trained staff are needed to manage the teens' behavior in the community and to sustain the program in community settings. Adolescents with serious behavior problems may be subject to psychosocial treatment and rehabilitation approaches, but also to incarceration and punishment.

Norway implemented the first TFCO team in 2009, in collaboration with the Norwegian State Child Welfare (Barne-, Ungdoms-, og Familieetaten, BUFETAT). The first team was located in Sandvika, approximately 20 kilometers outside of Oslo. The team has served 42 families with adolescents with severe behavioral problems, aged 12–18 years, with very good outcomes. In 2015, a second team was started in Norway, in Drammen, also in the southern part of the country. This team has now treated nine cases, and it is soon to become a certified TFCO team. Norway has strict regulations concerning children's rights compared to other countries. In connection with TFCO, this includes the right to control privileges, such as withholding their mobile phones and restricting access to the Internet. These interventions are defined as use of force and have to be reported to the judicial system every time they are used. Biological parents can without justification withhold their teenager's access to internet, telephone, and visits with friends, among other things, whereas when the teenager lives with someone other than his/her parents, these restrictions are seen as a violation of the youth's rights. Living in a foster home is a vital part of the youth's TFCO treatment, so this is a major challenge to solve during treatment. TFCO in Norway is defined legally as a residential care unit and can thus access, with limitations, the judicial exception to intervene with restrictions and thereby refrain a youth's rights. This judicial obstacle is continuously being investigated to find a solution for the long term to facilitate the possibility of implementing additional TFCO teams.

Controversial issues: punishment or treatment?

Adolescents over the age of criminal responsibility may be referred to rehabilitative treatment, but they may also be subject to legal sanctions and punishment. Preventive policies include interventions that seek to reduce the opportunities for offending through situational crime prevention, deterrent effects from better detection of crimes or heavier penalties when caught, and prevention by locking up adolescents (Rutter, Giller, & Hagell, 1998). Juvenile courts were established in the US and Europe to protect, support, and rehabilitate juvenile offenders through warnings, probation, and residential care rather than imprisonment. However, a sharp rise in the prevalence rates of juvenile delinquency led in some countries to a change of the view that emphasized control and punishment and that youths should be held accountable for their actions. As noted by McCart, Ogden, and Henggeler (2008), the justice philosophy has made countries such as the US, Canada, Australia, England, Ireland, and the Netherlands accept a lower age of criminal responsibility. Elsewhere, the welfare philosophy has been more prominent in countries such as Germany, France, and Belgium, which have a higher age of criminal responsibility, hand down prison sentences as a last resort, and place greater emphasis on treatment, mediation, and community alternatives. A mix of the justice and the welfare-based principles characterize Norway, Denmark, Sweden, and Scotland (McCart, Ogden, & Henggeler, 2008). Although justice-based interventions have become more common in the Scandinavian countries in recent years, these are typically reserved for older and more serious offenders. At present, Norway has no formal juvenile court or juvenile justice system, and the age of criminal responsibility is 15 years. Thus, no child or adolescent may be punished for a delinquent act committed prior to their 15th birthday. Juvenile offenders aged under 15 years are typically handled by the child welfare system, and youths aged 15–17 years are the responsibility of the adult criminal justice system.

Over the years, the research literature has continually dealt with the question of whether punishment versus treatment affects the rate of reoffending. In their review of research on correctional interventions, Lipsey and Cullen (2007) concluded that punishment was the less effective of the two. Generally, psychosocial or rehabilitative treatment seems to prevent reoffending better than measures based on punishment and control. The explanation may be that treatment engages young people in a supportive and constructive change process whereas punishment that is based on external control and sanctions rarely allows for such learning opportunities. Although no intervention was found to be universally effective, the most promising approaches were empirically supported treatments such as MST and FFT. However, Lipsey and Cullen (2007) also found that interventions did not necessarily have to follow a well-defined protocol to be effective. Generic interventions like family counseling also seemed to work well. Other successful interventions included educational and cognitive interventions. In a later meta-analysis, Lipsey (2009) set out to identify intervention types that were associated with the greatest reductions in recidivism and found that few empirically supported model programs were actually used and studied in the correctional system. For the few that existed, Lipsey's (2009) analysis showed that CBT, social learning and skill-building interventions were effective, and cognitive behavioral therapy had the largest mean ES. Generic programs included counseling interventions, skill-building and restorative programs and were found to be effective in some cases; success was highly dependent on the degree of implementation quality and whether the programs were directed toward high-risk offenders. Furthermore, most interventions were equally effective for younger and older offenders, males and females, and for populations of different ethnic backgrounds.

Diversionary policies are based on the fact that minor delinquent acts are almost normative in adolescence, transient in most cases, and that the majority of youths who commit them are neither in need of therapeutic interventions nor punishment. Empirically, data show that nine out of ten youngsters do not reoffend (Rutter, Giller, & Hagell, 1998). The most common measure is a formal warning by a uniformed officer. *Restorative justice* has also become a popular reaction to minor offenses and seeks resolution by having the offender face the victim and make up for the losses caused. In order to sum up restorative techniques, Rutter, Giller, and Hagell (1998) made the following list:

- Mediation – structured communication between the victim, offender and impartial intermediary to identify how the offense can be remedied.
- Reparation – "making good" the damage or injury by undertaking an act of reparation for the victim of their offenses.

- Compensation – redressing the loss by financial payment to the victim.
- Community service – undertaking tasks for the benefit of individuals or social institutions as recompense for the crime.
- Victim confrontation – confronting the offender with the pain, loss or suffering of the victim.
- Shaming and reintegration – shaming of the offender by the victim (and their family and friends), identifying the harm experienced and negotiating with the offender for acts of recompense.

(p. 358)

It is still not clear whether restorative justice leads to reduced criminality. Rutter, Giller, and Hagell (1998) recommend that restorative justice could be a supplement rather than an alternative to rehabilitative treatment. Some results do indicate, however, that the approach may work, particularly for girls and for offenders with a limited criminal career.

Concluding comments

Antisocial behavior is a multidimensional problem with aggression and norm- and rule-breaking behavior as its major characteristics. Problem behaviors exist on a continuum, ranging from the more trivial (e.g., not paying for a bus ride) to very serious acts of violence (e.g., physical attacks or rape). We have described several subtypes and discussed how both age and gender may modify the seriousness and comprehensiveness of antisocial behavior. On the other hand, CD represents a diagnostic and categorical approach that may be described as a cluster or pattern of externalizing behaviors (DSM-IV, International Classification of Diseases-10). As a behavioral syndrome, it consists of a selection of antisocial acts, and subtypes are defined according to the age of onset, the frequency, intensity, and stability of the problem behaviors. The inclusion criteria are more descriptive than causally related, and do not take into consideration contextual conditions such as family, peer, and school influences.

Research on risk and protective factors has identified numerous issues that influence the probability of antisocial careers, and the cumulative effect of such issues is widely accepted. Risk factors may occur at the proximal as well as the distal level and play a part in problematic transactions between the individual adolescent and her or his micro-, meso-, exo-, and macro-systems. It has been more difficult to identify protective factors that have a differential effect on externalizing behavior, and the buffering effects of most individual and environmental factors seem to be generally applicable across a broad spectrum of mental health problems.

Views on the treatment of these youths have changed from the optimistic "everything works" in the 1960s, via the more pessimistic "nothing works" in the 1970s (Martinson, 1974), to the cautiously optimistic "something works" in the 1990s. For some years, rehabilitative or psychosocial treatment was partly replaced and partly supplemented with alternative legal sanctions including conflict councils, community sanctions, and restorative justice. Increased emphasis on alternative sanctions produced encouraging outcomes but did not necessarily lead to less legal reoffending. At the same time, improvements were made in the structures, contents, and implementation of psychosocial treatments, and elicited increased optimism about the crime-prevention effect of psychological treatment.

4

INTERNALIZING PROBLEMS

This chapter starts with a description of the characteristics, definitions, prevalence rates, and diagnoses of internalizing problems. The emphasis is on anxiety and depression, which sometimes co-occur, along with both externalizing problem behavior and substance abuse. Included is a presentation of the development of internalizing problems and the risk factors associated with these. In their presentation of well-documented treatments of behavioral, emotional, and social problems, Weisz and Kazdin (2017) comment on the advances in the field of research-based interventions. They highlight the fact that treatment research has addressed an increasing range of social, emotional, and behavioral problems in children and adolescents and that research has begun to focus on disseminating and implementing evidence-based treatments in clinical practice settings. Also, advances in research have "[…] shown that factors such as comorbidity of disorders and complexity and stress in the family of clinically referred cases do not impede (or indeed even necessarily moderate) treatment outcome with EBPs" (p. 8) (see also Doss & Weisz, 2006; Kazdin & Whitley, 2006). Both prevention and treatment programs are included in the following review of promising or well-established interventions. Even if our main focus is on anxiety and depression, we acknowledge that the scope of problems to be included in preventive and treatment efforts is widening. For instance, the development of modularized and trans-diagnostic approaches combines separate research-based approaches into treatment packages (Scott, 2017). Even if the evidence base for some of these interventions may be questioned, they exemplify the process of integrating several programs or approaches into trans-diagnostic and research-based multicomponent interventions. We have added one example of this kind of modularized treatment approach in this chapter, namely, the Modular Approach to Therapy for Children (MATCH) with anxiety, depression, and conduct problems (Weisz et al., 2012) that is currently being tested in Norway.

Anxiety and depression

Mental health problems are most often associated with internalizing problems, particularly anxiety and depression (although somatic complaints, self-harm, and eating disorders may be included). Sad feelings and negative thought patterns dominate and internalizing behavior is often described as avoidant behavior, withdrawal, silence, and lack of communication. Mental health problems can be expressed in several ways, such as when youngsters retreat and isolate themselves, try to avoid social situations or activities, exhibit poor self-esteem, refuse to go to school, are unable to concentrate, complain of headache or have excessive concerns about school achievements, personal health, accidents, and disasters.

Internalizing problems are a broadband symptom category, encompassing symptoms of both depression and anxiety. They constitute internal emotional experiences (Weisz & Kazdin, 2017), usually characterized by negative emotionality. Depression and anxiety both reflect problems directed inward toward the self and signify over-controlled (dys)regulation of emotion. The undermining feelings and states of the anxious or depressed youth are typically accompanied by certain behavioral patterns. Left untreated, internalizing problems may rob the youth of meeting important developmental goals such as establishing positive relationships with friends and family, mastering schoolwork and social arenas, carving out a positive identity, and developing a sense of self-worth. Both anxiety and depression are associated with considerable suffering and personal distress, but they are also predictive of serious outcomes down the line such as school dropout, substance abuse, adult psychopathology, and suicide. We first present the characteristics and risk factors of anxiety and depression separately, and then go on to discuss comorbidity. Finally, we discuss evidence-based prevention and treatment programs designed to help alleviate these kinds of problems.

Anxiety

Symptoms of anxiety include feelings of fear, uneasiness, worry, restlessness and agitation, often accompanied by certain physiological responses. McClure and Pine (2006) make the distinction between anxiety and fear: whilst both result in similar responses in behavior, cognition, and physiology, anxiety—as opposed to fear—is experienced in the absence of overt threat or punishment. *Emotions* are reflected in neurophysiology and are linked to the reward and punishment systems in the brain. For example, individuals with higher anxiety sensitivity (that is, those who are more easily anxious) are more likely to engage in behavioral avoidance or escape. They tend to evade situations they expect will elicit uncomfortable or painful physiological arousal. Circumventing this distress by sidestepping perceived stressful situations in turn provides a reward for avoidant behavior that, in turn, may lead to a dysfunctional self-perpetuating cycle. *Feelings* are the subjective experience associated with the occurrence of an emotion (McClure & Pine, 2006). Thus, symptoms of anxiety have both a subjective and consciously felt component and a biologically based element to them, and they are often difficult to separate.

Anxious youths are often hypersensitive to stress or novel stimuli; they readily try to avoid perceived stressors and they frequently engage in pessimistic cognitions or self-talk that serves to reinforce anxious states. When trying to understand the anxious youth, clinicians should keep in mind that features of the disorder include biological, cognitive, and behavioral manifestations (Weisz & Kazdin, 1998), and all these expressions are targets for treatment. Treatment may therefore include strategies to calm oneself down (relaxing, breathing), reformulate negative self-talk, and practice being in situations that seem scary. It is also important to keep in mind that anxiety, like most other mental health problems, operates on a continuum. Diagnoses and cut-off scores, both of which aim to separate normal from pathological, are somewhat artificial and subject to bias. Assessors of adolescents' anxiety, whether they are school counselors, specialized clinicians, parents, teachers, or the adolescents themselves, rate behaviors and feelings differently and use different standards when evaluating problems. Furthermore, both symptoms and well-being fluctuate, and so how the youth feels "right now" may not be representative of his or her general level of functioning. Teens, like anyone else, will occasionally feel anxious or worried. An upcoming test, meeting new people, speaking in public, going on a date, and competing in sports are all situations that can bring about apprehension and nervousness. Most of the time, and for most adolescents, these are normal reactions. Some teenagers, however, react much more strongly to stressful situations than others and, for them, simply thinking about the situations may cause great distress. Anxious states become pathological when they are excessive and irrational and prevent a youth from taking part in normal and daily activities.

Prevalence and subtypes

Anxiety disorders are the most common psychiatric disorders among children and adolescents. Results from the National Comorbidity Survey on adolescent samples in the US indicated that lifetime rates of any anxiety disorder were 31.9 percent, of which 8.3 percent was characterized as severe impairment (Merikangas et al., 2010). In this epidemiological study, no other group of diagnostic disorders was more prevalent (behavioral disorders were at 19.6 percent; depression at 14.3 percent). Another large epidemiological investigation, the Great Smoky Mountains Study of Youth, reported 3-month prevalence rates to be 5.7 percent for anxiety disorders, more prevalent than any other disorders (Costello et al., 1996). In a cross-cultural comparison study of British and Norwegian 8–10-year-olds, clinician-assessed diagnoses for emotional disorder (depression and anxiety) were 3.0 percent and 3.2 percent, respectively (Heiervang, Goodman, & Goodman, 2008). The differences in prevalence rates from these studies are primarily explained by the fact that different time frames were under study (e.g., lifetime, 3 months, or point estimates). A frequency rate of a given disorder will be lower in shorter time frames (e.g., 3 months) than in longer ones (e.g., lifetime). It is important to consider, however, other features of prevalence studies as well, such as the age group and sample under study (children vs. adolescents), the informant (clinician, parent, or teacher), the type of assessment (diagnostic interview or questionnaire) and, in some instances, the cut-off score (or norm) applied. Nevertheless, anxiety problems are common and most adolescents who actually seek treatment demonstrate significant impairment. Unfortunately, anxiety disorders in youths often go unrecognized and anxious youths are less likely to be referred for treatment compared to, for example, youths with behavioral disorders (Emslie, 2008; Heiervang et al., 2007).

The *Diagnostic and Statistical Manual of Mental Disorders* (5th ed.) (DSM-V; American Psychiatric Association, 2013) recognizes multiple distinct anxiety disorders. Following is a brief description of the most common of these:

- *Separation Anxiety Disorder (SAD)* is defined by an unrealistic fear of separation from attachment figures and/or pervasive worries about losing or harm befalling the child's caregiver(s). SAD is common in children, but not in adolescents (American Psychiatric Association, 2013). Symptoms may also be somatic in nature, including headaches and nausea. By definition, SAD is the only disorder for which onset must occur before the age of 18. SAD may be related to panic disorder as clinical data suggest that adults with panic disorders commonly report having had childhood histories of SAD (Bandelow et al., 2001).

- *Specific Phobia* is evident when an individual has an extreme fear toward a specific animal, object, activity, or situation in a way that affects the individual's daily life. Simply thinking about the feared object may elicit anxious feelings. The disorder may have an onset in early childhood (Foa et al., 2005). According to the estimates from the National Comorbidity Survey, specific phobias are the most common of the anxiety disorders (Kessler, Chiu, Demler, & Walters, 2005).

- *Social anxiety disorder (Social Phobia)* is a pervasive and persistent fear of social and/or performance situations in which the person is exposed to unfamiliar people or to possible evaluation by others. The individual fears that he or she will act in a way (or show symptoms) that will be humiliating, embarrassing, or result in ridicule (DSM-IV, American Psychiatric Association, 1994).

- *Panic Disorder* involves repeated experiences of sudden and intense fear, fear of some catastrophic incident happening, feelings of being out of control, and by a persistent worry about when the next attack will occur. Physical symptoms during an attack include increased heart rate, sweating, breathing problems, dizziness, numb hands, chest pain, or stomach pain. It is sometimes accompanied by an avoidance of places where panic attacks have occurred in the past and may develop into a fear of leaving home to avoid future panic attacks (Foa et al., 2005).

- *Generalized Anxiety Disorder (GAD)* usually has onset in late adolescence and is characterized by excessive concern about daily activities, circumstances, and/or the future. Inflicted individuals are in a constant state of worry and often experience concentration difficulties, heightened startle responses, sleep problems, and somatic complaints such as headaches, muscle aches, and stomachaches.

- *Obsessive-Compulsive Disorder (OCD)* is characterized by having repeated, intrusive thoughts (obsessions) and/or engaging in repetitive acts or rituals (compulsions) that the person feels compelled to perform to avoid anxious states. Fear of germs, intruders, or hurting loved ones are examples of anxiety-provoking thoughts. Inflicted individuals have difficulties controlling their unwanted thoughts and behaviors. The disorder is frequently associated with tics and attention deficit disorder during childhood (Foa et al., 2005). Prevalence rates of OCD in youth samples vary from 1.9 percent to 4.1 percent (Stewart, Ceranoglu, O'Hanley, & Geller, 2005).
- *Post-traumatic Stress Disorder (PTSD)* differs from the other anxiety disorders in that the condition requires a specific and identifiable causal stressor. The stressor may be an acute traumatic event or it can be a prolonged period of stress or strain. PTSD symptoms are grouped into three categories: (1) re-experiencing the trauma (flashbacks with bodily symptoms and/or nightmares); (2) avoidance (staying clear of places and/or situations that are reminders of the traumatic event), numb feelings or feelings of guilt, loss of interest, and memory difficulties; and (3) arousal symptoms (being easily startled, feeling tense, or having angry outbursts). PTSD is co-morbidly and familiarly associated with major depressive disorder (MDD) and disruptive behavior disorder. Whether children exposed to trauma show all three groups of symptoms is still questioned. Young children typically display symptoms that are less distinguishable from other childhood conditions. Older children and adolescents may have symptoms similar to those of adults but may also develop oppositional and destructive behavior or have thoughts of revenge (NIMH, 2009). Unlike therapy for other anxiety disorders, which typically do not emphasize the possible causes of the symptoms, PTSD treatment often involves a focus on the traumatic event.

In the fifth edition of the DSM (2013), OCD and PTSD are now categorized as separate disorders (in the fourth edition, they were classified as subcategories of anxiety disorders). We list them here because they share both symptoms with the other anxiety disorders and components of the treatment approaches targeting anxiety in general (e.g., MATCH, CBT). The diagnostic criteria for anxiety disorders, with the exception of SAD, are similar for adults, children, and adolescents. It is, however, important to consider the age or developmental stage of the youth for both assessment and treatment purposes because different disorders may have common behavioral manifestations across the ages. For example, school refusal may be a result of separation anxiety for a school-aged child, but the very same reluctance exhibited by an adolescent may instead be a sign of social anxiety (Evans et al., 2005).

Whilst there is a considerable degree of overlap in symptoms and substantial comorbidity between the anxiety disorders, there are also some indications of their specificity. For example, symptoms of one specific anxiety disorder compared to another seem to cluster within individuals and, when studied over time, each sub-diagnosis develops somewhat differently. Furthermore, research indicates that each disorder and associated conditions aggregate within families. Finally, distinct anxiety disorders often relate to specific risk factors and they show differential responses to different pharmacological interventions. Social anxiety disorder, OCD and PTSD are the three subcategories of anxiety disorders with the strongest evidence suggesting specificity (McClure & Pine, 2006). Nevertheless, the majority of anxiety disorders share certain similarities including somatic symptoms, (e.g., increased heart rate, sweating, quivering, and nausea), behavioral symptoms (e.g., withdrawal, inhibition), and cognitive patterns (e.g., negatively biased thinking and exaggerated, unrealistic fear; McClure & Pine, 2006). Accordingly, anxiety disorders are part of a family of related, but distinct disorders.

Pathways to anxiety: risk factors

As in many other conditions, risks for anxiety disorders may exist on multiple levels of the ecological system, including the ontogenic system reflecting a genetic liability or temperamental qualities. Risk factors at the micro-system encompass parenting practices and transactions within close relationships, such as friends and teachers. Certain learning experiences (conditioning) and contextual influences may also trigger or exacerbate symptoms. Parental psychopathology has often been found to correlate with symptoms in youths. The effects of parental dysfunction, however, may be transmitted through both genes and upbringing environment and so the relative contribution of neither genetic nor environmental influence can be established on this association alone.

A temperamental characteristic often identified as a precursor to later anxiety disorders is *behavioral inhibition*, expressed as an overly shy and reticent demeanor. Approximately 15–20 percent of children can be characterized as behaviorally inhibited (Chronis-Tuscano et al., 2009) although many behaviorally inhibited children do not develop anxiety disorders. Stability of symptoms over time is more likely in children and youth who show higher levels of behavioral inhibition. Results from a longitudinal study of 126 adolescents aged 14–16 years who had been followed since 4 months of age, suggested that children who were consistently characterized as behaviorally inhibited across multiple assessments had 3.79 times increased odds of a lifetime social anxiety diagnosis (Chronis-Tuscano et al., 2009).

Parental psychopathology or symptomology especially related to symptoms of anxiety and/or depression has been found to place youths at risk of developing similar symptomology. Risk factors relating to parenting include parenting control (van der Bruggen, Stams, & Bogels, 2008), negativity, and a tendency to withdraw from interactions (Schrock & Woodruff-Borden, 2010). Mothers of anxious children, regardless of their own anxiety status, were found to be less autonomy granting and less warm (Moore, Whaley, & Sigman, 2004). Both parental and adolescent behaviors mutually affect each other via transactions, and so the parenting styles of anxious children may also be an effect of the behaviors of youths, not just a cause or accompanying factor. When children or adolescents withdraw from social situations or behave in an inhibited manner, they may elicit less constructive reactions in their parents. For example, parents may, in an effort to help or protect their anxious children, act overly solicitously (intrusive, directive, or excessively affectionate) toward their child in various social situations. This may in turn deprive the youth of independence, reduce the youth's confidence in him- or herself, and hinder the development of self-regulatory abilities that such situations can offer. It seems likely that, when parents and their adolescents enter into maladaptive cycles of interactions, they seem to self-perpetuate, that is, these transactions reinforce the dysfunctional patterns.

Contextual risk factors for anxiety include maternal stress (both prenatally and during childhood), family hardship, and violence exposure. These risk factors are not, however, unique to anxiety disorders; they are also predictive of depression, conduct disorders and other conditions. In a longitudinal study by Karevold, Roysamb, Ystrom, and Mathiesen (2009), results suggested that mothers' distress, family adversity, and social support assessed in early childhood were predictive of co-occurring symptoms of anxiety and depression in adolescence in both girls and boys.

Several potential candidate genes have been implicated in the manifestation of anxiety disorders. Social anxiety disorder (and Tourette's syndrome) has been linked to the number of ten-repeat alleles of the dopamine transporter gene (Rowe, 2012). Furthermore, Arbelle et al. (2003) found a significant effect of the long form of the 5-HTTLPR (serotonin) on shyness. What these studies show is that there likely is a genetic contribution to the development of anxiety disorders, or at least their behavioral precursors, and that some genes are more involved in the development of anxiety than are others. It is important to remember that the identification of genes involved in various disorders or the derived estimate from twin studies is an average approximation and not an individual characteristic. And for the treating clinician of an anxious youth, it does not really matter what his or her genetic make-up is or what the relative effect of genes versus environment is. What matters are the youth's own strengths and challenges, the resources available in the youth's surroundings that can prove helpful in treatment, and which techniques and methods are effective in helping the youth overcome or tackle his or her difficulties.

Whether symptoms of anxiety are within the normal, to-be-expected, range of responses or whether they are severe enough to satisfy criteria of a disorder depends both on the age of the child or youth and on the level of impairment that the child or youth suffers. For example, at age 15 months, separation anxiety is common and, to some degree, developmentally appropriate and can therefore hardly be classified as abnormal. When the same child is a few years older, however, the same elicited behavioral manifestations may be considered dysfunctional. During adolescence, socially oriented concerns increase and anxious feelings are near normal. The stresses and concerns that accompany entrance to puberty, as discussed in Chapter 1, may contribute to an exacerbation of anxious feelings and they may tip over to more pathological patterns for some adolescents. And, as noted earlier, in situations of a poor person–environment fit, vulnerable youths may be particularly liable to dysfunctional development and their anxiety may constitute a major hindrance to meeting important developmental milestones. Anxious feelings are common in youths, and most adolescents manage their concerns and worries without major threat to their development. It is when anxious feelings interfere with daily activities and ultimately impede normal developmental tasks (such as making friends, going to school) that the anxious feelings and emotions can be considered pathological.

Depression

It is only during the last few decades that the existence of depression in children and adolescents has been acknowledged. A commonly held belief well into the 1970s was that children and youths were incapable of experiencing depression as this condition was thought to require a certain level of personality maturity; specifically, a fully developed superego (Evans et al., 2005). The growing body of empirical and clinical observations made in recent decades has disposed of this myth. Childhood and adolescent depression is now recognized as a disabling and, indeed, real condition.

Adolescent depression is fairly common, although, as with anxiety, prevalence rates vary across studies. The National Comorbidity Survey, including over 10,000 US adolescents aged 13–18 years, reported a lifetime prevalence rate for mood disorder (major depressive disorder and bipolar disorder) for this age group to be 14.3 percent, of which 11.2 percent were characterized as serious symptomology (Merikangas et al., 2010). Results from this survey also indicated that prevalence rates for major depression are rising; they are higher for people born after the 1960s than for earlier cohorts. Moreover, the peak rise in prevalence rates is observed during the mid-teenage years (Kessler, Avenevoli, & Merikangas, 2001). A study with German adolescents aged 11–17 years found that about 11 percent of the sample scored above a set cut-off score for depressive symptoms (Ravens-Sieberer et al., 2008). Finally, the Great Smoky Mountains study reported 3-month prevalence rates of 2.2 percent, and higher for girls (2.8 percent) than for boys (1.6 percent). To sum up, whilst prevalence rates for mental disorders in general and depression in particular vary depending on the age group under study, diagnostic method used (e.g., self-report vs. diagnostic interview), and time frame set (e.g., lifetime rates vs. point estimate), most estimates suggest that more than one in ten adolescents will have suffered depressive symptoms during their lifetime.

Symptoms of depressive disorders can be categorized into affective, motivational, cognitive, behavioral, vegetative, and somatic indications (Evans et al., 2005). Affective symptoms include anxiety, melancholy, sad mood, and irritability. Motivational symptoms are expressed as helplessness, hopelessness, suicidal thoughts, and loss of interest in daily activities. Cognitive manifestations consist of low self-esteem, feelings of worthlessness and guilt, difficulty concentrating, and delusions or psychosis. Behavioral symptoms include preference for being alone, hot temper, opposition, and defiance. Vegetative and somatic problems include sleeping and eating disturbances, energy loss, headaches, stomachaches, and other bodily complaints. For symptoms to be indicative of depressive disorders, they must be clinically significant and represent major impairments in important areas such as home, social, or academic contexts. Furthermore, symptoms cannot be a result of substance use or a medical condition and should not be diagnosed if the symptoms are better explained as a result of other conditions or critical situations, such as bereavement.

Aron Beck introduced "the cognitive triad" to describe the typical thinking pattern of depression. Depressed individuals see themselves as inadequate, the world as unfair and hostile, and the future as hopeless. Adolescents who are depressed view the world through excessively negative lenses, and often lack the competence to make use of positive social interactions or to regulate their emotions. Depression in adolescence may lead to further problems later on, including social problems, academic or work-related difficulties, drug use, and a 30-fold increased risk of committing suicide (Horowitz & Garber, 2006). In a study examining the World Health Organization database with mortality rates for 15–19-year-olds from 90 countries, suicide was found to be the third leading cause of death among females and fourth among males.

Adolescent depression is characterized by a number of important features that have sparked research into the idiosyncrasy of the adolescent period and helped understand some of the mechanisms underlying the development of depressive disorders. What is it about the adolescent period that results in such a pronounced rise in the number of afflicted individuals? Why does the 2:1 female–male ratio in depression emerge in the adolescent years (Angold & Costello, 2006) when, during the childhood years, rates of depression are similar between boys and girls? Answering these questions requires an examination of the factors that have been shown to contribute to the emergence of depressive disorders, and to consider them within a developmental psychopathological perspective.

Pathways to depression: risk factors

The effects of puberty on depressive symptoms are evident almost exclusively in adolescent girls. This means that the sharp increase in rates of depressive symptoms seen in the teenage years are predominately explained by the increase in girls' depressive symptoms. The focus of much empirical work has been on the hormonal and physical changes that puberty is about for girls. This line of research includes many complicating factors. For one, the hormonal changes marking the onset of puberty actually start long before the emergence of visible and physical features of adolescence (Angold & Costello, 2006). Studies focusing on noticeable features (e.g., menarche or secondary sex characteristics) may miss the truly early markers of puberty and therefore often start too late. Second, puberty is a multiphasic process with no single unitary marker of its onset or progression. Thus, investigations of this association ought to include several markers of pubertal timing and progression (Angold & Costello, 2006). Third, puberty unfolds within a social environment, and features of the individual and the context influence each other.

When studying the potential impact of puberty on depression, Angold and Costello (2006) suggest three possible types of effects to be considered. First, the relationship could be a direct main effect, such that as sex hormone levels increase so does the likelihood of depressive symptoms. If this is the case, every girl is at risk by simply undergoing puberty. Second, the effects of puberty on depression could be evident only in girls who produce relatively high levels of certain hormones, in which case it is not puberty itself that places girls at heightened risk, but rather the relative level of end product of this transition. Finally, the effects may be a result of the timing of the process. In this scenario, the effect of puberty on depression is neither a result of the hormonal changes *per se* nor is it the comparative end levels of those changes, rather the effect emerges depending on *when* these changes occur, relative to peers and relative to the individual's maturity in other domains, such as cognitive and social development. To further complicate matters, there is the possibility that the onset of puberty and depression are both influenced by third factors. If this is the case, there is no causal effect of puberty on depression; they just happen to occur at the same time and are caused by characteristics of, and transactions with, the social environment.

Apart from the hormonal changes in puberty, none of these possible processes described above explain *why* adolescent girls show such marked increases in depression when entering puberty or why such increases seem to be almost absent in adolescent boys. Some empirically derived explanations have been offered, although most of these accounts need replications and further research to be considered consistent. One explanation may be that the coping strategies girls use to deal with either prior life stressors or strains associated with puberty may put them at risk for depressive symptoms (e.g., rumination). On the other hand, girls' entry into puberty is also more likely to co-occur with school transition (from elementary to middle school) than it is for boys. Such a major social change may place girls at additional risk. Finally, results suggest that girls tend to have a more negative body image, to mature earlier, and to experience greater relationship stress with their mothers, all associated with increases in depressive symptoms (Seiffge-Krenke & Stemmler, 2002).

The most salient risk factor for depressive disorder in adolescence, after female gender, is a familial history of major depression. Offspring of depressed individuals are three times more likely to themselves develop depression, anxiety, or substance use problems than are children of non-depressed parents (Weissman et al., 2006). The intergenerational transmission of depression may be due to several factors and their relative and unique effects are not easily separated. From twin studies, results suggest that genetics account for approximately 35 percent of the variance in the expression of unipolar depression. Depression seems to run in families and the increased risk may, in part, be due to family members' shared genetic make-up. It does not mean, however, that all depressed adolescents are genetically predisposed, nor that a genetic predisposition leads to depression. It does seem to indicate, however, that, on average, approximately 65 percent of the variance in depression is due to other factors than an inherited genetic liability. The behavioral and interpersonal patterns of parents who are affected by mental disorders in general, and depression in particular, often compromise optimal parenting practices, and so the fact that offspring of these parents themselves show dysfunctions in one area or another may in part be a result of less than ideal child-rearing contexts.

Another manner in which to examine the joint effects of genes and environment is what are referred to as gene × environment interactional (G × E) models. Such investigations ask the question of whether predictions can be enhanced by looking at the combined effects of genetic predisposition and contextual variables. Is the risk for depression greater in individuals with a certain genetic make-up coupled with exposure to certain environmental risks than when these influences are seen in isolation? In a series of studies by Caspi et al., the effect of the gene–environment interaction on depression has been supported. In one study, individuals with the long allele of the 5-HTT promoter polymorphism were less likely to develop depression and suicidality following stressful life events than were individuals with one or two copies of the short form of the allele (Caspi et al., 2003). In a more recent investigation, combining samples from both New Zealand and England, results were replicated for persistent depression. In both cohorts, individuals with two short 5-HTTLPR alleles, and who had experienced childhood maltreatment, evinced elevated risk of persistent depression (but not single-episode depression) compared to individuals with a history of childhood maltreatment but with the long form of the allele (Uher et al., 2011). A similar study, though with a cross-sectional design, conducted with Swedish teens, found that the G × E interaction effects on depression was evident in girls only (Aslund et al., 2009). Together, these studies suggest not only that some individuals demonstrate a genetic sensitivity to environmental influences but also that environmental influences play an important role in the development of depression. When individuals who are genetically susceptible to environmental stimuli do not experience maltreatment or other stressful life events, their risk for depression is not elevated. In other words, a person's genetic make-up does not by any means tell the whole story.

Dispositional risk factors at the individual level include biased cognitive patterns, temperamental characteristics such as emotion (dys-)regulation, attention control, and behavioral inhibition. Several studies have shown that negative affectivity, the tendency to experience negative emotions such as anger, sadness, and anxiety, is predictive of depression and chronicity of depressive symptoms (Clark, Watson, & Mineka, 1994). In a study by Caspi, Moffitt, Newman, and Silva (1996), results suggested that children who had been rated at age 3 as inhibited, socially reticent, and easily upset had elevated rates of depressive disorders at age 21. There is evidence to suggest gender differences in the association between early child behavior and later depressive symptoms. In one study, young women aged 23 years with higher levels of chronic depression were more likely to have been described as shy and withdrawn in the preschool years, whereas young adult males with chronic depression had been described as under-socialized, that is, less capable of following social rules and expectations. This study also found intellectual abilities to be negatively associated with depression in males, but not in females (Gjerde, 1995).

Several family variables have been found to predict adolescent depression, including maltreatment (Aslund et al., 2009; Donovan & Brassard, 2011), divorce (Rønning et al., 2011), harsh parental discipline (Bender et al., 2007), and lack of family support and low cohesion (Au, Lau, & Lee, 2009; Bean, Barber, & Crane, 2006). It is important to note that many familial risk factors are themselves associated with parental depression, including divorce, isolation, and lack of resources and they may similarly affect the youth who lives in the same household. Thus, the direction of effects between parental psychopathology, contextual risk, and adolescent depression is quite difficult to pinpoint. Furthermore, many of these risk factors are not predictive of depression alone. It is nevertheless important in the initial treatment setting that a thorough account of the family situation and difficult life circumstances be described. Risk factors, regardless of whether they are causal, concomitant, or resultant and regardless of whether they are of a relational, academic, or familial nature, should be kept in mind during the therapeutic process as they may hamper a youth's progress. Attending to the parent's own depression and their behavior toward the youth, for example, may in many cases be worthwhile. Academic assistance for a depressed youth who is more concerned about falling grades than their depression diagnosis, could also be an important aspect of the treatment. First, it shows sensitivity to the youth's own concern and thereby helps foster a good therapeutic relationship. Second, any improvement in an area important to the youth may bolster a belief that change is possible and can help motivate and engage the youth in treatment.

Adolescents who exhibit biased cognitions tend to attribute stressful life events to stable, global, and internal factors. That is, when something bad happens, the depressed youth blames him- or herself. They tend to believe that bad luck or unfortunate events are caused by their own shortcomings, and when good things happen, they believe these are due to some external fluke. Depressed youths are more likely to seek out or experience stressful events than are non-depressed individuals and tend to appraise neutral events as more negative. Either as a result of such attribution bias or as an accompanying factor, the typical correlates for these cognitive tendencies are helplessness, hopelessness, and feelings of low self-worth.

Interpersonal difficulties are also more common in depressed adolescents. Depressed youths have more trouble initiating and maintaining friendships, are more likely to be rejected or neglected by their peers, perceived as less likable, and are rated by peers as having more negative social behaviors. For many of the correlates of adolescent depression, the causal link is not well established. Whether lack of social skills on the part of the youth leads to peer rejection, which in turn leads to depression or conversely, the case may be that depressed youths act in ways that alienate peers (e.g., having a pessimistic, irritable, and complaining demeanor), leading to diminishing opportunities for learning important social lessons and further exacerbating the youths' negative self-perception.

As can be seen, many anxious and depressive symptoms overlap, such as preponderance toward negative (and irrational) thinking patterns, negative emotionality, social withdrawal, and low self-esteem. The risk factors associated with anxiety and depression are also similar, as are their long-term effects. Hence, the fact that these types of internalizing symptoms tend to co-occur is not surprising.

Comorbidity

Comorbidity in adolescence is the rule rather than the exception. Symptoms of depression are frequently comorbid with symptoms of anxiety, and vice versa. This seems to hold true in both clinical and community samples. Anxiety disorders are the most commonly comorbid disorders for depressed youths, with over 60 percent of depressed adolescents having a history of a concomitant anxiety disorder (Evans et al., 2005). In a review of the anxiety and depression literature, Brady and Kendall (1992) reported that 15.9 percent to 61.9 percent of the children identified as anxious or depressed had comorbid anxiety and depressive disorders. It is not clear whether the degree of comorbidity is a result of the natural sequence of initial anxiety followed by depression, or whether presenting either disorder increases the risk for developing the other. Compared to non-comorbid presentation of anxiety or depression, the co-occurring depression and anxiety profile is typically associated with greater symptom severity. Tracking a sample of adolescents through the age of 30, Mathew, Pettit, Lewinsohn, Seeley, & Roberts (2011) reported that a shared etiology model best explained situations in which depression preceded anxiety, whereas a causation model best explained comorbid cases where anxiety preceded depression. Depressed youths sometimes present other disorders as well, most notably, CD, substance use disorder, ADHD, and eating disorders.

For both anxious and depressed youths, knowing where to draw the line between what is normal adolescent worry and gloomy demeanor on the one hand and pathological anxious and depressed symptomology on the other is difficult. Adolescents who struggle with internalizing problems can also come across as angry and opposing; they may experiment with alcohol or drugs, have problems concentrating, and their difficulties may result in somatic complaints such as aches and pains. Thus, their overt behavior may sometimes be mistaken for other problems as they mask an underlying condition. If these behavioral expressions persist over time, seem to represent a change in the youth's personality, and affect his or her everyday activities, treatment should be considered.

Prevention and treatment for adolescent depression and anxiety

In their presentation of treatments for internalizing problems, Weisz and Kazdin (2017) include: (1) child-focused treatment for anxiety, (2) CBT or interpersonal psychotherapy for the treatment of adolescent depression, and (3) exposure-based cognitive behavioral therapy for the treatment of obsessive-compulsive disorder in children. Weisz, Hawley, and Jensen Doss (2004) reported that widely used and well-tested treatment elements of internalizing conditions include modeling, relaxation training, systematic desensitization, reinforced exposure, social skills training, self-talk intervention and, more generally, CBT.

Cognitive behavioral therapy

Successful programs that are either preventive efforts or intervention programs for anxiety disorders and depression are typically based on CBT principles. CBT is the most commonly used treatment of both depression and anxiety. CBT is quite effective and has been evaluated in numerous RCTs in several different contexts, with various samples and in different countries.

Most treatment programs, although differing slightly in their protocols, base their treatment on cognitive behavioral principles. Core components in these treatments include a psycho-educative module (e.g., explaining physical reactions to stress), learning how to regulate emotions, altering cognitive patterns, identifying situations that trigger depressive or anxious feelings, and practicing desired behaviors. For programs developed to alleviate anxiety, exposure therapy is usually an added element.

The Teaching Kids to Cope program

The Teaching Kids to Cope (TKC) program is a mental health promotion program designed to reduce depressive symptoms and risk factors associated with depression and suicide ideation in youth. Typically delivered in 1-hour group sessions over a 10-week period, the program, through information and discussions, teaches adolescents a range of skills aimed at helping them cope with typical teen stressors, including self-image, communication, and family relations. Building on cognitive behavioral principles, TKC participants are guided through a process that helps them identify distorted thinking patterns, alternate ways of interpreting problems, problem-solving skills, and new ways of reacting to stressors or problems. Each session also involves experiential learning, role-play, group projects, and films. Participants are given homework assignments to help them practice skills between sessions. The program can be delivered in after-school settings, at summer camp, and in outpatient clinics or the like.

The TKC program has primarily been delivered to US samples, though one RCT was recently conducted with Jordanian college students showing positive effects (Hamdan-Mansour, Puskar, & Bandak, 2009).

Results from trials with adolescent samples in the US have also shown positive results. In their study of 14–18-year-olds with slightly elevated depression scores, Puskar, Sereika, and Tusaie-Mumford (2003) found that participants in the intervention group reported significantly fewer depressive symptoms and scored higher on the coping skill "seeking guidance and support" and problem-solving compared to participants in the control group. An earlier RCT targeting rural high school students reporting elevated depressive symptomology found similar results with regard to both depressive symptoms and coping skills, but only for girls (Lamb, Puskar, Sereika, & Corcoran, 1998).

Coping and Support Training

The Coping and Support Training (CAST) program targets middle and high school students (aged 12–18 years) and is designed to reduce emotional distress, depression, and suicide risk. CAST was developed by Leona L. Eggert and Liela J. Nicholas. Delivered as a small group prevention program, CAST seeks to identify youths who live with multiple risks for, and who have access to, few protective factors against depression and suicide. The aim is to enhance their personal and social resources (www.reconnectingyouth.com/cast/). Each group typically consists of six to eight students per group leader and meets twice a week over a 6-week period. The program sessions cover areas such as skills training, with a focus on building self-esteem, decision-making and personal control, and strategies for seeking help and support. It has been implemented in 60 middle and high schools throughout the US and Canada.

Empirical support for the CAST program has been provided by several RCTs. In a study by Thompson, Eggert, Randell, & Pike (2001), 460 youths who had been identified as being at risk for suicide, were randomly assigned (by school) to either the Counselors CARE (C-CARE) program only, a brief assessment and crisis intervention module, to Coping and Support Training delivered together with C-CARE (CAST plus C-CARE), or to a usual-services control group. Assessment at pre-intervention, post-C-CARE intervention (at 4 weeks), post–CAST intervention (10 weeks), and follow-up at 9 months showed declines in attitudes toward suicide and suicidal ideation in participants in the experimental interventions. Furthermore, the intervention was also effective in reducing depression and hopelessness scores and in enhancing and sustaining personal control and problem-solving. In another study with 341 high school students at risk for school dropout, comparing the same three treatment conditions results showed that participants in the CAST plus C-CARE intervention group reported increases in personal control, problem-solving, coping, and perceived family support. Participants in both the CAST plus C-CARE and in C-CARE alone showed reduced symptoms of depression, enhanced self-esteem, and more family goals met. There were no significant differences between the three groups in suicide risk behaviors, anger control problems, and family distress as participants in all three groups evinced reductions in these domains. The usual care condition was developed specifically to ensure participant safety that likely explains why decreases in suicide risk behavior was evident in this group as well.

FRIENDS

FRIENDS is a prevention and treatment program for children and youths at risk of developing anxiety or for children and youths who already have an anxiety disorder. Building on cognitive behavioral theory and on the Coping Cat program (Kendall & Hedtke, 2006, see below) FRIENDS was further developed in Australia by Barrett in the late 1990s. As a school-based prevention program, FRIENDS has both a child and adolescent version and can be delivered both as universal prevention and as selective prevention. The program has since then been implemented in several countries including New Zealand, Canada, the

UK, Ireland, Germany, Finland, the Netherlands, the US, Mexico, Norway, and Portugal. A school-based trial with German children (aged 9–12 years) showed that participants in the FRIENDS program were more socially competent and used more positive coping strategies than their matched controls (Conradt & Essau, 2003). In Norway, the program is delivered in outpatient clinics, an RCT testing its efficacy is underway and, thus far, results are promising (Wergeland, Fjermestad, Haugland, Öst, & Heiervang, 2011). To date, the FRIENDS' curriculum has been implemented primarily as a universal preventive program delivered to whole grade classes by trained teachers. The program typically consists of ten sessions in addition to two booster sessions and aims to enhance students' self-esteem, problem-solving skills, psychological resilience, and self-expression and to build positive relationships with peers and adults. There are optional parent sessions that can be run in parallel by the teacher using the program manual. Regular teachers are given a 1-day training session. In 2005, the FRIENDS program underwent revisions and is now called FRIENDS for Life.

The FRIENDS program has a solid research base supporting its effectiveness, though most of the empirical work has been conducted by the program developers. In a study of 594 children and young adolescents aged 10–13 years from seven schools in Brisbane, Australia, participants were randomly assigned to an intervention or control group on a school-by-school basis. Results suggested that students who had participated in the FRIENDS program reported fewer anxiety symptoms at post-test than those in the control group. For students who were classified as the high-anxiety group, the FRIENDS intervention was associated with significant improvements in reported levels of depression as well. At 12-month follow-ups, intervention gains were maintained and 85 percent of children in the FRIENDS prevention groups who scored above the clinical cut-off for anxiety and depression at the pre-test were diagnosis-free compared to only 31.2 percent of students in the control group (Lowry-Webster, Barrett, & Lock, 2003). Long-term preventive effects have also been demonstrated with significantly fewer high-risk students at the 36-month follow-up in the intervention group compared to the control group (Barrett, Farrell, Ollendick, & Dadds, 2006). Long-term treatment effects were also maintained in a sample of 52 participants (aged 14–21 years) who had completed treatment an average of 6.17 years earlier on several outcome measures, and of these youths, 85.7 percent no longer fulfilled the diagnostic criteria for any anxiety disorder (Barrett et al., 2006). Results from these effects studies also indicate that younger children (aged 9–10 years) and girls may have greater treatment benefit than older (aged 14–16 years) and boys (Barrett et al., 2006; Barrett, Lock, & Farrell, 2005).

Treatment programs

Adolescent Coping with Depression course

The Adolescent Coping with Depression (CWD-A) course is a psycho-educational, cognitive behavioral intervention for adolescent depression. The module-based treatment is based on and modeled after the adult Coping with Depression Course (Lewinsohn, Antonuccio, Steinmetz-Breckenridge, & Teri, 1984). For the adolescent course, the classroom material and homework assignments have been modified and practical learning opportunities (e.g., role-play) have been enhanced from the adult version. Moreover, problem-solving skills were added to the program. The therapy is delivered in a classroom-like context believed to reduce any stigma the participants may feel. CWD-A has been implemented with adolescents in diverse contexts including inner-city and rural areas, schools, and juvenile detention centers. Numerous therapists across the US and Canada have been trained in CWD-A (www.nrepp.samhsa.gov/). The therapy consists of 2-hour sessions delivered over an 8-week period (Clarke, Lewinsohn, & Hops, 1990) to groups of four to eight participants, though the treatment can be modified to be delivered individually as well. The first session presents the outline of the course and the course rules, and introduces the rationale of the program, including the social learning of depression. The remaining sessions focus on skills for gaining control over moods and feelings and for dealing with and recognizing situations that contribute to depressive symptoms. These skills include mood monitoring, social skills, pleasant activities, relaxation techniques, constructive thinking, communication, negotiation, and problem-solving (Clarke, Lewinsohn, & Hops, 1990).

CWD-A was compared with a life skills tutoring comparison condition in a sample of adolescents aged 13–17 years who met the criteria for both MDD and CD. Participants were recruited from a county juvenile justice department and were randomly assigned to the two treatment conditions (Rohde, Clarke, Mace, Jorgensen, & Seeley, 2004). Results suggested that recovery rates post-treatment were greater in CWD-A compared with the life skills/tutoring condition, and CWD-A participants reported greater reductions on two self-reported depression measures and improved social functioning post-treatment. Recovery rates for both MDD and CD were non-significant at the 6- and 12-month follow-up. Based on the same sample of adolescents, Kaufman, Rohde, Seeley, Clarke, and Stice (2005) tested several potential mediators of treatment effects of CWD-A. Automatic negative cognitions fully mediated the relationship between treatment condition and two separate measures of depressive symptoms: one self-report, and one clinician-rated. Two non-specific treatment factors, working alliance and group cohesion, along with three other specific therapeutic factors were also tested as possible mediators, but were not found to mediate the relationship between treatment and outcome.

Coping Cat

The Coping Cat (Kendall & Hedtke, 2006) is a manualized CBT for the treatment of GAD, social phobia, and/or SAD in children and youths aged 7–14 years. The program has been implemented throughout the US, and in several other countries such as Norway, Australia (now called FRIENDS), Canada (called the Coping Bear), and the Netherlands (Kendall, Crawford, Kagan, Furr, & Podell, 2017). The therapy usually consists of 16 sessions and is delivered either individually or in a group setting. The first eight sessions are psycho-educative, in that the youth learns to recognize cues that trigger anxious feelings, cognitions, and physical symptoms. The youth learns several coping skills and practices, both in session and as part of homework assignments. The latter eight sessions are behaviorally focused and involve exposure techniques, in which the youth faces his/her fears in a graded hierarchy (Beidas, Benjamin, Puleo, Edmunds, & Kendall, 2010). The Coping Cat program uses an acronym, FEAR (or the FEAR-plan), to help participants remember the skills learned and to cope with difficult feelings when they emerge. The **F** step (feeling frightened) emphasizes learning about somatic reactions to anxious states; the **E** step (expecting bad things to happen) helps the participant recognize anxious thinking patterns; the **A** step (attitudes and actions) affords coping skills for the youth to employ in frightening situations (e.g., coping thoughts, problem-solving, relaxation, breathing right); and, finally, the **R** step (results and rewards) allows the youth to rate their performance and effort and to be rewarded for facing their fears (Beidas et al., 2010).

The effectiveness of the Coping Cat program has been demonstrated in several RCTs with both child and adolescent samples. For example, Kendall et al. (1997) reported on 94 children and adolescents (aged 9–13 years) who were randomly assigned to either an intervention group or a wait-list control group. Results suggested that over half (53 percent) of those youths who received Coping Cat no longer met the criteria for the diagnosis of their primary anxiety disorder at the end of treatment, whilst this was the case for only 6 percent of the youths in the wait-list control group. In a more recent trial, Kendall, Hudson, Gosch, Flannery-Schroeder, and Suveg (2008) compared three groups of youths aged 7–14 years, randomized to either a child CBT condition, family CBT condition, or a family-based education/support/attention condition. Children in the two CBT groups reduced the presence and principality of the primary anxiety disorder more than did children in the family-based education group. Also, the child CBT condition outperformed the other conditions on teacher reports of child anxiety. Long-term follow-up results were reported in a study by Kendall and Southam-Gerow (1996), showing that clients who had undergone treatment had maintained their treatment gains on an average of 3.35 years later. This study also reported that the components most readily recalled by study participants were therapeutic relationships, games, activities, and discussions of problems. Furthermore, in a recent study by Kendall and Treadwell (2007) both community children and adolescents, and children and adolescents with an anxiety disorder, were assessed. Results suggested that anxious children and youths reported greater frequency of anxious self-statements (e.g., "I am very nervous"), than did their non-anxious counterparts. In the second part of the study, results showed that the frequency of anxious self-statements partially mediated the effect of treatment status on several measures of treatment outcome. The mediator and outcome variables were measured at the same time in this study and so the temporal order of the mechanisms involved is difficult to pinpoint (e.g., which comes first?). The finding nevertheless implicates anxious self-talk as a possible mechanism through which anxious feelings are sustained.

A CASE DESCRIPTION OF THE COPING CAT PROGRAM FOR YOUTH

Astrid is a 14-year-old girl. Her parents are divorced and she stays with her father every other week. He has a history of alcohol abuse but is now receiving treatment. Her mother works part-time due to chronic back pain. Astrid has always been described as a shy and gentle girl with a high degree of empathy for other children. She prefers the company of her family but has two good friends that she also likes to spend time with. The family is described as isolated.

Ever since Astrid started school, her parents have struggled to get her to participate in sports and social activities such as going to birthday parties. Prior to social events, Astrid would start complaining about stomachaches and if her parents pushed her further, she would start crying and refuse to go. Sometimes she responded with angry outbursts. In sheer frustration, sometimes Astrid's father would carry her outside and into the car, which she would then refuse to leave. Eventually, her mother stopped trying to get her to go to social events, because she was afraid that forcing Astrid might traumatize her. During school performances, Astrid would always stand in the back, not visible to the audience.

In seventh grade, Astrid's parents divorced. The family breakup was accompanied by a difficult custody battle between the parents. At that time, Astrid started to stay at home on days when there were presentations or group assignments at school. She did not form any friendships with other youths in school. Once or twice a month she would, however, meet up with an old friend from elementary school. Because of her apprehension about working in groups with other children, she was allowed to sit alone in an adjacent room, working on assignments by herself. This increased her isolation and offered her little opportunity to improve her social skills.

Referral

The school nurse contacted Astrid's mother and father and asked them to contact their general practitioner to get a referral to the local youth community mental health clinic. Astrid's teachers had become increasingly concerned about her mounting school refusal.

Assessment

When Astrid and her parents entered the youth mental health clinic, they were interviewed about their background, Astrid's behavior, and the family situation in general. Several formal assessments were administered, including the Anxiety Disorders Interview Schedule for parents and youths, the Wechsler

Intelligence Scale for children, the Achenbach System of Empirically based Assessment (ASEBA) for parents, youths, and teachers, and the Beck depression inventory for youths.

Both parent and youth assessments indicated symptoms of social anxiety disorder. Astrid scored normally on intelligence. Astrid's responses to the ASEBA questionnaire also revealed depressive symptoms, a low self-esteem and feelings of hopelessness about the future. Astrid explained that she had always been scared of what other people thought of her and that she did not want to do presentations in school because she was afraid of acting stupid in front of the class. She said she would tremble so much that she was afraid someone would notice and laugh at her. During the first year of junior high school, Astrid had developed acne and was embarrassed about showing herself in front of other people. She never took the bus to school, but had her mother drive her instead. She was afraid of what the other people on the bus would think of her.

Treatment structure

Astrid received 20 treatment sessions, 1 hour a week (and four more than the normal treatment structure in the manual of 16 sessions). Her mother and father met with the therapist during three sessions. With the parents, the therapist focused on psycho-education, forming a common understanding of the anxiety disorder and how it had developed. Furthermore, the therapist helped the parents build skills to encourage constructive coping mechanisms for Astrid and how to support and reinforce brave behavior. The mother also attended the latter part of every session with Astrid to be informed about treatment progress.

Therapeutic process

Astrid had, in addition to her anxiety, lost hope that she could do anything about her problems. She was also concerned about the therapist's evaluation of her. An important feature of the treatment was to build an alliance by evoking a belief in Astrid that symptoms could be improved by normalizing anxious responses and by building a common ground. In the sessions with the parents, the therapist focused on parent behavior that would encourage coping mechanisms other than avoidance. Talking about the parents' own anxieties was important for understanding their daughter's behavior.

Treatment sequence

The first eight sessions with Astrid were focused on psycho-education about anxiety, recognizing anxious feelings and thoughts, and about normal physical reactions to anxiety. During these sessions, the therapist also helped Astrid to develop more constructive coping strategies, such as the use of positive self-talk, and they made a plan for determining what coping actions might be useful in different anxiety-provoking situations. Astrid was also introduced to alternative interpretations of social situations and she practiced positive self-talk. In this treatment, Astrid learned the acronym FEAR by heart to help her remember how to cope with anxiety.

In the remaining sessions, Astrid practiced her skills in role-plays with the therapist and she gradually took part in *in vivo* exposure tasks ranging from low-anxiety to high-anxiety situations. These exposure situations included reading from a book in front of the therapist (low anxiety) to buying some-thing in the store without having enough money (high anxiety). Between sessions, Astrid was given two home assignments that included skills training or exposure. Her parents participated in some of these. Some of the exposure tasks were conducted in the school setting with the school nurse and the ther-apist. The therapist modeled brave behavior and used social reinforcement during exposure tasks. At the end of each session, the therapist and Astrid explained to the parents what she had accomplished.

Outcomes

At the end of treatment, Astrid was able to attend school on a regular basis, and she started to participate in group assignments again. She began talking to her peers, and formed a friendship with another girl, who had herself struggled with anxiety. Astrid also started to take the bus in the morning.

MATCH: a modular approach to therapy for children with anxiety, depression, and conduct problems

Since the intake criteria of most evidence-based programs focus on a single problem syndrome like conduct problems, anxiety, or depression, they appear to have limited flexibility when facing children with several co-occurring problems. The challenge of many standard evidence-based treatments to deal with the complexity and comorbidity of presented problems and with the shifting needs of children and families during treatment has been met with modular approaches to treatment. MATCH combines evidence-based treatments for anxiety, depression, trauma, and behavioral problems. These are well-established treatment components from cogni-tive behavioral therapy for anxiety, depression, and traumatic stress, and for parent training for families with behavioral problems. In the protocol, components are grouped into 35 different modules or intervention elements. Therapists trained in MATCH learn how to combine these modules based on the child's needs and problems as they progress through treatment. Added to the treatment is a measurement feedback system which on a weekly basis informs clinicians through brief assessments of treatment response provided by the family. The children and their caregivers report separately on internalizing, externalizing, and their identified top problems. This information is used by the therapists to adjust and personalize the intervention. Flowcharts are used in MATCH to guide clinical decision-making during treatment, and the weekly feedback from clients are summarized and posted on a web-based platform or a "clinical dashboard" for each client. The dashboards are accessed by clinicians and consultants in weekly case consultations and used to measure treatment response and plan adjustments in treatment.

The aim of the new intervention format is to integrate the therapeutic procedures into a uniform system that can be used in a flexible way. This approach makes it easier for the therapist to address comorbidity, to handle changes in needs and symptoms, and allows for more relational continuity with the referred children.

A CASE DESCRIPTION OF MATCH

William is a 10-year-old boy who lives with his parents. He has no siblings. He is doing well in school and has no academic challenges. He likes to play the piano. He is also a Boy Scout but is reluctant to join group gatherings when they entail staying overnight and away from home. In his leisure time, he prefers to be at home, wanting his parents to take part in his games or play. He seldom seeks contact with peers but is happy when friends come over to visit him. He does not enjoy sports like soccer, volleyball, etc. like most of his schoolmates do.

William's parents have struggled with his sleeping routines ever since he was an infant. Today, the main problem is that William refuses to go to bed in his own room; he demands to go to sleep in his parents' bed and insists that one of the parents is present until he has fallen asleep. In the last couple of years, the parents have become increasingly concerned. Their hope that William would grow out of his bedtime problems has been thwarted and each time they try to talk with William about it, he cries and becomes very anxious and angry. The time it takes for William to fall asleep is increasing, the parents spending 2–4 hours each evening by his bedside. At the same time, the parents perceive that the boy expresses new anxious thoughts in connection to falling asleep. This prevents the parents from leaving him to himself when he is going to bed. By the time of referral, the parents are exhausted and worry that their child will neither be able to sleep by himself at home nor to stay overnight with relatives or friends. The father is also afraid that William's anxiety will worsen if they challenge him to go to bed or sleep alone.

Referral

The parents turned to their general practitioner to ask for assistance in how to remedy these persistent sleep problems and William's increasing bedtime anxieties. Because the severity of William's problems is also affecting the family as a whole, the general practitioner referred the family to a child mental health outpatient clinic.

Assessment

In addition to a regular clinical interview about family history, the child's level of functioning, and his developmental challenges, several questionnaires were administered, including ASEBA for parents and youths and a traumatic events checklist. Finally, both the child and the parents were asked to formulate separately the three main problems they thought were relevant for William's psychological treatment (Top Problem Assessment). Both parent and child assessments indicated symptoms of separation anxiety disorder. The details showed that the problems were primarily connected to falling asleep and that they prevented him from staying overnight with his cousins and friends. William himself was concerned that he might not dare to attend school camp in the spring. In addition, William expressed a general fear of being left alone, occasionally imagining that a person or an animal would come into his room at night. The parents reported that they both felt compelled to accommodate William's anxiety in order to alleviate his fears and avoid an escalation of a potential conflict and concede that his fears had now taken control over the entire family's evening routines.

Treatment structure

The MATCH treatment model consists of four different treatment protocols, one for each of the problem areas: anxiety, depression, trauma, and conduct problems. The results of the assessment give direction for what the initial treatment focus and the primary treatment protocol should be. Although the therapist starts out with one protocol, he or she can still pull modules from one of the other treatment protocols during the course of treatment. This can be done to deal with different forms of interference that can occur during treatment (e.g., aversive events, low motivation). For children with comorbidity (exhibiting symptoms from two or more diagnostic categories), modules from different protocols can be combined. Both the parents and the child fill out a short assessment form on a weekly basis asking them to rate the severity of the top three problems identified at the initial phase and the child's internalizing and externalizing symptoms. The scores on these assessments guide the therapist in selecting relevant treatment modules in the continuation of the treatment. In William's case, the primary treatment protocol was the anxiety protocol. The family had 18 weekly meetings at the clinic, switching between parent sessions and child sessions, about half of each. In the child sessions, the parents always took part in the last 15 minutes to learn what the child now understood about his anxiety and how to deal with it. The focus in the parent sessions was psycho-education about anxiety, supporting the parents to follow the plan developed in the sessions and developing strategies in how to deal with the challenging situation at home.

Every session with William started with a review of the agenda. Next, he scored "The fear ladder" and reviewed the home assignment together with the therapist, followed by planning how to practice at home. Each session ended by giving a practical home assignment. Before the child left, time was always set aside for a pleasant activity. Normally, exposure training would take place during sessions, but since this case involved sleeping problems, the exposure consisted of William having to try and go to bed alone and sleep by himself at home.

The parent sessions followed much the same structure. First, the parents scored the fear ladder to assess the last session. Second, a review of the home assignment was done. If there had been difficulties in any of the steps of the exposure, the therapist and the parents problem-solved. The therapist evaluated whether any of the difficulties experienced with following the exposure plan were about the parents or the child himself. If the problem was about the child, the therapist had to decide if the step was too difficult or if the child needed extra motivation. When it was parents who struggled to get out of their pattern of rescuing the child, the therapist had to review their psycho-education about anxiety.

Treatment sequences

The ordinary sequence of modules for the anxiety protocol is as follows: Engagement–Fear Ladder–Psycho-education for the Child–Psycho-education for the Parent–Exposure–Maintenance–Cognitive Stop–Wrap Up. The treatment may be adapted to the individual child and family's needs.

In the first session with William, the therapist sought to establish positive and safe relations with him, define goals, and give an overview of the treatment. William learned to use a fear thermometer to differentiate between low and high intensity of his anxious feelings. Then, the family completed a fear ladder together, identifying and rating situations that evoked anxious feelings. This fear ladder was rated in the beginning of each session throughout the therapy. The second session consisted of psycho-education about anxiety in which William learned to recognize the three parts of anxious feelings: bodily reactions, anxious thoughts, and anxious behavior (e.g., avoidance). He was also introduced to the concepts of true and false alarms and the importance of exposure. The third session consisted of psycho-education to the parents. Here, the importance of following through was emphasized to the parents, to stay in the situation during the child's exposure to ensure that he gets the chance to experience that he can tolerate his anxious feelings and that what he fears is going to happen, does not happen. In the following sessions, the therapist, the child, and the parents together planned in detail what William should practice at home during bedtime routines and how the parents should monitor and follow up the plans. It soon became apparent, however, that William would need extra motivation to continue practicing. At this point, the therapist decided to pull in modules from the treatment protocol for conduct problems, specifically the module "praise" for brave behavior and the module "rewards" when the child followed the exposure practices. After having introduced these skills to the parents, the remaining sessions consisted of continuing with increasingly challenging exposure.

Therapeutic process

Despite his anxiety about going to sleep without his parents in the evening, William was, at the start of treatment, also very motivated to be able to go on sleepovers and make the evenings more pleasant for the whole family. However, as treatment progressed and the exposure started, William became more ambivalent about facing his fears and started refusing to practice. William's strong protests toward exposure training at home was challenging for the parents who tried to stick to the therapeutic plan, and it made them unsure as to whether it was right to have the child exposed to the new sleeping routines. The therapist acknowledged how hard it was for all of them to follow through the exposures, but at the same time she communicated that this was necessary in order to obtain the treatment goals. The therapist succeeded in reassuring the parents that this was not harmful to the child, though it was painful, but it was essential to support their son to overcome his anxiety about sleeping alone. This supportive and authoritative attitude displayed by the therapist strengthened the parents' abilities to follow through the plan for exposure training at home. Throughout the whole treatment process, the parents needed substantial support and reassurance to maintain this way of responding during the child's exposure.

Outcomes

At the end of the treatment, William was able to go to sleep alone and stay in his bed throughout the night. He was comfortable about the idea of going to a school camp in the spring. He succeeded in staying on sleepovers with his friends and cousins. The parents developed new skills with a high mindfulness about encouraging their son to expose himself to situations that he had avoided earlier and also to participate in new situations that he would normally have met with great reluctance.

MATCH was tested in an RCT in the US with 10 outpatient service organizations, 84 community clinicians, and 174 clinically referred youths aged 7–13 years (Weisz et al., 2012). The modular approach outperformed usual care and standard evidence-based treatments on multiple clinical outcome measures. A second study reported on the outcomes from the same study but focused on the longer-term impact on the effectiveness of the treatment (Chorpita et al., 2013). MATCH outperformed usual care in the first 6 months of treatment, and also at the 1-year observation period. Rates of change were close to zero for all conditions for the second year of observation, which meant that gains were maintained. A Norwegian effectiveness trial of MATCH is in progress and 280 children aged 6–14 years referred to six child and adolescent psychiatric outpatient clinics will participate in the study (Amlund Hagen, et al., 2018). Recruitment started in 2016 and will continue until December 2018.

Concluding comments

Even if CBT has proven to be quite effective and has been evaluated in numerous RCTs in several different contexts, with various samples and in different countries, the large-scale *implementation* of the therapeutic approach remains a challenge, even though a widespread dissemination has taken place in many countries, including Norway. Most of the CBT training in Norway has been delivered by the Norwegian Association for Cognitive and Behavioral Therapy (NACBT). Feedback to NACBT indicated that trained therapists struggled with obstacles to the clinical use of CBT that may have led to lack of use of the approach in the treatment of eligible clients. A survey was conducted among 562 practitioners trained in CBT (Kjøge, Turtumøygard, Berge, & Ogden, 2015). In line with international research outcomes, the most important obstacles were workplace-related, e.g., lack of regular supervision, lack of opportunities to maintain skills, not enough time to learn the method, too little time for each client, and lack of continuity in CBT training when new staff were recruited. None of the training programs offered by the NACBT were program packages, but rather more general training programs addressing therapeutic skills that were applicable in the treatment of different diagnoses and in different contexts. Compared to the training and supervision in some of the evidence-based programs presented earlier in this chapter, the general CBT training did not have routines for monitoring and measuring treatment fidelity, implementation, and quality control.

Given the fact that both depression and anxiety are frequent mental health problems in general and in adolescence specifically, and considering the fact that they are associated with significant distress and poor outcomes, great efforts should be made to try and prevent these problems. Effective treatment and preventive components that have proven effective in numerous studies and across samples ought to be subject to widespread implementation accompanied by continuing quality assurance. Testing of how treatment and prevention methods can be refined and sharpened, the examination of a method's active ingredients (the mechanisms of the treatment or the treatment kernels), and subgroup analysis (identifying for whom and under what conditions treatment works or does not work) are all important research aims as the answer to these questions will help in tailoring future treatments to individual adolescents and their families.

Selected and indicated prevention approaches appear to be more effective than universal prevention approaches in preventing depression (Gillham, Shatte, & Freres, 2000). Policymakers should consider methods that can be widely used and easily taught, in addition to more specialized approaches, depending on the symptom and risk level of the youth. Moreover, prevention programs utilizing cognitive behavioral and/or interpersonal approaches, and family-based prevention strategies, seem to be the most helpful (Gladstone, Beardslee, & O'Connor, 2010). When adolescents enter into treatment or are the targets of a prevention program, they are simultaneously and always part of a family and a community. When the characteristics of these systems work to worsen or maintain problems in adolescents, they too need to be targets of treatment and prevention initiatives. Finally, prevention or treatment ought not to be concerned with the reduction of problems or risks unilaterally; equally important is the strengthening and identification of the resources and competencies of the youth and his or her environment. Whilst this is likely true for most adolescents who struggle in one area or another, it may be particularly important for anxious and depressed youths as experiences of success and mastery for them may be especially rewarding.

5

ALCOHOL AND DRUG USE

Background

This chapter deals with adolescent alcohol and drug use and with the prevention and treatment of substance use problems. We start with a description of the characteristics of substance use, followed by a brief review of the risk factors for the development of such problems. The emphasis in this chapter is on alcohol and soft drugs such as cannabis and marijuana. Whilst some adolescents unfortunately have advanced to heroin and other hard drugs, they rarely start out using these kinds of substances. Rather, the typical substances used and experimented with by teenagers are alcohol and marijuana. Nevertheless, these "soft drugs" are often considered gateway drugs, a risky stepping stone into full-fledged addictions of harmful substances and devastating lifestyles.

Certain issues covered in this chapter overlap with some of the topics discussed in Chapter 3 on externalizing problem behavior. There are considerable similarities between delinquency and drug abuse, both in the underlying individual and contextual risk factors and in the characteristics of successful interventions. In his discussion of predisposing risk factors in childhood, Rutter (2005) recommends that a main focus should be on conduct problems, as they are among the strongest risk factors for substance use and abuse. Still, there are some differences between the two domains. For one, individual treatment approaches seem to work better in the treatment of drug problems than in the treatment of externalizing behavior. Compared to Chapter 3 on externalizing problem behavior, this chapter goes deeper into the multi-theoretical foundation of interventions. As we see it, no single theory is sufficient to capture the process of successful drug treatment, though several theories are directly relevant for practice, and have contributed to our understanding of the onset and desistance of substance use. Following the section on theoretical perspectives, we review empirically supported family- and community-based treatments, but also promising individual treatments. We discuss the encouraging main effects of selected evidence-based interventions, but we also present characteristics that seem to moderate clinical outcomes. In sum, the main topics of this chapter are: (1) definitions and descriptions of adolescent drug abuse, (2) the risk factors of drug abuse and dependence, (3) the theoretical basis of promising interventions, (4) approaches to drug prevention, (5) approaches to family-based and individual treatments, (6) moderators and predictors of successful treatment, (7) controversial issues, and (8) summary and concluding thoughts. Before we proceed, we would like to stress the importance of *early intervention* in the prevention and treatment of drug abuse. Unlike many types of externalizing problems, drug abuse starts almost exclusively in adolescence. Thus, early intervention may take on a different meaning in this regard. Combating substance abuse in early adolescence is difficult because of the immediate gratifications of drug consummation; the serious and negative consequences appear at a much later stage and may therefore be difficult for the adolescent to grasp. When and if the adolescent crosses the line to heavy drug use, it has proven extremely difficult to change his or her pattern of behavior. Research suggests that the long-term prognosis is better if treatment is initiated as soon as possible after drug use or experimentation has been acknowledged (Dennis & Scott, 2007; Rowe, 2012). Therefore, preventive or early treatment interventions are of utmost importance.

What is drug abuse?

Adolescent drug abuse can be defined as the frequent use of alcohol or other drugs during the teenage years to such an extent that it leads to personal dysfunction and social problems (Hawkins, Catalano, & Miller, 1992). The most frequently used drug is alcohol. Indicators of dependence include affective symptoms, blackouts, reduced activity level, risky sexual behavior, and cravings. Compared to adults, occupational impairment, physiological dependence, and legal problems are rarer. Alcohol abuse progresses in quite predictable stages from initiation, experimental, or occasional use, to regular or escalating use and finally problem use and dependence (Chassin, Ritter, Trim, & King, 2006; Petraitis, Flay, & Miller, 1995). The prevalence figures vary considerably from one country to the next and it is a general finding that adolescent substance use seldom occurs alone (Fuller, 2008). One of the most consistent findings in the literature is that it accompanies disruptive behavior disorders (that include opposition, conduct problems, and ADHD). Several large-scale epidemiological studies of drug use and abuse in young people have been conducted in both the US and Europe, and some of the key findings are reported by Weinberg, Harper, and Brumback (2005), including:

- alcohol and nicotine are the most frequently used substances, followed closely by marijuana;
- only about 1 in 12 who have taken drugs are heavy users;

- drug use is uncommon in children under the age of 12, with the exception of inhalants;
- overall drug use is about as common in girls as in boys, but alcohol abuse is more common in males;
- association with social background varies according to the type of drug, but is more frequent among young people with poor academic achievement; and
- among current approaches to the prevention and treatment of drug problems, those addressing risk and protective factors appear to be the most promising.

The risk factor approach

A risk factor is by definition statistically associated with increased probability of unfavorable outcomes. Consequently, the goal of a risk-focused approach is to prevent drug abuse by eliminating or reducing the precursors. In other words, risk factors increase a young person's chance of using drugs, but they are present or occur before the actual drug problems are manifested. In adolescence, association with drug-abusing peers and peer pressure are highly influential factors (Robertson, David, & Rao, 2003). When entering high school, adolescents are faced with new social, emotional, and educational challenges, and they participate in more social activities that may involve drugs and alcohol.

Individual and interpersonal risk factors

Individual and interpersonal risk factors operate in the micro- and meso-systems, particularly in the adolescent's family and proximal social networks. Hawkins, Catalano, and Miller (1992) mention poor impulse control, sensation seeking, and low harm avoidance as highly profiled risk factors. Drug problems are also related to early and persistent childhood antisocial and aggressive behavior, difficult temperament, school misconduct, and ADHD. In addition, academic failure seems to predict adolescent drug abuse, but it is not clear at what time achievement problems become a stable predictor. In fact, social adjustment problems in early elementary grades seem to be a more important predictor of later drug abuse than are academic difficulties. But in late elementary grades, academic problems may contribute independently to a subsequent initiation of drug use. Moreover, a low degree of commitment to school, including truancy, negative attitudes toward schooling, and indifference toward homework, particularly among older students, place adolescents at risk for drug initiation.

Several risk factors likely operate simultaneously, such as genetic transmission of vulnerability, family modeling of substance-using behavior, and permissive parental attitudes toward drug use. Having parents with a history of alcohol and drug problems increases the risk of developing the same kind of problems, particularly for boys. Poor and inconsistent family management, including unclear expectations and poor monitoring of behavior, few and inconsistent rewards for positive behavior, combined with excessively severe and inconsistent punishment for unwanted behavior practices, increase the risk of drug use. Peers matter too; both peer rejection and association with drug-using peers are among the strongest predictors of adolescent drug use. Alienation and rebelliousness may describe adolescents who have weak bonds to society and who appear to resent or reject social values and norms.

In sum, according to Petraitis, Flay, and Miller (1995), adolescents are most at risk for substance use if they: (1) are detached from their parents, and are more influenced by deviant peers than their parents; (2) have friends who use and endorse substances; (3) have positive attitudes toward substance use; (4) devalue academic achievement; and (5) are socially critical, alienated, rebellious, and seek independence from conventional society. The risk factors listed here operate in the micro- and meso-system, but individual and peer group consumption of drugs are nevertheless influenced by the general attitudes toward and the availability of drugs in society at large.

Contextual risk factors

Contextual risk factors of the exo- and macro-system include such factors as laws and norms of a society. Laws reflect social standards and regulate how and where alcohol is sold, the minimum drinking age, the consequences of driving under the influence and, indirectly, the price of alcohol through the level of taxation. A related risk factor is the availability of substances; increases in the availability of legal drugs such as alcohol generally lead to increased consumption of legal and, possibly, of illegal drugs. Decreasing the availability and advertisement of drugs and increasing the cost of legal substances such as alcohol may have preventive effects (Biglan et al., 2004). Exposure to extreme economic deprivation in childhood may place some individuals at risk for later substance use, but on a general level there does not seem to be a consistent negative relationship between socioeconomic status and adolescent drug use. On the contrary, parental occupational prestige and education have in some studies actually shown to be positively related to teenage drinking (Zucker & Harford, 1983).

The identification of risk factors is important to develop intervention programs that can target core predictors of substance use. Like intervention and prevention programs for other mental health issues, drug prevention and treatment should have a strong theoretical rationale explaining mechanisms and trajectories of adolescent drug use.

Theories of drug use

Theories of the development, prevention, and treatment of substance use are numerous and to a certain extent overlap with theories of externalizing behavior problems. Consequently, most intervention programs that have shown to be effective in the prevention and reduction of drug use are multi-problem programs that also successfully target co-occurring problems such as disruptive behavior problems (Biglan et al., 2004). Because the treatment components are often combined across programs, it may be difficult to decide which elements specifically address the drug problems. Some of the most influential theoretical explanations of the development and mechanisms through which drug abusers' behavior is changed have been reviewed by Petraitis, Flay, & Miller (1995).

Behavior theory

The essence of behavior theory is learning from contingencies in interpersonal transactions. Behavior is viewed as a function of past and present environmental and genetic variables. But the focus is predominately on environmental influences since these are more dynamic and more easily changed than are genetics. In dysfunctional families, excessive aversive parent behavior toward the adolescent is typically combined with weak or ineffective consequences. Rather than enter into dialogues with their teenagers, some parents criticize, blame, and preclude constructive problem-solving. These reactions may promote the development of drug problems, but they may also be reversed through treatment in such a way that they contribute to the reduction or elimination of drug abuse. Effective treatment components of this theory include increased negative consequences for drug use and the systematic use of rewards and encouragement for abstinence.

Cognitive–affective theories

Cognitive theories seek to explain how adolescents' behavior is affected by their thoughts and beliefs about the consequences of drug use. Drug-specific expectations and attitudes influence whether an individual decides to try drugs. Individual characteristics such as personality and cognition and external influences such as peer influences are mediated through the adolescent's thinking, evaluation, and decisions. So, if a young person expects the advantages to be greater than the disadvantages, she or he is more likely to try drugs. This theory has clear implications for practice by recommending that interventions strengthen the messages about health risks and, if possible, help reduce the positive expectations about drug use. Moreover, adolescents seem to have a strong tendency to overestimate how many of their peers actually use drugs and interventions should therefore aim at changing biased perceptions about the prevalence of drug use among adolescents. Finally, refusal skills ought to be reinforced through information and skills training. A limitation of the cognitive theory is that it does not explain whether the beliefs are the cause or the consequence of substance use, nor does it clarify why some adolescents develop positive expectations about substance use whilst others do not. The reason why some adolescents develop negative attitudes toward drugs may be explained by social learning theory.

Social learning theory

Social learning theory emphasizes how adolescents learn deviant behavior from their role models of choice, usually their parents and friends (Bandura, 1986).

According to this highly influential theory, substance-specific attitudes and behavior of adolescents are learned by observing and imitating role models with whom the youth interacts. After observing how significant others relate to drugs, a young person may feel socially encouraged and supported to use drugs, and finally develop expectations of positive social and physical consequences of substance use. Social learning theory conveys a long-term perspective on the importance of role models, their attitudes, and behavior. Among recommendations for treatment are interventions that emphasize role models who abstain from drugs and the teaching of refusal skills.

Social attachment and bonding

Attachment theory explains how the emotional attachment or bonding to peers who use drugs may cause substance use, and alternatively, how a lack of positive relationships with caring adults may do the same. Closely related is Gottfredson and Hirschi's (1990) control theory, which claims that impulses in all people are affected by strong bonds to conventional persons and groups, and that this social control gradually becomes internalized. Adolescents who have weak social bonds and fragile attachment to conventional role models (e.g., parents and teachers) have little to lose when joining deviant peer groups. The lack of internalized social control may be due to "strain," that is, a discrepancy between a person's aspirations to succeed and his or her perceived opportunities. Youngsters growing up in disadvantaged families or neighborhoods may lack the social and academic skills necessary for coping with demands at home and at school. As a consequence, they may look for drug-using environments in which they have a greater probability of experiencing rewarding interactions, because conventional rules and norms in these contexts are lax or absent. The practical implications of the theory are that interventions should promote academic and social skills, build stronger social bonding with the family, with teachers, and with pro-social friends. Interventions in this tradition do not target substance use directly, but address factors that promote attachment to pro-social role models and commitment to conventional values (Petraitis, Flay, & Miller, 1995).

Intrapersonal theories

Several of the theories presented above share the assumption that within a social setting, adolescents differ in their motivation to use drugs and in their bonding with substance-using peers. These individual differences in motivational and attachment patterns have their basis in negative self-concept, stress in school, emotional difficulties, lack of social interaction, and dysfunctional coping skills. Elaborating on the theoretical perspective emphasizing intrapersonal characteristics, Sher (1991) formulated a theory of *vulnerability* based on models of the genetic basis for alcoholism. According to this theory, most risk factors for the development of drug use are of biological origin and explain why some families have a history of drug abuse whilst others do not. Sher claims that drug abuse develops because of differences in the biological foundation of the personality, the cognitive functioning, and in pharmacological sensitivity to substances. For example, children of alcoholics may inherit a difficult temperament or personality and they may have reduced cognitive functions (e.g., planning skills and attention). Additionally, they may have an increased pharmacological sensitivity to alcohol, an increased tolerance for alcohol, and a reduced sensitivity to the negative effects of alcohol. The practical implication of individual vulnerability theory is that substance use can be prevented by targeting personality traits and affective states of the youth rather than the substance-specific behavior of their peers. Longitudinal studies have found, however, that these factors are relatively weak predictors of substance use because intrapersonal (or individual) characteristics influence drug use primarily through drug-specific attitudes (Petraitis, Flay, & Miller, 1995).

Integrative theories

Compared to the theories presented so far, integrative theories try to combine the influence of: (1) social and interpersonal factors from family and social networks, and the modeling of substance-specific behavior by friends and parents; (2) cultural and attitudinal influences including commitment to conventional values and attachment to parents; and (3) personal or individual characteristics such as substance-specific cognitions and attitudes, personality traits, dispositions, emotional problems, and skills (Petraitis, Flay, & Miller, 1995). One such theory, *the problem theory* (Jessor & Jessor, 1977), addresses the risk factors underlying a host of different problem behaviors in youth. The theory explains that adolescents who are at risk for one problem behavior are also at risk for other problem behaviors. Accordingly, the interactions between the person and the environment that predict substance abuse are also strong predictors of other problem behaviors such as aggression and antisocial behavior.

Another example is *the social ecology of misuse*, which combines social learning, social control theory, and Bronfenbrenner's (1979) overarching social ecological perspective. To test this theoretical framework, Ennett et al. (2008), examined whether attributes of the family, peer, school, and neighborhood contexts predicted the development of alcohol misuse in adolescents aged 11–17 years. The study confirmed the joint relevance of social learning and social control theories by finding that the influence of alcohol use by others was usually conditional, depending on the nature of the social bond between the youth and significant others. In other words, interactions rather than main effects were the best predictors of alcohol use. And even though a youth's social contexts generally were found to be relevant to the development of alcohol misuse, *the family* seemed to be the most important predictor. And interestingly enough, the influence of the family did not wane over time.

In the next section, we turn to the issue of prevention of drug abuse. Most prevention strategies have a multi-theoretical basis, although at present the social learning theory and the Cognitive–affective theories seem to dominate the field. The field of drug prevention is also heavily influenced by research on risk and protective factors pertaining to drug use under the theoretical umbrella of social ecology of misuse.

Approaches to drug prevention

Studies of the causal pathways to drug abuse indicate that prevention policies with steps to constrain access to substances that carry risk for abuse or dependence are useful (Rutter, 2005). Bloom and Gullotta (2009) offer a broad perspective on prevention and recommend the inclusion of preventive, protective, and promotive actions in a *dynamic ecological perspective* on evidence-based approaches to adolescent substance abuse:

> Primary prevention involves actions taken by individuals and groups to prevent predictable problems, protect existing states of health and healthy functioning, and promote desired states of being and functioning within supportive or benign physical and socio-cultural environments.
>
> *(p. 155)*

In their review of general strategies for the prevention of substance use with adolescents, Bloom and Gullotta (2009) include *education* as the most common, although not the most effective, strategy when used alone. They stress that information alone does not affect attitudes, and therefore probably not behavior either. A second commonly used strategy is the promotion of *self-competency*, which starts when an adolescent enters a group, the group accepts the new member, and the individual makes a meaningful contribution to the group (e.g., Hawkins, Catalano, & Miller, 1992). The third strategy is *natural caregiving*, which may include mutual self-help groups led by laypersons and trained teachers, youth leaders, coaches, or others. Another example of natural caregiving is simply *friendship*, in which social support is offered to another person to promote health and social competence. Summing up the general preventive strategies, Bloom and Gullotta (2009) state: "Thus the full circle is completed–education informs, natural caregiving unites, social competency enables, social institutions create, and the physical environment supports" (p. 165).

The broad perspective on drug prevention is further supported by Hawkins, Catalano, Kosterman, Abbott, and Hill (1999) in their summary of how research targeting risk factors of drug use has inspired the development of prevention approaches such as: (1) early childhood and family support programs, (2) programs for parents of children and adolescents, (3) social competence skills training, (4) academic achievement promotion and alteration in classroom instructional practices, (5) organizational changes in schools, and (6) youth involvement in alternative activities. Some comprehensive risk-focused programs target several problems and combine several of the interventions listed above, whilst others have a more restricted range and address drug use only or even just a single substance.

The most frequently used drug prevention programs emphasize teaching of refusal skills, and the promotion of restrictive parent norms toward drug use (Koutakis, Stattin, & Kerr, 2008).

School-based prevention

Two major groups of effective school-based prevention programs were identified in Tobler et al.'s (2000) meta-analysis: (1) social influence programs emphasizing skill building, persuasion, and norm setting; and (2) comprehensive life skills programs teaching problem-solving, assertiveness, decision-making, coping, goal setting, and refusal skills. Both groups of programs stress the importance of interaction between teachers and students, and between students: "The message is clear: relying on information or persuasion alone is unlikely to affect teen behavior. Additional skill building that involves rehearsal and engagement by teens seems to be required to produce changes in substance use" (Biglan et al., 2004, p. 134). In line with the general recommendations for preventive efforts, most school programs address risk factors for drug abuse such as aggressive behavior, poor social skills, and academic difficulties. For older students, it is important that prevention programs aim at improving academic and social competence, including improvements in: (1) study habits and academic support, (2) communication, (3) peer relationships, (4) self-efficacy and assertiveness, (5) drug resistance skills, and (6) the reinforcement of anti-drug attitudes and strengthening of personal commitments against drug abuse. Three examples of universal school-based prevention programs will be described next: life skills training, preparing for the drug-free years, and the Örebro prevention project.

Botvin and Griffin's *Life Skills Training (LST) program* is a universal classroom curriculum based on social learning theory that targets risk and protective factors associated with drug-use initiation and teaches skills related to social resistance and social competence (Botvin & Griffin, 2004). Components of social influence resistance training are combined with skills such as problem-solving, decision-making, self-control, and assertion (Botvin, 1990). Findings from more than two decades of evaluation research are summarized by Botvin and Griffin (2004) and include small-scale efficacy studies as well as large effectiveness trials with a variety of adolescent populations. The studies indicate that LST has positive behavioral effects on smoking, alcohol, and marijuana use with prevention effects lasting up until the end of high school. Significant results are reported up to 6 years post-baseline (Botvin, Griffin, Diaz, & Ifill-Williams, 2001).

Preparing for the Drug Free Years is a program that helps parents and their middle-school-aged children prepare for a developmental period when children are vulnerable for initiating use of and experimenting with drugs. The program has five sessions. Four of these involve the parents, only. Parents are encouraged to use persuasion and consequences, and to monitor the children's behavior and whereabouts. In order to prevent drug use, parents receive information about typical family management problems, family drug use, peer drug use, alienation, and rebelliousness. Parents learn how to conduct family meetings to improve parent–child communications and parent–child interactions in children aged 8–14 years (Kosterman, Hawkins, Spoth, Haggerty, & Zhu, 1997). Hawkins et al. (1999) reported that interventions with teachers, parents, and children throughout the elementary grades had enduring effects on reducing heavy drinking and violent behavior by age 18 among multiethnic urban children.

The Örebro prevention program (ÖPP) is a 2.5-year prevention program working with parents and targeting drinking among 13–16-year-olds (Koutakis, Stattin, & Kerr, 2008). Parents are recruited through school meetings and mailings. The intervention primarily involves information to parents delivered through the schools. Teachers are asked to support the program publicly and to allocate time in parent meetings for parents to learn about the program. The parents are advised to communicate a zero tolerance attitude toward youth drinking and to enforce clear rules to their children. At the meetings, the parents are asked to formulate and sign agreements about their positions on drinking, and most parents comply. The agreements are mailed to all parents, including those not present. In all, five parent meetings are held: one in seventh grade, two in eighth grade, and then two in ninth grade. In addition, parents receive three mailings each semester repeating the key message from the meetings and stressing the importance of formulating and communicating strict rules against alcohol and drug use. In a quasi-experimental study, 900 students entering junior high school at age 13 and their parents participated. The project succeeded in bolstering the parents' strict attitudes and at the end of the program, self-reported drunkenness and frequency of drunkenness were lower in the intervention group compared to the control group. Another aim of the project, increased participation in organized activities, was not achieved. The authors speculate that the key to the success of the program may have been that it simply encouraged parents to maintain their positions, assuming that most parents of seventh-graders were against youth drinking (Koutakis et al., 2008; see also Ryan et al., 2011).

Overall, school-based drug prevention programs seem to be more effective than family-based programs, even if family focused interventions may supplement universal programs for adolescents who show emerging drug problems. In a meta-analysis of school-based substance use prevention, Ennett et al. (2003) found that school-based programs typically showed short-term effects on adolescent drug use, but that long-term effects were more difficult to achieve. In another meta-analysis, cognitive behavioral programs that emphasize social influencing approaches, refusal skills, and general social skills were most effective, particularly if combined with interactive teaching (Gottfredson & Wilson, 2003). The most successful school prevention programs according to Robertson, David, and Rao (2003) are interactive with peer discussion groups and role-playing, in addition to teacher training of classroom management practices that foster positive behavior, achievement, academic motivation, and school bonding.

When the evidence-based approach to drug prevention started in the US in the mid-1990s, the National Institute of Drug Abuse sponsored a booklet entitled "Preventing Drug Use Among Children and Adolescents" (Sloboda & David, 1997).

In the second edition from 2003 (Robertson et al., 2003), 16 prevention principles were presented intending to help parents, educators, and community leaders to plan and implement research-based drug abuse prevention programs. Based on the finding that the risk of drug abuse depends on the relationship among the number and type of risk factors (e.g., deviant attitudes and behaviors) and protective factors (e.g., parental support), the first prevention principle read: "Prevention programs should enhance protective factors and reverse or reduce risk factors" (p. 2). The other principles emphasized that prevention programs should address all forms of drug abuse, alone or in combination. Family programs should enhance family bonding and relationships, parental monitoring and supervision, and enforcement of family policies on substance abuse.

Next, we turn to the topic of treatment interventions. Although the strategy of addressing risk factors is relevant to the domain of treatment as well as to prevention, there are some important differences. Certain preventive tactics do not seem to work in interventions targeting adolescents who have already embarked on a "career" of substance use. They are in need of more individualized and comprehensive treatment methods, preferably individual-, family-, and community-based interventions.

Approaches to treatment

One group of treatment approaches can be categorized as *family- and community-based*, many of which have demonstrated promising outcomes in controlled evaluation trials (Calix & Fine, 2009; Rowe, 2012). Another approach is *individual treatment*, which emphasizes the importance of influencing the adolescents' behavior, cognition, attitudes, and values through the modification of contingencies and through cognitive and social skills training. The overall message from research is that family- and community-based approaches should be the number one priority in treatment of drug problems, although there is some evidence to suggest that individual treatment may work for some. There are several possible reasons for why effective home- and family-based treatments of externalizing problems overlap with effective treatment of substance use. One is that externalizing behavior and substance use often co-occur in adolescence. Antisocial adolescents are often keen to experiment with substances, and youths who are under the influence of drugs often act out. Another reason is that many of the underlying individual and contextual risk factors are shared by drug use and externalizing behavior. A third reason is that youths at risk have a tendency to associate with peer groups that support both drug use and disruptive behavior. This co-occurrence of problems may also help explain why some of the same treatment models or programs have been equally successful, regardless of whether drug use or acting-out behavior has been identified as the main problem.

Family- and community-based treatment models

Family-oriented approaches have only recently arrived in the field of drug treatment and rest upon two assumptions:

The family plays an important role in the creation of conditions related to adolescent drug use, and certain family environments and parent-adolescent relationships can both protect adolescents against drug use and offer an antidote for drug use that has already begun.

(Liddle & Dakof, 1995, p. 218)

Drug use and family interactions seem to be inextricably linked and addressing family issues can be critical to short- and long-term treatment success (Rowe, 2012). The term "family-based treatment" often replaces the term "family therapy," such as when treatment goes beyond the family system and views individual drug abuse as an eco-systemic problem (Stanton et al., 1982). Most family- and community-based treatments are short term and target adolescents aged 11–18 years. In the following section, we present some of the family-based approaches to treatment of drug abuse in adolescents. Some of these programs have also demonstrated positive treatment outcomes in the treatment of externalizing problem behavior, and were presented in Chapter 3. FFT and MST belong to this group of effective intervention programs. In this chapter, we will therefore not repeat the general structure and contents of these two programs but stress their appropriateness in the treatment of drug problems. We start by reviewing some of the intervention programs developed specifically for the treatment of drug problems.

Family Behavior Therapy

Family Behavior Therapy is based on systemic family theory and behavioral theory and explains that drug use is maintained by physiological as well as situational contingencies. The aim is to reduce the use of drugs and alcohol in individuals specifically, even if they may have co-occurring problems such as depression, behavior problems, and family difficulties (Donohue & Azrin, 2001). The treatment typically consists of 15 sessions spanning 6 months. Interventions may include: (1) use of behavioral contracts to reinforce behavior associated with abstinence, (2) implementing skill-based components to spend less time with persons or situations eliciting drug use, (3) skills training to reduce the desire to use drugs, (4) training in communication skills to establish social relations with people who do not use drugs, and (5) job-seeking training or school application skills (Azrin et al., 2001). Motivational strategies may also be included.

The treatment model takes a *family systems approach* by studying the characteristics of the family system in which the drug problems occur. Among the family characteristics examined are: (1) clarity and permeability of boundaries, (2) flexibility of interactions, (3) proximity of the family members, (4) autonomy of the family members, (5) degree of interdependence between the family members and the surrounding systems, and (6) repetitive behavioral sequences that maintain the family homeostasis or status quo (Bry, 1988). The therapist both observes and interacts with the family with the aim of discovering behavioral sequences, alliances, and unspoken family rules that maintain the family status quo and the adolescent's problem. The adolescent's behavior is changed by changing the parents' behavior (Bry, 1988). It is made clear to the parents that the therapist is not going to "fix the child," but she or he can help parents "fix the environment." The target behavior should be one that the parents are most concerned about, and the therapist analyzes the functional relationship between the problem behavior and its antecedents and consequences. In collaboration with the parents, the therapist selects a particular measurable problem behavior, establishes the base rate of that behavior per unit of time, changes the environment, and reports the impact of the change on the targeted behavior. Principles and skills of behavior change can be taught to caregivers in several ways, for instance by providing reading material, interactive instruction, modeling, behavioral rehearsal, providing reinforcement, and assigning homework. The parents are taught how to pinpoint behavior and then to analyze and change the antecedents and the consequences of that behavior. For instance, they are supported in how to communicate the new rules to the adolescent in a calm manner, reduce their frequency of demands, nagging, and commands. They are also advised to consistently praise or provide a tangible reward for desirable behavior and consistently punish or withdraw attention or rewards for undesirable behavior. Among the options is the use of contingency contracts, written documents specifying which behaviors are to be changed and the reinforcement arrangements that have been agreed upon by the members of the family. Such contracts specify that the adolescent and the other members of the family will obtain something desired through compromise. The model has shown to result in a significant reduction in drug use and related mental health problems and an increase in school attendance (Austin, Macgowan, & Wagner, 2005).

Adolescent Community Reinforcement Approach

The Adolescent Community Reinforcement Approach (ACRA) treatment has much in common with the previous model and builds on behavioral theory and Bronfenbrenner's (1979) social ecological theory. The target group is adolescents between 13 and 18 years of age with a low to moderate drug problem and their families. During therapy, the adolescent is reinforced and rewarded for staying drug-free, and he or she is taught how to take advantage of resources in the community to support positive change and to develop a positive support system within the family (Azrin, 1976). Functional analysis is used to help the youth to identify antecedents to drug use, to partake in social activities, establish positive friendships, and improve family relations. The approach also encourages the caregivers to participate in the treatment. Parents learn how to promote abstinence from drugs, and to improve their parenting skills. The treatment model has demonstrated significant reduction in drug use in youth at the termination of treatment (Kaminer, 2002).

Brief Strategic Family Therapy

Most family- and community-based treatments have a flexible treatment length, but Brief Strategic Family Therapy (BSFT) is less intensive and is limited to 12–16 sessions (Szapocznik, Hervis, & Schwartz, 2003). BSFT is based on systemic family theory, structural and strategic family therapy and relies on three core strategies to alter family interactions (Minuchin, 1974). The three main elements of the model are the engagement phase (*joining*), the diagnostic phase, and the restructuring phase. The therapist tries to establish a new system in the family in which the therapist is both an observer and a change agent. The approach is limited to the family system and does not include the wider social network as the latter task is left to the family itself. A great deal of outreach should be expected to access families who have an adolescent with substance use problems. Home visits are carried out to recruit families and the therapist "joins" the family by accepting the goals and values of each family member. The therapist makes a promise that if the family will engage in therapy for a limited period, she or he will help the family reach their goals. Joining the family may also include regular telephone contact between sessions. In order to clarify boundaries within the family system, rules should be established allowing family members to finish talking without being interrupted and prohibiting family members from speaking on others' behalf. The caregivers are encouraged to set limits of their young adolescent's freedom, and both limit setting and marital problems are discussed when the youth is not present (Kaufman, 1985). The model has been evaluated in several studies (Szapocznik & Williams, 2000), including one by Santisteban, Muir, Mena, and Mitrani (2003) which demonstrated that BSFT was superior to group therapy in reducing marijuana use.

Multidimensional Family Therapy

Multidimensional Family Therapy (MDFT) is based on developmental psychology, social ecological theory, and partly on family therapy. The treatment approach communicates that adolescent substance abuse develops along pathways that involve peer relationships, family relationships, individual psychological issues, and the extra-familial system. The therapy is manual-based and focuses on the youth, the family, and their social network. The treatment has three stages, each consisting of several modules. In stage one, the aim is to engage the family. The therapist meets with the adolescent and the caregivers separately; the therapist then meets with the whole family before their wider social network is contacted. In stage two, the primary interventions are initiated in which the goal is to be insight oriented, skills oriented, and solution focused. When interventions are targeting the parents, family discussions of conflicts are emphasized. In stage three, changes in the family are acknowledged and reflected back to the family members, and the termination of the therapy is planned. MDFT has a strong empirical track record in the treatment of substance abuse (Hogue, Henderson, Ozechowski, & Robins, 2014; Liddle, 2010). The program has shown to be effective in reducing drug consumption both at termination of treatment and in follow-up studies. In previous reviews, MDFT demonstrated consistent reductions in adolescent drug use (Austin et al., 2005; Becker & Curry, 2008; Brannigan, Schackman, Falco, & Millman, 2004; Waldron & Turner, 2008). Liddle, Rowe, Dakof, Henderson, & Greenbaum (2009) tested MDFT in an RCT with 83 young minority adolescents (aged 11–15 years) referred to drug treatment. MDFT youths showed greater decreases in marijuana use compared to youths receiving a manual-based CBT peer group treatment. MDFT youths were also more likely to stop using drugs and to report no drug problems in the 12-month follow-up study. Youths' and families' functioning improved during treatment in several domains and the gains following treatment were also maintained in the follow-up period (Liddle et al., 2009).

Functional Family Therapy

The Functional Family Therapy (FFT) intervention program has the same eco-logical and family therapeutic basis as other multisystemic models and was ini-tially designed for the treatment of adolescents with serious behavior problems (Sexton & Alexander, 2005). We described this treatment intervention program in Chapter 3. Since its introduction in the early 1970s, FFT has been extensively researched and has made way for the subsequent development and study of family-based treatments for drug-abusing adolescents. Several studies have shown encour-aging results in the treatment of substance use problems (e.g., Rowe, 2012; Waldron, Brody, & Hops, 2017; Waldron, Slesnick, Brody, Turner, & Peterson, 2001).

Multisystemic Therapy

As presented in Chapter 3, Multisystemic Therapy (MST) is based on Bronfenbrenner's (1979) ecological model. Among the inclusion criteria for MST treatment is substance use in combination with antisocial behavior. Summarizing the research outcomes of MST, Sheidow and Henggeler (2008) reported on four studies that targeted substance-using adolescents (Borduin et al., 1995; Henggeler, Melton, & Smith 1992; Henggeler et al., 1999; Henggeler, Clingempeel, Brondino, & Pickrel, 2002). MST has demonstrated encouraging results on substance-related outcomes. In order to increase the effectiveness in the treatment of substance-using adolescents, however, more recent approaches have integrated CM and CBT into MST (Henggeler et al., 2006; Randall, Henggeler, Cunningham, Rowland, & Swenson, 2001).

Multisystemic treatment and contingency management

The CM/CBT model has been successfully and separately evaluated as a treatment approach for substance use, and previous studies indicate that CM/CBT probably adds to the effectiveness of the ecologically oriented MST program (Randall et al., 2001). The CM and CBT approach has therefore been integrated with MST in the treatment of youth drug problems both in the US (Henggeler et al., 2006) and in Norway (Holth, Torsheim, Sheidow, Ogden, & Henggeler, 2011). The Norwegian MST/CM study is presented here in some detail because it illustrates the prob-able gain of adding empirically supported components to the MST model. The characteristics of CM, including the frequent, but random, collection of biological drug screens and the delivery of positive reinforcers, may add to the effects of MST. During treatment, vouchers or points can be exchanged for specific, individualized goods or preferred activities contingent upon clean screens. Also, detailed functional analyses of interrelations between drug-related behavior and its antecedents and consequences are easily integrated into the MST model. Self-management training and planning may also be delivered based on the results of the functional analyses (Cunningham et al., 2003).

MULTISYSTEMIC THERAPY: A CONTINGENCY MANAGEMENT CASE

Brad is an acting-out adolescent who regularly abuses drugs, stays out at nights, and bullies his parents. At home, there are serious conflicts marked by verbal abuse, vandalism, and violence. Brad stays out at nights two or three times each week, and some weeks on a daily basis. He uses marijuana, alcohol, and pills once or twice each week. He is very persistent and is totally unwilling to comply with his parents' demands. When pressured or denied something, he may become threatening and violent. On occasions, he has chased after his mother and father, punching and kicking them and destroying property in the house.

On the positive side, Brad usually gets along with others and he is good with children, for instance his little brother who he cares about a lot. And even if he bullies and tyrannizes his family, he occasionally helps out at home doing household chores. Brad's mother is a caring person and she's good at organizing things at home. The father has a generally good and supportive relationship with his son, and he uses humor to solve conflicts. Brad also has a few positive friends with whom he likes to spend time, and a good network of relatives. The local community is generally safe, with a well-developed service system, and the family is on good terms with their neighbors. On the downside, Brad is easily drawn into negative activities that lead to drug consumption and conflicts at home. He has some negative peers who are involved in illegal activities and who also stay away from school. Apart from weekly visits to the local community center, there is not much for him to do besides hang out at a mall with an arcade in which drugs are being traded and older youths buy alcohol for the younger ones. The parents are usually uninformed about where Brad is, what he is up to, and who he is spending time with, particularly at night. They admit that they have little overview and control of the situation. The parents often disagree on how to set limits and the use of consequences for rule-breaking behavior; his father is strict and his mother more lenient. The father wants to be less short-tempered and irritable and wants to argue less with Brad in minor confrontations. The mother wants to be firmer and calmer in difficult situations.

Brad's mother wants him to stop taking drugs, attend school every day, come home every night, and stop being threatening and destructive. These goals are also supported by his father, who also wants him to be involved in positive activities with pro-social friends. The extended family want to help Brad get rid of his drug problem, and to put an end to the conflicts at home. Brad himself wants help to stop taking drugs. The Child Welfare Services want Brad to attend school more regularly, reduce conflicts at home, and help the parents change their ways of setting limits to Brad's behavior. The therapist wants to help the family interact with less conflict and to help Brad stop taking drugs and come home at night.

In order for the parents to monitor Brad's whereabouts, they committed themselves to increase their monitoring activities by collecting information about who his friends and their parents were, and where he spent his time away from home. They also established clear rules about what was allowed and what was not accepted at home, and also clear contingencies for following or breaking rules.

A contingency contract was written between Brad and his parents in which he agreed to come home every night at 21:30, except for Fridays when he should return after the club at 23:45 at the latest. On Saturdays, he should be home no later than 23:00 and his parents should have approved of his whereabouts. In return, he would receive 10 kr every day he came home on time and, when he had earned 150 kr, he would get a phone card. If he did not come home on time, he would be fined 10 kr and would have to come home 1 hour earlier for the next 2 days. If he did not comply, he would get a 1-day curfew. Brad committed himself to stop taking drugs, documented by negative urine screens and the absence of negative reports from the parents and the police. When he came home in the evenings he agreed to taking a urine screen test which his father administered. For every week with no negative urine screens and no fines, he earned 300 kr, which he could use to buy clothes of his own choice. If he had taken drugs or was fined, he did not earn money to buy clothes, but only received functional clothes as deemed necessary by the parents. Brad also agreed to stop using threats and violence, documented by reports from parents, family, and police.

The reward system was a three-level escalating voucher-based schedule in which more points could gradually be earned to attain successive levels after consecutive weeks with clean urine screens. Points could be exchanged for rewards that were identified by Brad and his parents and described in a rewards menu. Rewards typically included activities (e.g., driving), social events (e.g., having friends visit), items (new clothes, cell phone or CDs), or privileges (e.g., extended curfew, favorite meals). Negative consequences of positive drug screens included being dropped down to a lower level on the reward system as well as the loss of privileges (e.g., restrictions on transportation, new clothes, and curfew) (Holth et al., 2011).

The cognitive behavioral component consisted of a detailed functional analysis of substance use that served as a basis for self-management planning. The functional analyses were performed by the parent and the therapist together, and they also collaborated in planning of interventions and in monitoring of the self-management and the substance use outcomes for Brad. He was instructed in how to tell others that he did not want to use drugs, how to react to drug-use triggers according to a trigger list, and how to avoid situations that typically involved drug use. Finally, Brad was trained by the therapist in drug-refusal skills practice.

Next, the parents discussed the contract with the therapist to assess the need for adjustments. The parents gathered information about Brad's friends and contacted their parents. A social network map was drawn and potential support persons were invited to a meeting. Possible barriers for the achievement of the treatment goals were also discussed.

Evaluation of advances in the treatment showed that Brad had started with urine screens and followed the parents' instructions with only one exception. New intermediate goals were set, in which the parents should modify their reactions to Brad's rage when he was denied what he wanted. The mother contacted a homework mentor for a first appointment. The father was still responsible for supervising Brad's urine screens.

The Norwegian Multisystemic Therapy: a contingency management project

The Norwegian project of integrating CM and CBT into MST was a transcultural replication of a US study that investigated therapist adherence to behavioral interventions as a result of an intensive quality assurance system (Holth et al., 2011). During the project period, 21 therapists treated 41 cannabis-abusing adolescents and their families. The youths eligible for participation to the project ranged in age from 13–17 years and met diagnostic criteria for cannabis abuse or dependence. During the workshop, therapists were taught CM/CBT intervention skills and were prepared for the challenges of working with substance-using adolescents (Cunningham et al., 2003). In addition to the training and resources supplied during the workshop, intensive quality assurance included manual-based components related to treatment, supervision, expert consultation, organizational support by the supervisors, and ongoing training. The outcomes of the study were encouraging, albeit not all in the expected direction. Results suggested that CM skills improved over time for the Norwegian therapists, irrespective of condition. This indicated that the CM workshop followed by clinical practice and monthly reminders through assessment of fidelity was sufficient for the MST therapists to establish skills in CM. Cannabis abstinence increased as a function of time in treatment for all participants. The study demonstrated how MST in combination with cognitive behavioral and contingency management procedures could be effective in the treatment of drug problems, although the outcomes for the intensive adherence measure used did not live up to expectations.

In the following section, we present research on individual treatment approaches. Cognitive behavioral, motivational, and operant learning theories help explain why individual treatment of drug abuse may be effective. Some examples also follow.

Individual treatment

Individual treatment includes interventions that help adolescents recognize triggers of substance use and develop drug-refusal skills. Cognitive behavioral approaches in which the youth is taught how to identify and change disturbing or intrusive thoughts and perceptions that may lead to drug use are related interventions. Another group of individual interventions focuses on the adolescent's knowledge and awareness of her or his own drug abuse and helps motivate behavioral change.

Cognitive Behavior Therapy

Cognitive Behavior Therapy (CBT) is among the most frequently cited empirically supported individual interventions and aims at reducing problems related to dysfunctional feelings, behavior, and thinking patterns by changing the youth's cognition or skills (Dembo & Muck, 2009). The model is based on classical, operant, and social learning theory in which drug use is functionally related to the youth's problems. The treatment is usually manual-based with emphasis on specific cognitive and behavioral strategies and techniques. Irrational and dysfunctional thoughts are identified and challenged by cognitive restructuring and by using modeling and role-play to learn functional skills. Most CBTs have the following characteristics in common: (1) they build on a cognitive model for emotional reactions, (2) they are short-term and time-limited treatments, (3) a therapeutic relation is necessary but is not the main focus, (4) they emphasize a collaborative union between therapist and client, (5) they are structured and partly directive, and (6) the youth is encouraged to do homework tasks. CBT principles are discussed in more detail in Chapter 4, as CBT is the treatment method of choice in treating anxiety and depression. CBT has been found to help reduce drug use among adolescents (Azrin et al., 2001; Becker & Curry, 2008; Kaminer, 2002). CBT has been compared to MDFT in the treatment of adolescent drug abuse treatment (Liddle, Dakof, Turner, Henderson, & Greenbaum, 2008). Both treatments produced significant decreases in cannabis use and there were no treatment differences in reducing frequency of cannabis and alcohol use (although MDFT demonstrated higher sustainability of treatment effects over time).

Motivational enhancement therapy and motivational interviewing

This individually oriented treatment approach was developed by Miller and Rollnick (2002) to help individuals who struggle with their motivation and who are ambivalent toward engaging in treatment. Motivational interviewing (MI) is based on the assumption that behavioral change is intentional and contingent on constructive participation from the client. In order to get "in sync" with their clients' motivation, the therapists follow five principles: (1) express empathy, (2) develop discrepancy, (3) avoid argumentation, (4) roll with the resistance, and (5) support self-efficacy. The three stages of therapy are thought to facilitate motivation for change, strengthening commitment to change, and secure follow-through. Therapeutic techniques include active listening, reflections, and the use of questions with an empathetic attitude. Coping strategies for high-risk situations are proposed and discussed with the client, and the therapist monitors change and encourages decisions to terminate drug use. If relevant, the client is asked to bring along significant others such as parents or friends to the treatment sessions. Evaluation studies have shown that motivational interviewing is most effective when used in combination with other forms of intensive drug treatment (Becker & Curry, 2008; Kaminer, 2002).

Treatment moderators, predictors, and core components

In a review of research on drug treatment, Kristoffersen, Holth, and Ogden (2011) examined research on potential moderators that may influence the association between treatment approach and outcomes. Examining moderators can help answer the question of "what works for whom," but few moderators have been identified in research on drug use thus far. The review concluded that current research has not indicated whether certain treatment models are more effective for boys than for girls, for different ethnic groups, or for different forms of drug abuse. Family- and community-based treatment models seem to produce positive outcomes regardless of groups, type of drugs, comorbid disorders, age, gender, and ethnic background. Thus, to a certain extent, the question remains open as to whether gender-sensitive or culturally sensitive treatments may moderate outcomes in future studies.

A rather consistent finding in the research literature is that youths who have drug-abusing friends are themselves at much greater risk of abusing drugs (e.g., Connell, Dishion, Yasui, & Kavanagh, 2007; Dishion & Loeber, 1985). Almost all research examining *therapeutic alliance* with adolescent drug abusers has investigated family-based models and several studies have linked the lack of alliance to premature dropout (Hogue & Liddle, 2009; Robins et al., 2006; Rowe, 2012). Therapeutic alliance seems to predict the probability of retaining youths in treatment and also reducing the amount of problem behavior, including drug abuse (Diamond, Mensinger, Kaminer, & Wintersteen, 2006; Hogue, Dauber, Faw, Cecero, & Liddle, 2006). In a meta-analysis, therapeutic alliance was associated with positive treatment outcomes across treatment models and for clinical subgroups of children and adolescents (Shirk & Karver, 2003). The prevention of premature dropout and positive treatment outcomes were also predicted by a positive thera-peutic alliance in an MST study (Cunningham & Henggeler, 1999). Moreover, well-developed, intensive, and family-based *motivational techniques* demonstrate better results compared to standard motivational practice regarding retaining the youth or the family in treatment. Other promising predictors of treatment par-ticipation are low levels of drug abuse, fewer behavior problems, less psychopath-ology, good school functioning and achievement, holding a job, being motivated for treatment, fewer previous drug treatments, and social support from friends and parents (Williams, Chang, & Addiction Center Adolescent Research Group 2000). Plant and Panzarella (2009) add that positive self-perceived competence, problem awareness, strong social network, good general functioning, academic abilities, less serious behavior problems, and family involvement in treatment are precursors of successful residential treatment of drug abuse. Most of these relationships are correl-ational, which means that even if variations in these predictors co-vary with staying in treatment, it is not necessarily the case that therapeutic modification of these variables actually *causes* reductions in drug use.

Effective drug treatment methods may share common underlying change mechanisms that affect adolescent drug use. So far, no study has been able to estab-lish a clear relationship between possible mediators of change and outcomes for young drug users (Waldron & Turner, 2008). Rowe (2012) reviewed two studies that used mediational analyses to link mechanisms of change in family-based treatments to outcomes (Henderson, Rowe, Dakof, Hawes, & Liddle, 2009; Henggeler et al., 2009) and wrote: "Both studies highlight the importance of altering negative parenting practices and bolstering parenting skills to change adolescent problem behaviors" (p. 71). Even if it is assumed that increased involvement of the family in drug treatment is an active ingredient, no research study has so far been able to demonstrate that variations in family involvement significantly influence the amount or seriousness of drug use.

Recent meta-analyses and systematic reviews

A comprehensive meta-analysis of adolescent substance use treatment was conducted by Tanner-Smith, Wilson, and Lipsey (2013). Based on 45 randomized and quasi-experimental studies, they found support for previous study findings that family-based treatments produced the best outcomes, even in comparison with other manualized treatments. Individual and group-based CBT, other behavioral models, and models based on MI did reasonably well, but not with sufficient con-sistency to declare superiority compared to other approaches. Less encouraging results were found for non-CBT group or mixed treatments, psycho-education, and treatment as usual when compared with non-treatment control.

One year later, another update on the evidence base on outpatient behav-ioral treatments for adolescent substance use was reported by Hogue et al. (2014) in which substances such as alcohol, cannabis, and other drugs were included as examples of adolescent drug use. Of the 19 studies included, 11 were efficacy studies. They concluded that the ecological approach of family-based treatment (Slesnick & Prestopnik, 2009), which targets both family and interacting systems such as schools and peers, was "well established," as were more specific ecological models. Among programs with the strongest evidence base were Brief Strategic Family Therapy (BSFT), Ecological Based Family Therapy, and MST. Hogue et al. (2014) mention that the three branded programs were all managed by purveyor organizations that provide implementation support internationally, and that decisions about which program to adopt should be based on organizational and financial fit as well as purveyor availability.

Cognitive behavior therapy was also deemed "well established," whether it was delivered in group or individually. MI was deemed "probably efficacious," but it was commented that the approach was difficult to label as a stand-alone intervention because successes and failures were reported in almost equal proportion. But MI is often used in combination with other interventions like the Family Check-Up model (Dishion, Nelson, & Kavanagh, 2003). Integrated models combined more than one evidence-based approach and they performed well based on proven effectiveness in several trials. One example was the MST/CM approach (Henggeler et al., 2006), whilst others were based on the CBT approach. According to Hogue et al. (2014), this suggested that increasing the scope and intensity of treatments by combining evidence-based interventions can yield positive returns. In other words, the authors argue in favor of multicomponent treatment for adolescent substance use, and particularly for clients with co-occurring disorders. In general, stronger fidelity to evidence-based treatment predicted better outcomes and, contrary to previous reports, treatment effects were found to be moderated by age, ethnicity, comorbidity, level of impairment, and affiliation with delinquent peers. Even if the reviewers identified several group-based interventions as "well established," they caution that group interventions may harm youths by increasing their exposure to deviant peers. However, such iatrogenic effects were not corroborated by the studies included in their review.

Future perspectives and the way ahead

Most substance-abusing adolescents receive expensive day treatment or residential treatment rather than research-based outpatient treatment in their communities. During the last decade, there has been a steady increase in outpatient treatments for adolescent substance use outside traditional clinic, school, drug court, or shelter settings. There has also been a development in which treatment type and approach (e.g., cognitive behavior therapy) rather than treatment model or brand (e.g., MST and FFT) have come into focus. In several countries, practice guidelines in behavioral health care favors on-site treatment over referrals, and behavioral therapists should be prepared to manage common adolescent substance use problems (Hogue et al., 2014). The field of research-tested intervention now represents almost every form of treatment format (individual, group, family) and orientation (behavioral, client-centered, cognitive behavioral, drug counseling, and family systems). Given the richness of the field, Hogue et al. (2014) argue that rather than developing more brand-name models, the efforts should target the scaling-up of evidence-based interventions in large-scale implementation efforts. The authors therefore argue in favor of introducing behavioral interventions for adolescent substance use into various community settings to reach underserved groups. And because it has proven difficult to import research-developed models into community settings with fidelity, there is a great demand for quality assurance methods that can sustain evidence-based approaches in routine care. They also emphasize that even the top treatment models have much room for improvement; the best performing family-based treatment proved to have an ES of $d = 0.26$ which is quite low (Tanner-Smith et al., 2013).

Controversial issues

Several meta-analyses of prevention programs of drug use were summarized by Sloboda (2009) and included components such as addressing the normative beliefs that adolescents hold about the prevalence of substance use by their peers, reinforcing negative consequences of substance use, especially as related to adolescence, and providing life skills such as communication, decision-making, and resistance along with opportunities to practice these skills in real-life situations. Programs that seemed to work better than others:

- had a multicomponent and integrated focus to create system-wide changes in schools and in the community;
- provided sufficient doses of program activities and follow-up using multi-year programs or boosters;
- established norms that supported non-use of alcohol;
- trained parents on monitoring and supervision, particularly around access to alcohol;
- were interactive and required active participation of students;
- were implemented with fidelity;
- focused heavily on youth access to alcohol;
- ensured that non-use norms and restricted access to alcohol were institutionalized;
- avoided focusing on information-only and/or group interventions for youths at high risk; and
- provided interventions that supported social and emotional skills development.

Critics have questioned, however, whether such programs are in fact effective in that outcome studies have presented mixed results (Gorman, 2003). Although the outcomes of prevention programs are encouraging, the results also indicate that there is considerable room for improvement. In many ways, the question of "what works" in the prevention of alcohol and drug abuse remains unanswered. Moreover, several studies indicate that although many schools are familiar with the evidence-based principles of drug prevention, and many schools use evidence-based curricula, the programs are not always implemented effectively (Sloboda, 2009). In order to be successfully implemented, preventive interventions should retain core elements of the original research-based intervention with emphasis on *structure* (how the program is organized and constructed), *content* (the information, skills, and strategies of the program), and *delivery* (how the program is adapted, implemented, and evaluated) (Robertson et al., 2003). Several of the principles of effective substance prevention are also relevant for treatment of drug abuse. But there are also concerns that preventive interventions do not translate into treatment of those who have started to use drugs, and that they may have little impact on multi-problem youths or on those who are heavily involved in substance use (Biglan et al., 2004).

Concluding comments

In asking which treatment models or programs produce positive or promising clinical outcomes, the best answer we can give at this point is that treatment works better than no treatment, and that family-based approaches ought to be prioritized. Which theoretical basis of promising treatments one should go with is probably a bit more complicated to answer. Several theories are relevant to the development of effective treatment models of drug abuse. The theoretical components include social and interpersonal variables, cultural and attitudinal variables, and last but not least, variables at the individual level. Multi-theoretical and integrative foundation of drug treatment programs seem to be superior. Separately and in combination, the theories presented in this chapter may help explain how the complex interactions between individual and environmental risk factors drive substance abuse. The same theories are also helpful in the process of developing prevention and treatment programs. Family-, school-, and community-based treatments typically take on an ecological or multisystemic perspective on youth and family. Additionally, the therapists working with these programs aim at engaging the whole family in the treatment process by joining the family perspective and emphasizing the importance of increased cohesion, monitoring, and social control of the youth. Across theories, family therapy approaches to drug use have similar goals. They: (1) utilize the support from and leverage of the family to reduce the individual's drug use and implement other important lifestyle changes, and (2) alter problematic aspects of the family environment to maintain positive changes in the individual and in other family members to promote long-term recovery (Fals-Stewart, Lam, & Kelley, 2009; Rowe, 2012).

Calix and Fine (2009) summarize, in their review, that treatment should engage not only the adolescent, but also the whole family. Second, rather than dealing with the past, the therapy should have a present- and problem-focused approach based on family interactions that take place during and between therapy sessions. Third, the therapy should have a multisystemic orientation, aiming to change the system or the ecology in which the youth and the family is embedded. The reason for this approach is that an adolescent's drug problems often are maintained by factors in the family's social network that, in turn, influence the behavior of the youth and the family members.

Family-based models for adolescent drug abuse may impact other problems as well because they address underlying risk factors common to related problem behaviors (Rowe, 2012). Few attempts at comparing empirically based programs were identified, so their effectiveness relative to each other could not be determined. In a recent review of family therapy for drug use, Rowe (2012) concludes:

> The overarching conclusion is that family-based models are not only a viable treatment alternative for the treatment of drug abuse, but are now consistently recognized among the most effective approaches for treating both adults and adolescents with drug problems. Adolescent-focused family-based models that attend to the ecology of the teen and family show the most consistent and strongest findings in recent studies.
>
> *(p. 59)*

The answer to the question about important individual and contextual moderators of clinical outcomes seems to be that most treatment models have shown to be more effective than no treatment or regular treatment with no treatment protocol. They are typically flexible enough to address gender, ethnicity, and the type of drug issues. Motivational approaches, teaching cognitive and social skills in combination with positive reward systems, have turned out to be particularly promising. Research on core components or effective treatment kernels of drug treatment is more tentative, thus more research is needed to answer this important question and, more importantly, help alleviate the devastating effects of drug abuse.

6

SOCIAL COMPETENCE AND SOCIAL SKILLS

In the previous chapters, we focused on some of the common mental health problems in adolescence under the headings of internalizing and externalizing problem behavior and substance use. In writing these chapters, we have emphasized how individual and contextual risk factors may be addressed in preventive and treatment efforts. In this chapter, we apply a resource perspective when we turn to the issue of competence promotion, and how this approach may be applied to prevent and reduce mental health problems. There was an increase in the interest of research on social competence in the 1960s when it turned out that social competence was associated with children's mental health, problem behavior, and substance use (Asher & Renshaw, 1981). It was assumed that social competence could protect against stress and psychosocial strain, and that it could contribute to successful inclusion of disaffected youths in schools and in the local community. During the next three decades, numerous research studies have supported the finding that there is a dual relationship between mental health and social competence (Beauchamp & Anderson, 2010; Beelmann, Pfingsten, & Lösel, 1994; Burt, Obradovic, Long, & Masten, 2008; Garmezy, 1989; Schneider, 1993; Spence, 2003). Closely related to the social competence approach is the Social and Emotional Learning model (SEL) that is particularly relevant for schools and has a lot in common with "social competence and skills education," although the authors of this book prefer the latter approach. SEL program developers combine the teaching of social and emotional skills to promote the integration of emotion, cognition, communication, and behavior. From our point of view, it is more difficult to define what "emotional skills" are compared to "cognitive and social skills." Although it makes sense that social and emotional problems should be prevented or reduced by using social and emotional interventions, we prefer to focus on social learning and the concept of "social competence and skills education." Still, we think that a lot of what is written about social and emotional learning overlaps with and is relevant for the domain of social competence and will therefore be included in this chapter (Weissberg, Durlak, Domitrovich, & Gullotta, 2015). In recent years, the OECD organization has taken great interest in the measurement and promotion of social and emotional skills. Inspired by both James Heckman and the CASEL organization, OECD has supported and published several reports on the topic of social skills under the heading of "Skills for the 21st Century" (for a summary, see OECD, 2015).

The chapter opens with a review of definitions of social competence and social skills, and a description of important skill dimensions. The concept of self-regulation is underlying and closely linked to social competence and is central to the understanding of adolescent social functioning. We review theoretical approaches that have contributed to the understanding of social development and functioning, and the most influential among these are the social information processing model (SIP; Crick & Dodge, 1994) and social learning theory (Bandura, 1986). Next, we focus on preventive and treatment interventions. A distinction is often made between the social–cognitive approach and the interpersonal or social skills approach to training, although they are increasingly combined in practical applications. Later in the chapter, we present selected universal programs for the promotion of social competence and programs for adolescents who have developed mental health problems in the externalizing or internalizing domain. In the review of research on social skills training, we address interpersonal and academic outcomes along with influences that may moderate adolescents' benefits from intervention programs. Next, we introduce recent developments that are promising programs with multilevel interventions (Gresham & Elliott, 2008), and the idea of expanding from programs to strategies (Jones & Bouffard, 2012). We end this chapter with OECD perspectives on the importance of promoting children and adolescents' development of social and emotional competence to succeed in the educational system, in work life, and social life in families and communities (OECD, 2015).

Social competence and social skills: definitions and descriptions

Children who grow up in modern societies face some important overall *developmental tasks* such as making and keeping friends, performing adequately in school, and complying with norms and rules in different contexts (Masten & Powell, 2003). As children grow into adolescents, they need new age-appropriate skills and competence to cope with new developmental challenges. In adolescence, these include the successful transition to secondary school and high school, academic achievement, involvement in extracurricular activities like athletics and clubs, forming close friendships within and across gender, and forming a cohesive sense of self or establishing an identity (Masten & Coatsworth, 1998). But there are also qualitative differences in performance of skills, such as when adolescents are expected to communicate empathy or exercise self-control in other ways than children. The competence and skills that are required for the successful accomplishment of developmental tasks are also associated with good mental health. Most of the definitions offered emphasize social competence as an organizational concept in which the individual takes full advantage of internal and external social resources to achieve personal goals. A frequently cited definition reads: "Competence is viewed as an integrative concept which refers broadly to an ability to generate and coordinate flexible, adaptive responses to demands and to generate and capitalize on opportunities in the environment" (Waters & Sroufe, 1983, p. 79). A closely related definition emphasizes competence as an active and skill-based *coordination* of processes and resources that individuals may use to comply with social demands and achieve goals in social interactions in defined contexts (Beauchamp & Anderson, 2010). Moving from competence to social competence, one definition highlights the complex process of *integrating* thinking, feelings, and behavior to succeed socially (Weissberg & Greenberg, 1998). Another frequently used definition refers to social competence as "an evaluative term based on judgments that a person has performed adequately" (Gresham 1986, pp. 145–146), indicating that it is a capacity for behavior that is positively *evaluated* by significant persons in the individual's social context or by the person her- or himself. But even if several definitions are at hand, no single one seems to be universally accepted. This lack of consensus has not reduced the practical relevance of the concept that has been demonstrated in studies of social skills training (Beelmann et al., 1994), the development of friendship and social acceptance (Schneider, Attili, Nadel, & Weissberg, 2012), successful social inclusion in school (Gresham, Elliott, & Black 1987), coping with stress and crises (Garmezy 1989), and in the prevention of psychosocial problems in general (CSPSC, 1994). There is a general lack of prevalent data on social competence problems and this may be due to the fact that social problems are often described as a symptom or secondary consequence of other conditions, and may also appear in different forms as problem behavior (e.g., CD) or psychological distress (e.g., depression). Beauchamp and Anderson (2010) refer to Asher's (1990) estimate that approximately 10 percent of all children have social problems, but they also claim that the figures are much higher in high-risk groups. Moving from social competence to social skills, an elaborated definition explains that they:

> Include the abilities to (a) accurately select relevant and useful information from an interpersonal context, (b) use that information to determine appropriate goal-directed behavior, and (c) execute verbal and non-verbal behaviors that maximize the likelihood of goal attainment and the maintenance of good relations with others.
>
> *(Bedell & Lennox, 1997, p. 9)*

A distinction is often drawn between cognitive skills and interpersonal skills as verbal and non-verbal behavior by which individuals take social initiatives or respond appropriately to initiatives from others. In the Social Skills Rating System, Gresham and Elliott (1990) distinguished between five skill dimensions:

- *Cooperation* is helping others, sharing materials, and complying with rules and directions and has much in common with pro-social skills. Children and youths cooperate with peers on a symmetrical basis, but with adults in a more asymmetrical relationship in which the older person has more authority.

- *Assertion* is initiating behavior such as asking others for information, introducing oneself and responding to the actions of others. Assertive children and youths express their opinions and rights in a positive and explicit way—and are able to resist negative group pressure. Being assertive may be explained as finding a mid-way point on the dimension between submissiveness and aggressiveness.
- *Responsibility* is about being accountable or dependable according to adults, and showing regard for belongings or work, e.g., asking permission before using the property of someone else.
- *Empathy* is to be able to adapt to another person's perspective and to show concern and respect for others' feelings and viewpoints like in forgiving others, or feeling bad when others are sad.
- *Self-control* is the ability to bring feelings under cognitive control and examples are staying calm when teased and making a compromise during a conflict. It also relates to the ability to resist temptation and postpone rewards.

The integration of social skills and the timing of their execution are at the heart of social competence and defined in the following way by Gresham and Elliott (1984; 1990): "Social skills are socially acceptable learned behaviors that enable a person to interact effectively with others and to avoid socially unacceptable responses" (p. 1). They are specific behaviors that an individual exhibits to successfully accomplish social tasks like having a conversation, entering a peer group, or making a friend.

Self-regulation

Self-regulation is an important aspect of social competence and refers to the ability to concurrently regulate attention, emotion, and behavior in social contexts (Shields, Cicchetti, & Ryan, 1994). The link to social competence goes through higher self-control of attention and behavior and through the tendency to express positive emotions (Eisenberg et al., 1997). Examples of self-regulation skills are paying attention, taking turns, waiting in line, persevering with a task that is boring or difficult, and refraining from actions that are considered inappropriate in social situations, such as shouting out in class. Even if such regulation is described as non-cognitive, it has proved to depend on an individual's level of intellectual functioning (Nisbett et al., 2012). The development of self-regulation skills is influenced by both genetic and environmental factors and takes place when adolescents adapt their feelings and actions to what is expected in a situation and when he or she internalizes social standards and norms (Berger, 2011). Such skills are highly important for the development of competence and start emerging as children become increasingly skilled in controlling their attention, emotions, and behavior (Masten & Coatsworth, 1998). Skills in recognition, changing and sustaining behavior and mood to improve cognitive achievements may be described as self-discipline, but also as the ability to delay gratification, or as self-regulated learning (Nisbett et al., 2012). Self-regulation has been linked to positive outcomes such as good social relations with peers and adults, and regulation problems are associated with various problems like ADHD, antisocial behavior, and school failure. The increased capacity for self-regulation is related to maturation of the prefrontal lobes in adolescence, and neurostructural changes occur at the same time as the adolescent is exposed to many new social situations. An increase in practicing opportunities may lead to an increase in the effectiveness and precision of performing social skills (Beauchamp & Anderson, 2010). This developmental pattern is summed up by Masten and Coatsworth (1998) who argue that the successful development of social skills depends on normal maturation of the brain and cognitive regulation of behavior within a supportive environmental context. In other words, socially competent children have adults who care for them, a good cognitive development with brains that are developing normally, and adaptive skills necessary to manage their attention, emotions, and behavior. Self-control and compliance are important aspects of self-regulation and seem to be the outcomes of consistent caregiving and a warm but firm parenting style.

The development of social competence

One way or another, most theoretical models describe the development of social competence as a dynamic interplay between individual characteristics and the environment to achieve an optimal match between genes and context (Beauchamp & Anderson, 2010; Iarocci, Yager, & Elfers, 2007; Odom, McConnell, & Brown, 2008). Some theories stress the importance of individual and genetic factors whilst others emphasize the importance of environmental influences. Individual or intrapersonal factors that influence social development include temperament, personality, or physical characteristics that determine how the individual interacts with others. Social skills seem to be associated with the development of expressive language in such a way that adolescents with good language abilities are better at communicating information that promotes the quality of social interactions. Included among the early developmental building blocks of social competence are also basic sensory/perceptual, cognitive, and emotion processes such as sociability, face and emotion recognition, and "theory of mind" (Beauchamp & Anderson, 2010). High or low sociability seems to a large extent to be inherited, whilst the ability to recognize faces is more dependent on experience and learning. *Emotion recognition* is the ability to interpret emotional states of others based on their facial expressions. Another important milestone in the development of social competence is "joint attention" or shared intentionality (Tomasello & Carpenter, 2007), such as when two persons are experiencing the same thing at the same time and knowing together that they are doing this (Tomasello, 1995). Such an awareness of the social partner is also called social cognition or social perspective taking. *Theory of mind* is the ability to attribute mental states (beliefs, intents, desires) to oneself and others and to understand that others have mental states different from one's own (Frith & Frith, 2005). It is closely related to empathy, which may be defined as the emotional reaction in the observer to the affective state of another (Blair, 2005). Theory of mind can be seen as a form of "cognitive empathy" requiring an understanding of the mental state of another individual, but without the emotional involvement that characterizes empathy. From a developmental perspective, social competence originates from personality characteristics such as sociability or extraversion, but further development is highly reliant on the particular social models children are exposed to and on the social learning opportunities offered at home, among peers, or in kindergarten and at school. Socially skilled behavior has to be learned and enables individuals to regulate their own feelings, but also the behavior and feelings of others. Social maturation in adolescence is a function of increased personal independence and interactions with peers, combined with the increased importance of friendships and other relations. Cerebral maturation and increased social contact may influence the brain's capacity for managing social environments and interactions. Underlying social skills are cognitive abilities such as executive functions, and important changes in social behavior in adolescence are attributable to changes in the brain's social information processing network (Nelson, Leibenluft, McClure, & Pine, 2005). The two most influential theoretical approaches to the development of social competence are social learning theory (Bandura, 1986) and the theory of social information processing (Crick & Dodge, 1994).

The Social Information Processing model

The Social Information Processing (SIP) model has been highly influential in the process of analyzing and understanding how individuals solve problems and behave in social situations. According to the SIP model, individuals develop social interaction skills as a function of complex social–cognitive operations that may be described by the following steps: (1) encoding of cues, (2) interpretation of cues, (3) clarification of goals, (4) response access or construction, (5) response decision, (6) behavioral enactment or implementation, and (7) peer evaluation and response (Crick & Dodge, 1994). The model does not assume, however, a linear relationship between the processing at one step and the processing at the next step. Rather, the steps take place simultaneously, but still the path from a particular stimulus to a certain response follows a logical sequence. A hypothesis of parallel processes requires feedback loops among the steps. For example, an aggressive response is not only a function of the level of hostility as assessed by the individual, but a multivariate and non-linear aggregation of many factors. Mental processes that integrate past behaviors into memory and guide future behaviors are cyclical and transactional:

> It is proposed that (a) social experiences lead to the generation of latent mental structures that are stored and carried forward over time in memory in the form of social knowledge, (b) these mental structures constitute the "database" in processing models and influence a child's on-line processing

of social cues, (c) on–line processing directly influences social behavior, and (d) the child mentally represents social behavior and its outcomes and stores them in memory, and they become part of his or her general social knowledge that will influence future actions.

(Crick & Dodge, 1994, p. 79)

The adolescents' social knowledge (or latent mental structures) that may guide future processing are also referred to as schemata, scripts (Shank & Abelson, 1977), or working models of relationships (Bowlby, 1969). Past experiences such as social rejection may be stored in long-term memory and influence future social information processing and behavior. Development is characterized by increased acquisition of cognitive skills and experiential knowledge that increase the individual's database of social knowledge. As children grow into adolescents they demonstrate improved attention, greater mental organizational skills, and increases in capacity or speed of processing. Compared to children, adolescents will typically develop more efficient, skillful ways of representing, organizing, and interpreting social information. Greater accuracy in social information processing is achieved because adolescents focus on relevant rather than irrelevant social cues. Their information processing is more efficient because they waste less time on irrelevant cues and also more complex because both obvious and subtler social cues are taken into consideration. Cognitions have a primary organizing role in the model, but the model also takes into consideration non-cognitive influences on social adjustment like emotions, social experience, and relations (Crick & Dodge, 1994). A strength of the SIP model is that it enables the identification of deficits in social information processing and may be used as a guide for the development of interventions like cognitive skills training (Fraser et al., 2005). Still, a limitation of the model is that the model's social–cognitive variables have accounted for a limited amount of variation in social adjustment in empirical studies. The generally weak association between social information processing and social adjustment implies that there are small differences in cognitions between youths who vary in terms of social adjustment (Crick & Dodge, 1994). Still, social–cognitive learning programs have proven to have a positive preventive effect on antisocial behavior.

Social Information Processing and problem behavior

The Social Information Processing (SIP) model is based on the assumption that social behavior builds on social cognitions and has to a large extent been developed by studying cognitive bias or deficits that may lead to social adjustment problems. Social information processing bias and deficits are typical of antisocial adolescents, but also of adolescents with internalizing problems. Both groups tend to overlook important social signals or selectively attend to certain cues, for instance signals of rejection or disinterest. Depressed children are likely to engage in self-blame; they expect failure and their social responses tend to be irrelevant and ineffective. Adolescents with internalizing problems often struggle in the social arena, though their specific challenges may be different in nature and they may be in need of other types of social skills training than their peers with externalizing types of behavior (Cartledge & Milburn, 1995). Most studies of bias and deficits in social information processing have focused on aggressive and violent behavior; antisocial adolescents seem to lack social–cognitive as well as interpersonal skills (Fontaine, Yang, Dodge, Pettit, & Bates, 2009). Aggressive individuals attend to fewer cues and are more sensitive to hostile cues from others. Because they are less able to understand the emotions of others and more likely to misinterpret neutral signals, they more often attribute hostile intent. Their responses are repeatedly coercive, ineffective, and inflexible or even rigid. Furthermore, antisocial individuals are often impulsive; they fail to consider the consequences of behavior or they anticipate that aggressive behavior will lead to positive outcomes (Cartledge & Milburn, 1995). According to teachers and parents, they generally have a lower level of social competence than their age-mates, and skill deficits are particularly evident in the domains of self-control and cooperation (Ogden, 1995). Their social goals have a tendency to undermine pro-social relations, such as when they are too concerned with dominating others in social contacts and interactions. They also tend to overestimate their own competence compared to age-mates, even in the face of repeated rejections from peers. Not all antisocial adolescents are socially unskilled in all domains, however, and some aggressive individuals are controversial, that is, both liked and disliked by others (Price & Dodge, 1989). Coie and Dodge (1998) found that approximately half of the aggressive children were not rejected by their peers.

Social competence and problem behaviors are not merely opposites on the same continuum. The lack of social competence does not necessarily mean the presence of antisocial behaviors. And as is exemplified with controversial children, some youths demonstrate both certain social skills (they are well liked and admired by some children) and problem behaviors (unruly or bullying). As we have discussed above, social competence and problem behaviors are nevertheless linked, and may *over time* become more strongly associated with each other. The question then becomes, which comes first? In a study of 391 eighth-graders, parents, teachers, peers, and the adolescents themselves were asked to rate both the youths' levels of social competence and antisocial behavior. Assessments were repeated 2 years later. The main results from the study are depicted in Figure 6.1.

The results from this study showed that, as expected, adolescents who scored high on social competence in eighth grade generally continued to score high on this dimension 2 years later, in tenth grade. And, unsurprisingly, the same pattern was found for youths who scored high on antisocial behavior; these youths tended to receive similar scores in both eighth and tenth grade. What is interesting, however, is that low social competence in eighth grade significantly predicted elevated scores on antisocial behavior in tenth grade, whereas antisocial behavior in eighth grade was not significantly (n.s.) related to lower social competence 2 years later. So, the main result from this study gives at least preliminary support to the notion that lack of social competence seems to precede antisocial behavior, rather than the other way around (Sørlie, Amlund Hagen, & Ogden, 2008).

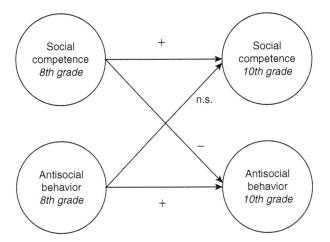

FIGURE 6.1 Four-factor structural equation model predicting social competence and antisocial behavior. *Journal of Research on Adolescence*, 18(1), 121–144. (Reprinted with permission.)

Because of their social information processing problems, antisocial adolescents seem to be in need of social–cognitive and emotional regulation skills that might help them navigate better in social situations (Bierman, 2004; Fraser et al., 2005). In treatment settings, social–cognitive and social skills training have proven effective in interventions aimed at reducing antisocial behavior, often in combination with parent or family treatment (Kazdin, Siegel, & Bass, 1992; Tremblay, Pagani-Kurtz, Mâsse, Vitaro, & Pihl, 1995; Webster-Stratton & Lindsay, 1999). A significant increase in social competence has also been demonstrated in MST of antisocial behavior in adolescents, even if no explicit skills training was involved (Ogden & Halliday-Boykins, 2004).

Social learning perspective

The *social learning perspective* is concerned with how environmental influences contribute to individual differences in social competence. The approach stresses how social competence and skills may be learned through observation and imitation of models, but also through practice and feedback. Among the contextual variables that empirically have shown to promote the development of social competence are parent–child attachment (Cohn et al., 1990), the quality of parenting and, at later stages, influences from peers (Englund, Levy, Hyson, & Sroufe, 2000; Masten et al., 1995). Social learning takes place in both formal and informal settings, and authentic learning experiences can actually be more influential than organized and structured learning that is a part of education or intervention programs. Therefore, training program developers often emphasize the importance of integrating formal and informal learning by giving the adolescents homework and requesting parental support.

Contextual influences are of particular interest in the social learning approach because they may promote pro-social development or make corrections when problems have occurred. Among the important proximal contextual influences in the micro- and meso-systems are family climate and interactions, school, classroom and teacher influences, and peer influences. Among the distal contextual influences in the exo- and macro-system is culture that impacts how children "learn the rules" for social behavior in multiple social contexts from both peers and adults and through media (Odom et al, 2008). In a review of family influences on peer-related social competence, McCollum and Ostrosky (2008) underscore the importance of family interactions and relationships. Family members may influence a child's social behavior directly by teaching social skills, but also indirectly by providing opportunities for and encouraging positive interactions. Additionally, the socioeconomic level of the family, the stability of the home environment, and resources available in the home environment affect children's social development. Well-educated and resourceful parents in a stable relationship seem to foster children's social competence. Peer-related social competence in school seems to increase when students have a positive relationship with their teacher, and this positive influence seems to be mediated by a positive classroom climate (Brophy-Herb, Lee, Nievar, & Stollak, 2007).

Social skills training based on social learning theory makes a clear distinction between learning skills and practicing them. This means that some adolescents have social interaction problems because they lack the necessary skills. Others have acquired social skills but lack the motivation to use them (Gresham & Elliott, 1990). Thoughts, attitudes, or beliefs may come in the way of demonstrating socially skilled behavior, such as when boys think that social skills are too feminine or a young person is socially inhibited by the fear of being rejected. Some do not find socially competent behavior to be sufficiently rewarding or think that it is incompatible with their self-concept as being "macho," "rebel," or "non-conformist."

Social skills and social competence interventions

A considerable number of training programs have adopted the SIP model of Crick and Dodge (1994) with the following core components: (1) social perception, (2) perspective taking and engagement in others, (3) effective problem-solving, (4) making decisions and considering consequences, (5) acting, and (6) evaluating the outcomes. The first step, social perception, stresses the importance of being attentive and perceptive in the process of receiving and interpreting social cues. The second step addresses skills in social decentering and empathy, that is, to understand the perspectives and feelings of others. The third step centers on how to effectively solve social problems or handle conflicts, but also to consider what consequences the alternatives may have, and to predict potential barriers and negative reactions. The next step is concerned with turning social decisions into goal-directed behavior, for instance to make social contact or communicate effectively (Spence, 2003). Several structured social skills and competence programs have been developed and have produced encouraging results in controlled trials (Beelmann, Pfingsten, & Lösel, 1994; Durlak, Weissberg, Dymnicki, Taylor, & Schellinger, 2011; Lösel & Beelmann, 2003). Viewed within a developmental context, training programs should focus on age-appropriate skills (Cartledge & Milburn, 1995). Beyond programs, the resource-focused perspective may impact policy and practice in a direction where the promotion of adolescent competence becomes more influential in public health and education (Dodge, 2008).

The promotion of social skills and social competence has been singled out as a promising preventive approach toward several types of problem behavior in children and youth, including externalizing and internalizing behavior problems, and drug use. Some social skills interventions universally address all children or youths, but there are also some programs that target those who are at risk. The two main approaches to social skills training are the *social–cognitive approach*, which emphasizes learning of cognitive skills such as social problem-solving, means–end thinking, and understanding of consequences, and the *social skills approach*, which emphasizes teaching practical communication skills aimed at increasing youths' abilities to interact with others. Usually, practical, concrete skills have been emphasized in training with children, whilst cognitive skills have been more central in interventions targeting adolescents. But even if the approaches emphasize different areas, they may be used in combination, and often are. The *social–cognitive approach* aims at improving social behavior through cognitively based skills training that influences how the individual perceives, codes, and experiences the world (Kazdin, 2003). The training leans heavily on the social information processing model (Crick & Dodge, 1994) and participants are taught how to generate alternative solutions to social problems and analyze the consequences of different choices of action. By acquiring cognitive skills, children and youths are in a good position to regulate their own behavior, but the emphasis is more on thought processes than on observable skills. On the other hand, the *social skills approach* emphasizes how the learning and practicing of verbal and non-verbal skills contributes to social success. Learning of interpersonal social skills takes place through the observation and imitation of role models and through the encouragement and reinforcement of pro-social behavior. The skills are taught through instruction, coaching, discussions, role-play, and practical exercises. Participants learn how to make contact and communicate with other people, how to introduce themselves in a group context, how to compliment others, and how to be self-assertive in positive ways.

Some individuals have problems in translating social knowledge into practice because of strong interfering emotions like anxiety or aggression. Social anxiety or shyness hinder some adolescents from interactions with others, whilst others are rejected or avoided because they appear overly aggressive in social encounters. And finally, some lack practice in integrating new skills into their behavioral repertoire (Mize, 1995). On the other hand, overt training of social skills alone is insufficient to achieve long-term changes in social competence. Interfering thoughts and feelings, a lack of motivation, and non-social individual characteristics, as well as the behavior of others, may influence the social behavior of adolescents (Spence,

1995). Permanent changes of social competence also seem to require changes in the underlying social–cognitive skills, attitudes, and values that are stored in long-term memory. So, unless the entire cognitive–affective behavioral system is permanently changed, new skills will not be integrated and applied in new situations (Johnson & Johnson, 2006).

Over the years, competence-promotion programs have changed in nature and scope (Masten & Coatsworth, 1998). First-generation efforts were characterized by child-focused definitions of competence and emphasized building singular or core sets of skills (e.g., Spivack & Shure, 1974). The programs documented that skills could be changed, but the benefits of adjustment turned out to be small in magnitude. The next generation of competence-enhancement programs are more complex; they train a variety of more elaborate skills over longer periods of time, and link the teaching of skills to the developmental stage of children and youths and to their developmental contexts (e.g., The Seattle Social developmental project, and the Fast Track project, CPPRG, 2010a, b).

School-based social competence promotion

Schools are often considered to be the ideal learning arenas for primary prevention efforts such as social skills training (Boxer, Goldstein, Musher-Eizenman, Dubow, & Heretick, 2005; Fraser et al., 2005). Reviewing research syntheses of school-based prevention and promotion programs, Durlak et al. (2011) found positive outcomes on a wide range of outcome variables including academic performance (Zins, Weissberg, Wang, & Walberg, 2004), antisocial and aggressive behavior (Wilson & Lipsey, 2007), depressive symptoms (Horowitz & Garber, 2006), drug use (Tobler et al., 2000), mental health (Durlak & Wells, 1997), problem behaviors (Wilson, Gottfredson, & Najaka, 2001), and positive youth development (Catalano, Berglund, Ryan, Lonczaak, & Hawkins, 2002). Most programs, however, are social skills programs that target young children in order to prevent problems from occurring in adolescence. Examples are: Interpersonal Social Problem Solving (Spivack & Shure, 1974; Spivack, Platt, & Shure, 1976), Second Step (Committee for Children; Beeland, 1991), Positive Alternative Thinking Strategies (Greenberg et al., 2003), and the Coping Power program (Lochman & Wells, 2004). Some of these programs, such as the Coping Power program, have shown to lower the rate of delinquent behavior, substance abuse, and teacher-reported difficulties at a 1-year follow-up.

Selected and indicated social competence programs

Few competency-promoting programs are directed at adolescents but there are exceptions. Two program examples are Reasoning and Re-acting (Fabiano & Porporino, 1997) and ART (Goldstein, Glick, & Gibbs, 1998) that target externalizing problem behavior in young people.

CASE EXAMPLE OF SOCIAL SKILLS TRAINING: PATRICK

Patrick is quite a challenge in class because he talks a lot and often interrupts the teacher or other students. He appears quite bossy, and often confronts those who disagree with him. He gets frustrated easily and, in such situations, may appear threatening and rude. When angry, he is quite intrusive and stares other people down. Still, he is quite happy with himself, and does not seem to notice the negative signals and feedback he gets from his peers. He is both liked and disliked in class. Some peer students admire him because he stands up to teachers, and his dominant interactional style earns him status in class. Over time, Patrick has been involved in criminal activities and drug abuse, and for these actions he was referred by the police to the Child Welfare Services. They enrolled him in a treatment program in which he and his parents received family therapy. In addition, Patrick was to receive social skills training by a coach or a personal trainer. The coach observed him in several social situations and tried to single out his main social skills deficits. One problem was obviously that he was not aware of his own and other people's emotions, and that he did not register social signals. When he addressed or confronted others he gazed away, and therefore did not register any feedback. He also interrupted others whilst they were speaking and made rude comments about them. According to his coach, his main problem was his lack of social sensitivity and self-control. He did not perceive social signals from others and became easily upset. Helping him to read social situations more accurately became an important goal in the social skills training, the other being learning techniques of anger management. After a period of getting to know each other, the coach gradually introduced some of his training goals. He knew that Patrick sometimes felt socially excluded and talked with him about the goal of making friends. They also talked about the problems that conflicts with parents, teachers, and other adults led to, and how these could be avoided by being in better control of his temper. How to reduce frustration and prevent angry outbursts were discussed and demonstrated in role-plays with the coach. He also learned how to read expressions on other people's faces by looking at pictures or watching the coach as he simulated different emotional states. Problem-solving techniques were also an important part of the intervention, and the coach demonstrated how to be creative when facing a problem and to think about the possible consequences of alternative responses. Simple tactics of greeting others and saying "thank you" were also introduced during training.

Aggression Replacement Training and skillstreaming

The skillstreaming program consists of a' curriculum of 50 skills that aim at the promotion of pro-social skills, coping with interpersonal stress, and planning skills in youths at risk. Starting in 1973, skillstreaming was gradually transformed into Aggression Replacement Training (ART) that, in 1988, was itself transformed into the Prepare Curriculum with ten course-length interventions: (1) skillstreaming, (2) anger control training, (3) moral reasoning training, (4) problem-solving training, (5) empathy training, (6) situational perception training, (7) stress management, (8) cooperation training, (9) recruiting supportive models, and (10) understanding and using group processes (Goldstein, Glick, & Gibbs, 1998).

Skillstreaming is described by its authors as a psycho-educational intervention designed to enhance the pro-social, interpersonal, stress management, and planning skills of adolescents who have behavior disorders or are "normal" but developmentally lagged. Three categories of adolescent behavior disorders were addressed. The first was aggression, and the second was withdrawal including depression, feelings of inferiority, self-consciousness, shyness, anxiety, hypersensitivity, reclusiveness, and timidity. The third category was immaturity, including short attention span, clumsiness, preference for younger playmates, passivity, and daydreaming. The program takes as its point of departure several life tasks that all adolescents should be able to master at home, in school, and in the community in interactions with family, peers, and authority figures. The following six skills groups are included: (1) beginning social skills, as in having a conversation, listening, introducing oneself, and giving a compliment; (2) advanced social skills, as in asking for help, joining in, giving or following instructions, apologizing, or convincing others; (3) skills for dealing with feelings, as in coping with fear, expressing feelings, and understanding the feelings of others; (4) skill alternatives to aggression; (5) skills for dealing with stress, as in coping with embarrassment, responding to failure, or preparing for stressful meetings; and (6) planning skills. Each skill is broken down into behavioral steps that are modeled by the trainer and role-played and practiced by the participants. A typical skillstreaming session starts with the trainer defining and modeling the skill that the trainee is found to be in need of. Then, role-players are selected and a role-play conducted, and performance feedback is provided to the participants. The session ends with the assignment of homework (Goldstein, Glick, & Gibbs, 1998). The four components that make up skillstreaming are modeling, role-playing, feedback, and transfer training.

Each skill is broken down into sub-skills, such as *"starting a conversation"* (i.e., greet the other person, make small talk, decide if the other person is listening, and bring up the main topic) or *"giving instructions"* (i.e., decide what needs to be done, think about the different people who could do it and choose one, ask that person to do what you want done, ask the other person if he or she understands what to do, and change or repeat instructions if necessary).

Individual social competence training in small groups

Individual social skills training is also referred to as coaching and is designed to teach youths behaviors needed for social acceptance and friendship through techniques such as discussion, rehearsal, and feedback from the coach (Asher & Wheeler, 1985). Individual treatment should be based on selection of social skills to meet individual needs and after consideration of the most important skills for the young person to learn. Behavioral objectives should be stated in positive terms and social behavior analyzed into subcomponents. The essential steps for the trainer are to specify the desired behavior and identify the sub-skills it comprises. The sub-skills should be stated in terms of observable behaviors and listed according to sequence of instruction. Then, the appropriate instructional strategies should be identified and implemented and the results evaluated (Cartledge & Milburn, 1995). Individual social skills training usually takes place in small groups of 4–8 participants led by a trainer (Elliott & Gresham, 1991; Goldstein, Glick, & Gibbs, 1998). Individual social skills training has not been accepted as a stand-alone intervention among aggressive children and should preferably be combined with parenting skills training (Kjøbli & Ogden, 2014). Adolescents may be more receptive to social skills training, and even if training adolescents is different from training children, some programs developed for children may easily be adapted to older participants. One example is Susan Spence's (1995) program for enhancing social competence with children and adolescents. The following components make up the program: (1) training in performance of specific basic social skills, for example eye contact; (2) social perception skills training; (3) training in social problem-solving skills; (4) training in the use of self-instructions to guide behavior; (5) replacement of unhelpful thoughts with positive, helpful thinking; and (6) application of these skills to specific social problems, for example making friends, dealing with teasing, or dealing with disagreements. Under the heading of social perception, her program deals with micro-social skills like eye contact, posture, facial expression, and tone of voice. Under the heading of friendship skills, she includes identifying friendly behavior, offering help, giving compliments, asking to join in, and giving invitations. And among skills needed to deal with conflict situations, she includes "saying no," dealing with teasing and bullying, arguments, and disagreements with peers, siblings, and adults. She observed that most sessions worked equally well for children and adolescents, but examples should be adapted to the age and developmental level of the participants. Adolescents were usually more aware of and troubled by interfering negative thoughts and feelings, and focusing on these negative thoughts and feelings could be important when older kids were learning about and carrying out social skills like problem-solving and friendship skills. A lot of the time in the training groups of adolescents is therefore devoted to identifying unhelpful thoughts and introducing helpful thoughts. Time is also spent on integrating social skills in social perception, self-instruction methods, and problem-solving. In line with several other programs, behavioral skills training includes instruction, discussion, modeling or demonstration, practice, role-playing, giving feedback, and setting home tasks.

CASE EXAMPLE OF SOCIAL SKILLS TRAINING: GWEN

Gwen is an extremely shy and withdrawn adolescent who always stays in the background. When her age-mates eagerly discuss their topics of interest, she never says a word unless she is asked to do so by one of the others. In class, she is not fond of attention and never volunteers to answer when teachers ask questions. Her fellow students are nice to her, but even if she is accepted, she is easily overlooked when activities are planned in class. When she feels observed or evaluated she becomes embarrassed and seems to look for a way to escape from the situation. She is also uncomfortable in informal situations such as school breaks or when she is expected to have a chat with classmates. Ordering food at a restaurant or asking for help in a shop is also difficult for her. The school counselor has tried to talk to her, but her polite approaches only seem to make things worse. In such situations, Gwen avoids eye contact, answers with a no or a yes, and is visibly uncomfortable with the situation. When asked if she has any questions for the counselor, she quickly replies, "Am I allowed to go now?" Her classmates can tell that she feels rather lonely, and that she would like to have more friends. She fears that no one likes her and never takes the initiative like asking other students for company out of fear of being rejected. When other students ask her for favors, she finds it difficult to say no and sometimes she gives in to peer pressure. She spends far too much time on her homework and is always well prepared for class. She is almost a perfectionist but complains about the heavy workload at school and is terrified of tests and exams.

Gwen accepts an invitation from the school counselor to join a small dis-cussion group of five students who will meet on a regular basis to talk about things that adolescents are concerned about. Her main motivation for joining the group may be the fact that one of her friends in class has agreed to join it too. The group meets once a week at the counselor's office for about an hour, and whilst three of them are rather shy and withdrawn, two of the participants are rather outgoing and socially competent. In the first meeting, they address concerns that are of interest to them all, like music, books, parents, and school-work. Then they continue to talk about social relations, about friendships, and about having boyfriends (there are only girls in the group). They start talking about and practice rules of communication like taking turns, listening atten-tively when others speak, making eye contact, and responding clearly to what others say. They sit in pairs, take turns practicing saying "no" to each other and learn how to express disagreement in conversations. They talk about posi-tive ways of making contact with other adolescents, such as greeting them, tuning in to the way they speak, and talking about things they agree on before expressing any disagreement. They also practice refusal skills, both verbally and non-verbally, and talk about how to handle peer pressure. Working in pairs, they take turns saying "no" in a clear loud voice, and also demonstrate how crossing arms, turning away, or walking out of a situation may send strong signals to their partner. What takes place in the group sessions are exposure training, and Gwen learns to speak out in the small group and, more than anything, she learns how to be assertive in a positive way. Practicing difficult situations in a safe setting and a positive atmosphere is quite conducive to increasing Gwen's social competence. In one of her last exercises, she enters the headmaster's office to ask him to join the social skills training group's final meeting and tells him what she has learned during the semester.

Research on program effectiveness

Social competence training in general has produced varying results in outcome studies. Some have reported positive effects and others have found no effects on adjustment. Meta-analyses have shown social competence training to have a moderate short-term effect on a broad range of behavioral and mental health problems, but the long-term outcomes have been more modest (Beelmann & Lösel, 2006). The effect sizes were higher for increases in social competence outcomes than for the diminishing of antisocial behavior. Meta-analyses have also indicated that social problem-solving training primarily strengthened social–cognitive skills compared to social skills training that primarily improved social interaction skills (Denham & Almeida, 1987; Lösel & Beelmann, 2003). Younger children, immature children, and aggressive children (Kjøbli & Ogden, 2014) seem to profit least from social skills training either because the content or the presentation is insufficient or inadequate. In a systematic review, social competence training seemed to be most effective for children who had been exposed to critical life events and lack of social stimulation, whilst children with externalizing and internalizing problems had approximately the same, moderate outcome (Lösel & Beelmann, 2003). There were indications, however, that children and youths who were anxious, isolated, and lonely benefited more than those who were acting out. A later meta-analysis also concluded that cognitive behavioral programs gave the most sustainable outcomes, particularly for antisocial children (Beelmann & Lösel, 2006).

Durlak et al. (2011) examined the effects of *universal school-based SEL programs* on several outcome variables. SEL programs aim at combining personal and environmental resources to promote: (1) competencies to recognize and manage emotions, (2) set and achieve positive goals, (3) appreciate the perspectives of others, (4) establish and maintain positive relationships, (5) make responsible decisions, and (6) handle interpersonal situations constructively (Durlak et al., 2011; Elias et al., 1997). The largest ESs occurred for social–emotional skill performance that included assessments of social–cognitive and affective competencies such as emotions recognition, stress management, empathy, problem-solving, or decision-making skills. The SEL programs also enhanced students' behavioral adjustment in the form of increased pro-social behaviors and reduced conduct and internalizing problems. SEL programs appeared to be effective across all educational levels from elementary to high school and in urban as well as in suburban schools. Aside from social and emotional skills, the average ES in the Durlak et al. (2011) meta-analysis were "small." The authors underline, however, that the results were similar to, or in some cases higher than, those achieved by other types of universal interventions in each outcome category (Durlak, 2003). In addition to the key outcome indicators like social and cognitive skills, social competence training may also positively impact outcomes like peer acceptance, positive self-esteem, quality of life and academic achievement (Durlak et al., 2011).

The reciprocal influence of social and academic competence has been documented in several studies. Wentzel (1991) found that socially responsible behavior was a critical aspect of classroom social competence and a powerful predictor of academic performance in early adolescence. An association was also found between social and emotional learning and school attitudes and performance in a study by Zins et al. (2004). And in a systematic review of meta-analyses, Hattie (2009) concluded that in addition to being important for the development of friendship and other social relations, teaching and learning social competence resulted in improved academic achievement. Jennings and DiPrete (2010) found in their study that good procedures for social learning increased the students' academic achievement by approximately 25 percent. Teachers influenced the students' academic development both directly through teaching of subjects and indirectly through teaching social and behavioral skills. Socially and behaviorally competent students seemed to take full advantage of the learning opportunities in the lessons. When teachers create learning opportunities in the classroom and encourage learning outside school, some students more than others take advantage of these, increasing their efforts and attention by controlling their impulses. According to the authors, such skills can be taught and learned much in the same way as reading and mathematics, particularly when such skills are valued both at home and at school. In other words, teachers who were able to promote social skills also indirectly boosted the students' academic skills (Jennings & DiPrete, 2010). But even if several studies have indicated that social and academic learning is interrelated and mutually reinforcing, there is a lack of studies that clearly demonstrate the combined positive interactions of social and academic competence on academic achievements.

Who benefits most from social and emotional learning programs?

Warnings are issued about unintended negative outcomes of skills training in homogeneous groups of acting-out youths (Arnold & Hughes, 1999; Dodge, Dishion, & Lansford, 2006). The most positive outcomes have been demonstrated for heterogeneous skills training groups in which there was a mixture of pro-social and antisocial participants. Both groups improved and no negative side effects were registered for the pro-social participants (Ang & Hughes, 2001). The most successful interventions also seem to be multi-year programs with multiple components and social–cognitive training combined with behavioral training for parents. The promotion of cognitive and social competence along with changing family interactions and increasing the quality of parenting can have long-term protective effects (Masten & Coatsworth, 1998).

Durlak et al. (2011) searched for variables that had a moderating effect on outcomes in their meta-analysis. They found that variables representing recommended practices for skills development and adequate program implementation increased the positive outcomes of studies (see also Topping, 2012). In other words, programs were more likely to be effective if they used a sequenced step-by-step training approach, used active forms of learning, spent sufficient time on skill development, and had explicit learning goals. Recommended practice was summarized in the acronym of SAFE: Sequenced with a connected and coordinated set of activities to achieve their objectives relative to skill development; Active forms of learning; Focused with at least one component devoted to developing personal or social skills; and Explicit in targeting specific SEL skills rather than skills or positive development in general terms. Programs that had adopted all four recommended training procedures (i.e., coded as SAFE) produced significant positive effects for all six outcomes (compared to only three for those not coded SAFE). Additionally, interventions without any apparent implementation problems yielded significant mean effects in all six categories. The fact that both SAFE and implementation quality moderated SEL outcomes was taken to mean that developing evidence-based interventions is not enough; beneficial programs must be well designed and well implemented (Topping, 2012). The findings are consistent with other reviews that conclude that more successful youth programs are interactive in nature, use coaching and role-playing, and employ a set of structured activities to guide youths toward achievement of specific goals (DuBois, Holloway, Valentine, & Cooper, 2002; Tobler et al., 2000; see also the next chapter on mental health interventions in school). In order to take social skills training programs a step further, multilevel approaches have been established to adapt the training to different student needs.

A multilevel social skills training program: the Social Skills Improvement System

Gresham and Elliott's (2008) school-based three-level Social Skills Improvement System (SSIS) model is an update and further development of an earlier version of the program (Elliott and Gresham, 1991). SSIS consists of a universal program for use in the whole school, a program of skills training in small groups, and one for individual learning skills. More than the previous version of the program, it focuses on adapting the education to the students' needs and risk levels. Attention is focused on risk factors for the development of social skills problems, such as lack of knowledge and practice, little stimulation and encouragement, lack of opportunities for practice and reinforcement, and interfering problem behavior. Interfering or competitive problem behavior is behavior that blocks the learning or the practicing of social skills. The program follows the subdivision into three levels according to the model of *Response to Intervention.* At the universal level, class-wide social skills training is described for 80–85 percent of the students, with emphasis on the learning of ten key skills. At the selected level, social skills training is described in small groups for the 10–15 percent of the students who do not adequately benefit from the universal education. At the indicated level, individual measures are described for the 3–5 percent of the students who did not receive sufficient benefit from the two preceding levels. At each level, an assessment of the students' social skills is also carried out with a combination of teacher, parent, and self-assessments (Gresham & Elliott, 1990; 2008). It may involve internalizing or externalizing behavior, possibly also hyperactivity and inattention. The new version of the program also focuses on collaboration, self-control, self-esteem, empathy, and cooperation, but has added the dimensions of communication and engagement. Theoretical SSIS builds on social learning theory, cognitive behavioral theory, and applied behavioral analysis, and to a lesser extent on the social information processing model of Crick and Dodge (1994). Neither the earlier nor the new version introduce specific training requirements for the practitioners, and the description in the handbook is expected to be sufficient to practice the program.

Level 1. Class-wide social skills training. The universal program is aimed at teachers in unified classes and combines methods of good teaching with social skills training. The instruction is divided into six steps and consists of: (1) to tell (coaching), where the goal of the skill is presented, the teacher asks questions, defines the skill, highlights the keywords, discusses why completeness is important, and shows how the skill is to be practiced; (2) to show (model), where the teacher gives positive and negative examples of completeness, presents the skills step by step, performs role-playing, and discusses alternative ways in which to reach the social goal; (3) to do (role-play), where the teacher asks students to define the skill and explain why it is important, and the student explains and shows the steps that the skill comprises, is a model in role-play, and gives feedback; (4) practice, where the teacher examines and uses the skill in the workbook, and the students practice and give feedback in pairs, and are encouraged to use the skill in other situations; (5) to evaluate progress, where the teacher asks students to think about how well they practice the skill and asks them to register their own evaluation; and (6) to generalize and sustain, where the teacher gives students home assignments in which they get the opportunity to practice skills together with others, such as family and friends.

The program is adapted to children in kindergarten and in elementary school and provides for ten social basic skills: (1) listening to others, (2) following instructions, (3) obeying rules, (4) not being distracted by fellow students, (5) asking for help, (6) waiting in turn, (7) cooperating with others, (8) controlling anger in conflict situations, (9) behaving responsibly toward others, and (10) showing friendliness. Teaching consists of ten units each lasting about half an hour, three times a week. The instruction is supplemented with video clips and workbooks for the students as well as supplementary material for parents.

Level 2. Teaching students who have limited benefits from the universal level. For students who do not benefit from the general program, education is carried out in heterogeneous small groups or as individual education. Here, the teacher re-examines the ten basic social skills, but also expands with ten new key skills. Overall, all the seven skills dimensions mentioned above are represented, and the teaching follows the same layout as mentioned above. In this teaching, one can also use students as teachers, and the teacher reminds the students to use the skills. As positive reinforcement for competent behavior, the teacher can use tangible rewards, points systems, behavioral contracts, and home report cards. If the problem is related to skills learning, the teaching will be conducted in small groups, but if the problem is lacking in the performance of skills, problem-solving consultation is undertaken in the classroom.

Level 3. Individual teaching and skills training. The third step targets students who do not seem to benefit from level two. The teaching of social skills is combined with interventions to replace competing problem behavior with pro-social alternatives. Based on functional behavioral assessment, the teacher tries to identify behavior that is a good alternative to the problem behavior, that is, positive behavioral options that are assumed to be reinforced as much as the problem behavior. Behavior that should be replaced is primarily behavior that competes with or blocks the learning or practice of social skills. The most common examples are externalized or internalized problem behavior as well as bullying, hyperactivity, and attention failure. Although the SSIS represents a refinement and improvement of previous programs, some authors have explored other avenues in their search for ways to improve social skills and competence in children and adolescents. Some authors, such as Jones and Bouffard (2012) in the next section, argue for a shift in focus from programs to strategies. They stress that they do not argue in favor of abolishing programs, but rather supplementing them with intervention strategies to promote students' social competence.

From programs to strategies

One way of thinking about a shift from programs to strategies is moving from "brands to essential ingredients" or, to use a food metaphor, from a focus on packaged, branded products (curricula) to essential ingredients like vitamins and minerals (essential and beneficial strategies) (Jones & Bouffard, 2012). This requires developing, applying, and testing essential ingredients to determine which ingredients or combination of ingredients are most linked with positive outcomes for children. The authors find the framework of evidence-based kernels useful: "fundamental units of behavioral influence that underlie effective prevention and treatment" (Embry & Biglan, 2008, p. 75). Like Embry and Biglan, they don't suggest that kernels should replace programs, but rather "supplement" and "strengthen" them and widen the dissemination of effective strategies, when full-scale programs are impractical. SEL programs are rarely integrated into classrooms and in ways that are meaningful, sustained, and embedded in the day-to-day interactions of students and teachers; typically, they only occupy a half-hour lesson on a weekly or monthly basis. Jones and Bouffard (2012) recommend that schools integrate the teaching and reinforcement of SEL skills into their mission and daily interactions with students, for example in the way that adults talk to students and consistent routines for situations like transitions and social problem-solving. Integrated, everyday approaches could add value to full-scale comprehensive programs that teach SEL during structured lesson blocks. The authors are not proposing the elimination of SEL curricula, but rather a continuum of approaches matched to the needs and contexts of each school and a commitment of all schools to make SEL part of educating students. The approach draws on "developmental–contextual models" that view development as taking place in a nested set of interactive contexts ranging from immediate (e.g., family, peer system, classroom, school) to more distal (e.g., cultural, political) (Bronfenbrenner & Morris, 1998).

At the center of the framework are the core domains of SEL skills, grouped into three categories: (1) emotional process, (2) social/interpersonal skills, and (3) cognitive regulation. *Emotional processes* include emotional knowledge and expression, emotional and behavioral regulation, empathy, and perspective taking. *Social/ interpersonal skills* include understanding social cues, interpreting others' behaviors, navigating social situations, interacting positively with peers and adults, and other pro-social behavior. *Cognitive regulation* includes attention control, inhibiting inappropriate responses, working memory, and cognitive flexibility or set shifting. These three domains of SEL skills are related to short- and long-term outcomes like academic achievement (e.g., grades, standardized tests of academic skills), behavioral adjustment (e.g., taking others' perspective, getting along well with other children, solving conflicts, and exhibiting less aggression and conduct problems), and emotional health and well-being (e.g., lower levels of depression and social isolation). The links between SEL skills and outcomes are influenced by several environmental factors and systems. The school context includes school culture and school climate as well as effective SEL implementation. Student skills and school context factors are influenced by teachers' social and emotional competence and pedagogical knowledge and skills, as well as community contexts and policy. In other words, SEL skills develop in a complex system of contexts, interactions, and relationships.

Integrated approaches to SEL in schools: continuity and consistency. Four principles of SEL development that can drive more effective school-based approaches are that: (1) continuity and consistency are essential for SEL skill development; (2) social, emotional, and academic skills are interdependent; (3) SEL skills develop in social contexts; and (4) classrooms and schools operate as systems. Like reading and math, some SEL skills are sequential. Just as children must learn to read before they can read to learn, they must be able to effectively read social cues to make sound judgments about how to react to challenging social situations. SEL skills therefore develop in an ongoing relational context. There are many ways SEL efforts can influence the broad systemic school context, and one of the most visible is by influencing school culture and climate.

School culture and climate. Culture and climate are the regular and consistent patterns that characterize how actors in the organization think, feel, interact, and behave. School culture refers to a school's set of norms, beliefs, and practices or "the way things are done around here." Culture is driven by the school's values and expectations that are embedded in structures and practices and transmitted both explicitly and implicitly. Climate, on the other hand, is the aggregate of individuals' perceptions of the environment's impact on the well-being and is influenced by their perceptions of the psychological environment. Together, culture and climate set the tone and focus of relationships and interactions between leaders, staff, and students. Schools' culture and climate are shaped by social norms and school staff can gradually shift SEL-related social norms, with students playing a powerful role in maintaining and strengthening them.

Shifting the approach

The principles of social and emotional development and learning are: (1) continuity over time, (2) interconnectedness with academics, (3) importance of relationships, and (4) importance of culture and climate. Changing students' daily behaviors and skills requires changes in daily educational practice, from staff–student interactions and norms for acceptable behavior to routines that adults and children use for regulating emotions and behavior. If school staff receive training and support in how to use specific SEL strategies and structures during daily interactions, these strategies can become habits of mind rather than an additional curricular burden. As mentioned above, Jones and Bouffard (2012) emphasize that SEL programs should not be eliminated from schools. On the contrary, programs should still play a very important role, but schools need a continuum of approaches that range from routines and structures to school-wide efforts to promote supportive cultures and positive climates.

Integrating SEL development into daily educational practice

Some of the strategies utilize, but do not constitute, kernels, because they are larger strategies that can be broken down into component parts (Jones & Bouffard, 2012). Some distill intensive efforts into simpler ones, whilst others broaden specific practices into larger or more intentional efforts. Key steps to successful integration of SEL into everyday practice are: routines, training, support, setting standards, and policy support.

Routines. Routines include emotional regulation and conflict-resolution strategies, games that hone attention skills, and class council meetings for resolving classroom issues. Reminders and tips about using the routines may be posted throughout the school. Routines include: "Stop and Stay Cool," a three-step process for staying in control of emotions, and "Decision Tree" that students use to guide choices. Brain games are short, easy-to-play games built on traditional games like Simon Says and Red light/Green light promoting memory and impulse control. The routines will be most effective when posted throughout the school building and used consistently by both staff and students every day.

Training and support for all teachers, staff, and leaders. Teachers and other staff need support that will help them learn how to interact positively with students, react effectively to emotional and social challenges and conflicts, communicate clear expectations for student's behavior, and set up the conditions for supportive school cultures and climates such as treating everyone with respect, seeking opportunities to help others, and acknowledging and improving on mistakes as part of learning.

Support for the adults' own SEL skills. It is difficult, if not impossible, for adults to help students build skills that they themselves do not possess. Adult SEL skills include: (1) modeling the use of these skills, (2) managing stress and modulating emotional responses to respond to situations effectively, (3) remaining aware in the present moment and being intent on working with students, (4) creating positive interactions with students, (5) using executive functioning skills such as focusing and planning, and (6) implementing SEL programs with fidelity and quality.

SEL standards. These represent a set of benchmarks and can be linked with assessment to help schools measure their progress. Whilst standards have traditionally focused on academic content, SEL standards provide guidance for schools in the kind of skills students should attain, how to align academic and SEL goals, and how to make SEL a core part of schools' mission.

Policy support. Research suggests the following additional strategies for integrating SEL into the school day: (1) adequate and flexible funding; (2) reviewing and consolidating standards; (3) integrating SEL into administrator, teacher, and staff training; (4) supporting assessment of SEL practices and skills; (5) creating opportunities for networking, learning, and continuous improvement; and (6) increasing connections between SEL and academics (Jones & Bouffard, 2012). A further development of the idea and importance of promoting social skills and competence in children and adolescents is represented by the OECD initiative "Skills for the 21st Century": the importance of social and emotional skills.

The larger picture: OECD and social and emotional skills for the twenty-first century

At the OECD's informal ministerial meeting on Skills for Social Progress in Sao Paulo, Brazil in March 2014, policymakers discussed the skills that drive individual well-being and progress. They agreed on the need to develop a balanced set of cognitive, social, and emotional skills so that individuals could better face the challenges of the twenty-first century. A report was published that summarized some of the aims of the initiative (OECD, 2015) and identified which social and emotional skills contribute to children's cognitive, social, and emotional development, thus: (1) both cognitive and social and emotional skills are important for children to improve their opportunities and for achieving positive results later in life, (2) families can play an important role in raising children's social and emotional development from birth, (3) schools can further enhance children's social and emotional skills by introducing innovations in teaching and learning through curricular and extracurricular activities, and (4) communities can further enhance social and emotional skills by providing valuable contexts for informal learning. Teachers and parents can help improve children's social and emotional skills by promoting good relationships and through practical learning experiences. Social and emotional skills are also important for the development of cognitive skills (cf. the relationship between endurance and mathematics). With reference to Heckman (2008), the report states that investing in social and emotional skills, especially among those disadvantaged in early childhood, is one of the best ways of reducing social and economic inequality—skills shortages may affect more than family income.

Miyamoto, Huerta, and Kubacka (2015) explain that researchers, parents, and teachers can all help to bridge the gap between educational research and practice. One reason for a gap between the two fields may be the perception that social–emotional skills are difficult to improve, particularly through formal schooling. A second reason may be the impression among school leadership and staff that promoting such skills involves significant additional efforts, training, and resources, although this is not necessarily the case. A third reason may be the perception that social and emotional skills are difficult to measure. However, recent developments in psychosocial assessments point to a number of instruments that can be used to reliably measure relevant social and emotional skills within a culture or linguistic boundary. Among the social and emotional skills that have been measured and tested, conscientiousness (responsibility and persistence), sociability and emotional stability were among the most important dimensions (OECD, 2015).

The OECD's Framework for Measuring Well-Being and Progress emphasizes outcomes that are relevant in the modern world, including education and skills, labor market outcomes, health, civic engagement, personal security, family and social connections, subjective well-being, environmental outcomes, and material conditions. The framework has evolved toward understanding not only economic, but also a wider range of factors that matter for individual well-being and societal progress. The broad skill categories include pursuing goals, working with others, and managing emotions. Social and emotional skills play a crucial role from an early age when children are pursuing goals by playing games, solving puzzles, or finishing homework. This becomes even more important when they become adults and strive for academic degrees, look for good jobs, or start a business. Learning how to show positive and negative emotions and managing stress and frustration is also important, for instance when dealing with life challenges such as divorce, unemployment, or long-term disability. The basic negative emotions are fear (anxiety), sadness (depression), and anger. Emotion regulation can be taught as self-confidence and control by introducing strategies for regulating temper, anger, and irritation.

In Durlak et al.'s (2011) meta-analysis of social and emotional training, it was suggested that children benefited in general from the interventions and that their social and behavioral skills improved in particular. Participating students also demonstrated higher academic achievement, with a gain in performance estimated to be equivalent to 11 percentile points across grades. Levin (2012) translates this gain into a measure equivalent to one third of a standard deviation, which is a significant increase from an education policy perspective. Interesting findings also come from studies of how executive function skills (self-regulation and self-control) are important predictors of achievement. For instance, self-control and self-discipline are predictive of better behaviors in the classroom that also correlate with improved report card grades and other measures of academic performance (Duckworth, Quinn, & Tsukayama 2012; Duckworth & Seligman, 2005).

Controversial issues

The critique of social competence training programs and their evaluations points at several opportunities for improvement. The greatest challenges to social competence training seem to be limitations in generalization or transfer of training, low sustainability of the program activity, and lack of environmental support (Beelmann, Pfingsten, & Lösel, 1994). For instance, in schools, social skills training may be offered to students in separate lessons, but these efforts are not supported by other teachers in other classes. In social competence classes, students may learn about the importance of cooperation, but in the next lesson they may compete for the best grades in math. Formal monitoring of the implementation of the programs is often missing and there is a lack of control of program integrity. It may also be difficult to confirm whether or not the program has been delivered with the dosage and engagement intended by the program developer. Moreover, the effects of the programs on teachers, peers, and parents are not evaluated, and these may turn out to be both larger or smaller than the effects on the adolescents going through training. In sum, outcome evaluations indicate that the results of social competence training programs have not been as good as expected. Skills that help adolescents deal with the developmental tasks and individual challenges they face when interacting with peers and adults have high social validity and should be prioritized. For example, skills that increase social competence with peers of both genders are self-rewarding and the probability of immediate and gratifying practice in authentic situations increases significantly. The impact of formal social skills training may also be neutralized by experiences that adolescents are exposed to in their daily lives, such as the loss of highly valued family members and friends, failure and rejection in social relationships, or unexpected negative life events.

Concluding comments

As a concept, social competence links behavior and environment because individuals are always competent in relation to something or someone. Usually, it relates to actions that are positively evaluated by parents, teachers, and peers. Youths may have positive goals, for example when they try to help someone or show concern for others. But they may also have goals that bring them into conflict with others, when they act against other people's wishes and expectations, for example. This may occur when they want to be with friends rather than with their parents, or when they compete for attention in a peer group. Socially competent youths are usually able to strike a good balance between their own and other people's interests when they strive to achieve social goals in an acceptable way.

Over recent decades, we have witnessed an increased awareness of the importance of social competence for children and adolescents' development and functioning. This may reflect a higher focus in current society, not only for the importance of intellectual, but also for interpersonal social competence to succeed in school or on the job market. People who lack social sensitivity or social antennae find it increasingly difficult to succeed academically, professionally, or in personal relationships. Adolescents organize and coordinate their own resources with those in their environment to achieve social goals. This is a dynamic process that starts with the perception of social cues from the environment and ends with goal-directed social behavior. Environmental influences include good learning opportunities with access to competent models and a social climate in which competent behavior is requested, promoted, and rewarded. Even if children differ in their individual sociability and social dispositions, their social development is also influenced by the environment in important ways. Opinions vary, however, with regard to how important the context is for the normative development as well as for the development of individual differences in social competence. The social learning of adolescents takes place in most social situations and relationships, and a myriad of environmental influences interact with individual dispositions. It is difficult to determine the relative impact of each factor, and it is also difficult to decide how much impact formal teaching and learning have on social skills and competence. Hence, systematic teaching or education has to compete with other major social influences in the ecology of the adolescents like family, friends, peers, and teachers.

Social skills and competence can be taught in school like other skills and subjects, using both structured and authentic learning situations. But what is learned and what is practiced are both influenced by the school culture and the classroom environment. Of equal importance is the social learning that takes place in the families and homes of children and youths. The ecology of social learning includes a high collective awareness of the importance of social competence in both family and school. Adopting a public health perspective, Dodge (2008) suggests that antisocial behavior should be framed as a form of social illiteracy and, therefore, a challenge to public education. He proposes a model in which chronic violence is described as social incompetence that is a failure of society to educate:

> Although our society would not deny a child access to public education and then incarcerate him or her at 18 for being illiterate [...] we fail to see the folly in denying a child access to appropriate instruction and opportunities for learning self-regulation and then holding him or her responsible for incompetent behavior that results in a violent act in young adulthood.
> *(Dodge, 2008, pp. 585–586)*

This perspective implies an educational model of antisocial development and opens up possibilities of new and different intervention approaches from childhood to adolescence. Short-term preventive or promotive interventions are probably not enough to reduce the prevalence of antisocial behavior in schools and communities, however a comprehensive system of social competence education with continued teaching and learning of vital social skills derived from social developmental research could hold great promise for the future.

In a complex and multicultural society, the socialization of children and youth represents new challenges. The family arena seems to decrease in importance when it comes to learning social and practical skills. Families are becoming smaller as the number of single parents increases and the number of siblings decreases. Parents and children spend less time together in practical and social activities, and children spend more time interacting with their computers and iPhones rather than in face-to-face peer interactions. Increased knowledge about the preventive and health-promoting potential of social competence is also a part of this picture. Adolescents are competent actors who shape their own environment and contribute to their own development in several ways. Socialization is now understood as a reciprocal process wherein children and youths are both influenced by and influence their context. In the process of growing up, children and youths need skills and competence to adapt, but also to change the environment. It is important to discuss the goals of social competence education and to identify which skills should be emphasized. Children need competence to cope with crises, conflicts, and negative life events, but they also need life skills and competence to take advantage of their abilities and talents, and to live a good life. Social competence predicts positive interpersonal relations like friendship and contributes to well-being and improved quality of life.

The concept of competence promotion demonstrates how problem- and risk-reducing approaches to prevention and treatment increasingly have been supplemented and replaced with *resource-focused interventions* that emphasize how youths may deal with developmental challenges and increase their emotional, psychological, and social well-being (Gustafsson et al., 2010). The prospect of fostering success in youth may also be much more appealing to parents and teachers than preventing mental health problems (Masten & Powell, 2003). Efforts to promote mental health and competence in several countries over the past 15 years have been commented on by the US Public Health Service (2000): "Fostering social and emotional health in children as a part of healthy child development must therefore be a national priority" (p. 3). This change of perspective implies that the search for competence, particularly social competence, will become more important than looking for risk factors or signs of psychopathology.

7

ADOLESCENT MENTAL HEALTH AND THE SCHOOL SYSTEM

This chapter is devoted to mental health problems as they relate to the school context and to academic failure. We review mental health delivery models and interventions that may prevent or reduce such problems in school. Besides the family and the peer group, the school is probably the most important developmental arena for adolescents. There are three important points to be made in this regard: (1) there is a reciprocal relationship between mental health and academic achievement; (2) the school context may moderate this relationship, making it particularly strong for some adolescents; and (3) the school context may work to ameliorate, maintain, or worsen both school performance and psychological and behavioral adjustment in its students.

The first part of this chapter discusses research that has contributed to the identification of risk and protective factors in schools. The second part of the chapter reviews models and intervention approaches that have produced encouraging results for mental health outcomes. The chapter further outlines how school staff may handle mental health problems and ends with an overview of research-based practices in school and common challenges to effective collaboration between school staff and mental health practitioners.

Adolescent mental health problems in school

As discussed in Chapter 1, the transition from childhood to adolescence and from primary to secondary school is characterized by important individual and environmental challenges. The prevalence of certain internalizing problems, such as depression, increases in adolescence, particularly in girls. In addition, problems such as delinquency and alcohol and drug abuse also escalate. Mental health problems reduce the quality of life for youths and are predictive of both short- and long-term developmental problems (Layard & Dunn, 2009). Behavioral and emotional problems also undermine academic achievement. They may lead to truancy, school dropout, and to difficulties in getting along with peers. In spite of the many challenges of adolescence, however, the period also opens up a window of opportunity for the promotion of mental health and for the prevention of adjustment problems. Moreover, prevention initiatives put forth at this developmental phase may also help reduce problem severity, thwart new problems from emerging, and avert the development of comorbidity (Slade, 2003). Vulnerable students and students with mental health problems often struggle in school, socially, academically, or both, and even more so in schools with high rates of bullying, inconsistent enforcement of rules, or unfavorable climates. The situation that these students find themselves in is probably one of the greatest unmet challenges to the school system at the present time and in years to come.

School risk factors

Ideally, school staff should be able to observe and identify students who experience difficulties, and they ought to have the skills to recognize the early signals of deviant development (Roeser, Eccles, & Strobel, 1998). Some students continue to manage their schoolwork and they get good results, even if they have considerable social and emotional problems. Thus, unless school personnel know what to look for, students' mental health difficulties may go undetected. At *the individual level*, Roeser et al. (1998) are concerned with indicators of risk, as well as with resilience and promotion. They list: (1) risks related to problems with attention, cognition, emotions, and self-regulation that may lead to academic or emotional problems; (2) protective processes that enable some students to adjust to demands in school against all odds; or (3) processes that might lead to academic and emotional well-being and functioning. At *the contextual level*, they recommend the assessment of teacher–student interactions, particularly how teachers support, interact, and struggle with students who show problems.

Longitudinal studies indicate that there are specific processes that underlie academic and social–emotional functioning, and that the social context of the school can prevent or reduce such problems (Roeser et al., 1998; see also Hinshaw, 1992). Four possible hypotheses were formulated by Roeser et al. (1998) in trying to explain the relationship between academic problems and emotional distress: (1) *the academic difficulties hypothesis* states that academic problems lead to emotional problems, (2) *the emotional difficulties hypothesis* explains how emotional problems may lead to academic problems, (3) *the reciprocal influence hypothesis* assumes that each type of problem reinforces the other in a reciprocal fashion, and (4) *the third variable hypothesis* in which the school context accounts for the development of both academic and emotional difficulties and also the association between them. The four hypotheses are considered to be complementary rather than competing explanations for why academic and emotional problems often go together in high-risk youths. Taken together, these hypotheses draw a rather complex picture of the development and relationship between mental health and academic difficulties. In the following section, we discuss each of the four hypotheses.

Academic difficulties may lead to mental health problems

The academic difficulties hypothesis states that academic problems cause emotional difficulties by generating feelings of frustration, anger, anxiety, incompetence, and disinterest. The main mental health problem caused by academic difficulties seems to be depression. Several studies investigating the effects of adolescent academic achievement on mental health show that school failure is related to development of internalizing problems (Buehler & Gerard, 2004; Goldston et al., 2007; Gustafsson et al., 2010), particularly in girls (McCarthy et al., 2008). According to Cole's (1991) *competency-based model of depression*, academic and social difficulties are stressors that can cause depression, anxiety, and related symptoms. Negative feedback and low expectations from teachers, parents, or peers may eventually turn into negative self-evaluations and unfavorable comparison with fellow students. Regardless of who the sender is, repeated negative feedback about performance in a specific domain inhibits the development of positive self-perceived competence and may set the stage for depressive symptoms (Cole, 1991). Adding a moderating factor—friendships—into the prediction of depression development, Schwartz, Gorman, Duong, and Nakamoto (2008) found that poor academic functioning was predictive of depressive symptoms, but not for children who had many friends in the classroom. A study following students aged 12–15 years over 1 year showed that three school-related factors predicted *change* in girls' levels of depressive symptoms (Undheim & Sund, 2005). The first factor was perceived school stress that may be caused by high expectations from the girls themselves or others, leading to a feeling of insufficiency and, as a result, depressive symptoms. The second factor was lack of teacher support: the findings indicated that the personal relationship with the teacher was more important for girls than for boys. The third predictor was low grades. The interpretation of the results was that low grades might be perceived as more stressful for girls than for boys and increase their depressive symptoms.

Academic problems may be transformed into emotional distress via cognitive and motivational processes. These processes include negative attributions, coping, and self-perception of competence, resulting in a devaluation of schooling and academic work. The consequences of academic problems may be emotional or social–cognitive, such as when adolescents compare themselves unfavorably with peers, or engage in negative self-evaluation. Cognitive and meta-cognitive skill deficits might undermine academic capacity and, for students at risk, eventually lead to school dropout and to drug use and delinquency later on. Summarizing relevant research on the topic, Frydenberg (2008) concluded that academic failure was one of the main sources of stress in the lives of adolescents. Stress was defined as a perceived imbalance between environmental demands and personal resources. Frydenberg (2008) also examined potential resources that could be cultivated through interventions. These included self-esteem, optimism, and problem-solving skills. Markham and Aveyard (2003) emphasized that the best ways for schools to promote health and to prevent problems is by improving pupil functioning through the school organization, curriculum development, and pedagogic practice. Put differently, in order to prevent mental health problems, teachers should primarily do what they are best at: taking good care of their students and doing a good job teaching them.

Mental health as a determinant of academic achievement

As described above, academic difficulties can lead to emotional and behavioral problems, but psychological maladjustment can also result in academic difficulties (Roeser et al., 1998). Negative emotions may have a detrimental effect on attention and motivation, such as when students blame themselves or others for their failures, and when their attention is drawn to task-irrelevant factors during learning. Repeated failures will eventually lead some students to feel helpless and to avoid schoolwork. When adolescents experience extreme disaffection with learning, they tend to get bored, lose academic interest, and devalue school. Negative emotions might also influence cognition by draining resources available for learning and by activating scripts for avoidance behavior and self-protection. Unpleasant feelings make it hard to concentrate on the task at hand and one way to cope is to escape from the situation or devalue the task. In this process, a distinction can be made between academic internalizing and externalizing reaction patterns.

Internalizing problems and achievement

In the internalizing reaction pattern, anxiety in particular seems to have a negative effect on attention exemplified by a student who is overly concerned about the risk of future failures and focuses too little on positive experiences and the impending task (Roeser et al., 1998). Chen and Lie (2000) found depressed children to be more prone to loss of concentration, lack of energy, and to exhibit cognitive distortions that interfere with the learning process. McLeod and Fettes (2007) found academic problems to be more prevalent among students whose mental health problems started in childhood. Those who developed mental health problems in adolescence, on the other hand, were primarily perceived as disruptive and were met with lower academic expectations. This latter process demonstrates a self-fulfilling expectancy effect on academic achievement imposed by low expectations from parents, teachers, and other students.

Externalizing problems and achievement

A wide range of problems such as dropout, low grades, truancy, bullying, property damage, and general disturbance typically accompanies externalizing problem behavior in school. For some students, academic failure generates negative perceptions and they blame others for their shortcomings. Angry students may be hypersensitive to hostile (or neutral) cues, they look for and perceive provocations, and they automatically respond with aggression. If the interaction with these students becomes aversive and difficult, teachers and peers may gradually withdraw their social and intellectual support (Roeser et al., 1998). Poor anger management may result in increased conflicts with classmates and teachers. Conflicts detract attention from learning and may lead to expulsion from school or truancy, further reducing opportunities for learning. In addition, acting-out students may be transferred to special education classes, reducing their opportunities for meeting normal developmental tasks still further (Aviles, Anderson, & Davila, 2006). One of the main academically related precursors of externalizing problem behavior is early reading instruction, and there seems to be considerable overlap between reading skills and behavior problems. Indeed, poor reading ability in adolescence has been found to predict school dropout at the secondary level (Daniel et al., 2006).

Gustafsson et al. (2010) identified three possible mechanisms that could account for the effects of externalizing problems on academic achievement: first, externalizing behavior problems may directly interfere with effective schoolwork and educational careers (McLeod & Fettes, 2007). Second, externalizing behavior problems cause maladjustment in the classroom by inducing peer rejection and teacher–student conflicts that, in turn, affect academic achievement (Ladd & Burgess, 2001). Third, externalizing problems lead to criminal activity and risk-taking behavior that are incompatible with academic success in secondary school (McGee, Prior, Williams, Smart, & Sanson, 2002).

The reciprocal relationship between mental health and academic problems

In Gustafsson et al.'s (2010) systematic review of longitudinal relationships between mental health and academic achievement, internalizing and externalizing problems were both found to be associated with low academic achievement and premature termination of schooling. The reciprocal relations between academic achievement and mental health may cause a negative spiral in which school failure leads to mental health problems that, in turn, lead to further school failure, and so on. These reciprocal relations could also create positive spirals of development because success in school could improve mental health that, in turn, improves chances of further success. Interventions ought to take into consideration the interactive nature of the psychological, educational, and behavioral processes that underlie co-occurring problems.

A stable relationship between mental health and academic functioning was reported in a follow-up study of 491 students through grades 8, 9, and 11 (Roeser, Eccles, & Freedman-Doan, 1999). One group of students, "the well-adjusted group," did consistently well over time. Another group, "the multiple problems group," did consistently poorly. The multiple problems group had difficulties in both the academic and emotional domains from elementary school to high school. But, contrary to expectations, their mental health actually improved after the transition to high school and there were no declines in self-esteem or achievement after that. Possible mechanisms for their sustained problems were the internalization of negative self-perceptions of academic competence and a perception of school as uninteresting and unimportant. It appeared that it was not a cognitive deficit that accounted for their long-term problems, but rather a lack of appropriate skills and behaviors. A third group, "the poor school motivation group," failed in school, which lowered their perceptions of their academic competence and caused them to devalue school over time, possibly to protect their self-image. A last group, "the poor mental health group," was likely to go unnoticed, probably because they behaved and managed their schoolwork adequately, in spite of their problems (Roeser et al., 1998). As high-risk students move through the school system, they may experience both academic and mental health problems. Consequently, schooling and mental health ought to be studied simultaneously in order to inform the design of interventions at both the individual and the contextual level.

Context matters

A third variable may influence both achievement and mental health and also the relationship between them. A likely candidate is the school context. The school context encompasses the psychological, social, academic, and physical characteristics of the organization and the collective environment provided by teachers, students, parents, and principals (Reynolds, 2001). Whilst many studies have analyzed the associations between school climate and academic achievement, few have actually examined how school climate impacts students' mental health (e.g., Rutter & Maughan, 2002). Still, schools are undoubtedly important suppliers of informal mental health services such as positive social interactions and learning opportunities, both of which contribute to improving students' well-being. Students need and benefit from secure and trusting relationships with teachers. Clearly, school personnel should not take on the sole responsibility for providing mental health services, nor should they work as clinicians, but they nevertheless play an important role by influencing the students' ability to learn through their engagement, behavior management, and instructional strategies (Weist & Albus, 2004).

Peer and teacher influences

Several studies show the importance of peer influences on school achievement. For example, friendships can reduce the negative impact of poor achievement on internalizing problems (Schwartz et al., 2008). School burnout—defined as exhaustion due to study demands, a cynical and detached attitude toward studies, and students' feelings of incompetence—was measured at two time points for 517 ninth-graders in a Finnish study (Kiuru, Aunola, Nurmi, Leskinen, & Salmela-Aro, 2008). The results suggested that being in a high-achievement peer group protected youths against an increase in school burnout. In a prospective study spanning 17 years, Brendgen, Bukowski, Wanner, Vitaro, and Tremblay (2007) found that verbal abuse by teachers during childhood predicted behavior problems for both boys and girls, even when childhood levels of antisociality, anxiety, school perform-ance, and peer preferences were controlled. Verbal abuse by teachers was defined as verbal putdowns, negative prediction, negative comparison, scapegoating, shaming, cursing, swearing, and threats.

Student perceptions of barriers and facilitators of mental health

Social and emotional problems may appear very differently from the perspective of an adult observer as compared to the perspective of the students themselves. Students' experiences, as well as their attributions, are central in the process of understanding which factors contribute to school failure and school dropout. In a systematic review of research on mental health in youth, Harden et al. (2001) found the school context to be both a risk factor and a facilitator of adjustment. The rather discouraging message from their review was that few school-related facilitators to mental health were identified by the youth, and many considered school to be a barrier to good mental health. Relationships with other students and teachers were particularly important for how students perceived their learning environment, but their relations with teachers were often described in negative terms. Lack of respect and support from teachers were often mentioned, and teachers were frequently reported to undermine the self-esteem of many students. Students who did not like to go to school or who did not show up for classes often claimed that they disliked their teachers (Cornelius-White, 2007). Some students reported that pressure to perform well in school often led to stress and anxiety. Moreover, some found the workload to be overwhelming, exams to be stressful, and homework to occupy too much of their leisure time. Lack of engagement in school was attributed to boredom, monotony, and poor results.

Nevertheless, teachers were also found to protect and promote the students' mental health. Harden et al. (2001) note that, in addition to teacher density, teachers' competence in classroom management and student care promote positive social and emotional functioning in school. Their review concluded that mental health interventions can give positive results. Rather than relying solely on the transmission of information, prevention programs ought to include skill-enhancing components through the use of behavioral techniques. Furthermore, according to the authors of the review, interventions should be evaluated on their impact on students' academic achievement as well as on their mental health as the two domains are both interrelated and important. The authors also warn that strat-egies applied to increase the level of academic achievement might lead to increased stress and anxiety in secondary school. Thus, it is important that the youths' own viewpoints and opinions are the starting point of all future mental health pro-motion initiatives. Interventions aimed at reducing the workload and pressure in schools should be further improved and tested in conjunction with interventions aimed at improving the social relationships between teachers and youth. Like several authors before them, they recommended mental health interventions that lead to changes in the *structural aspects* of the school (Harden et al., 2001). For instance, Roeser et al. (1998) were convinced that it is through institutional reforms rather than individual-level services that it is possible to address the many educational and mental health needs of students. System-wide interventions should include efforts to reduce truancy, the number of disciplinary referrals, and unnecessary special education placements. Such an approach requires the understanding of how school-level organizational practices may impact the emotional and behavioral functioning of individual students. And because students with serious emotional disturbances have the highest rates of school failure of all students with disabilities, Paternite (2005) recommends that schools take part in the mental health care of students and promote both academic skills and social–emotional competence.

The school setting is considered a good venue for the identification of children and adolescents in need of services (Aviles et al., 2006; Ringeisen, Henderson, & Hoagwood, 2003). Virtually all children and young adolescents go to school and they spend many hours of the day there. Looking for ways to approach the reciprocal relationship of academic and mental health problems, Roeser et al. (1998) recommend the use of behavioral interventions combined with helping students to reframe their biased perceptions of academic demands. Interventions aimed at increasing student motivation include meaningful learning tasks from the perspective of the students and, more generally, interventions delivered in a context of caring relationships and a supportive academic setting.

Mental health service models in schools

Traditionally, mental health services in schools have had a restrictive focus on assessment, clinical consultation, and treatment services for students in or referred to special education (Weist, 1997). The most common forms of service delivery are individual counseling, case management, and evaluation/testing. Some critics argue, however, that individual service delivery models may be inadequate (Adelman & Taylor, 1999). Most school-based mental health service programs have no evidence to support their effectiveness (Rones & Hoagwood, 2000). Therefore, mental health professionals may assist schools in capitalizing on their resources through their knowledge of empirically supported interventions (Ringeisen et al., 2003). Most of the evaluation research to date, however, has focused on universal programs in elementary school, and less has been evaluated with middle and high school students. The tremendous pressure on academics, to the detriment of much else, may explain why there are fewer evidence-based mental health programs for adolescents (Merrell, 2010). So, even if the need for mental health services probably increases from primary to secondary school, there are fewer opportunities for older students to get appropriate help. School staff should be prepared to counsel adolescents about mental health problems and refer them for treatment if needed, but they should also be able to provide a school environment that promotes well-being and good adjustment in all students. Teachers should therefore be trained to recognize the social–emotional needs of students and know how to care for and support them in the classroom (Aviles et al., 2006).

The integrated three-tiered public health model

Macklem (2011) is rather critical of traditional mental health services in schools. He proposes a preventive approach that, rather than conveying information, focuses on skill-enhancing components through the use of behavioral techniques. Moreover, such programs are likely to be more effective if they are delivered early in the students' academic careers (Rodney, Johnson, & Srivastava, 2005). Preventive interventions can either focus on reducing the probability of individual deficits and problems, or concentrate on improving the social contexts and systems (Hoffman, 2009) by creating and supporting positive emotional climates in schools (Macklem, 2011). Support for Macklem's approach comes from Harden et al. (2001) who suggest that preventive efforts should be strengthened by contributions from various levels such as the classroom, the school, the home, the neighborhood, and society at large. Macklem's alternative is a three-tiered public health model in which a "continuum of care" includes three categories: universal (Tier 1), selective (Tier 2), and indicated (Tier 3) (see also Chapter 2). Tier 1 concentrates on efforts to improve school climate and the implementation of evidence-based universal programs for all students. Tier 2 includes targeted interventions for students at risk of developing mental health problems, and Tier 3 contains indicated programming for students already manifesting emotional and behavioral difficulties. Students who do not benefit from Tier 1 interventions get a second chance at Tier 2 and another one at Tier 3, if they do not make progress. The differentiation in treatment is based on evidence-based components that progressively increase in intensity. Some students need both more time and greater intensity, so training becomes more explicit as students move through the tiered system. The delivery of intervention may also progress from large groups to small groups and then to individually delivered interventions. Of particular relevance to the current chapter is the comprehensive and systematic review of evidence-based mental health programs and interventions undertaken by Weare and Nind (2011). As a part of the European Union's DataPrev project, they identified 52 systematic reviews and meta-analyses of mental health interventions in schools under various headings, including "mental health," "social and emotional learning," "emotional intelligence," "resilience," "life skills," and "character education."

A systematic review of mental health promotion and problem prevention in schools

The aim of the systematic review was to "[...] clarify the evidence for and create a database of key evidence-based principles, approaches and interventions that are relevant to Europe and produce policy and practice guidelines to assist policymakers as they select approaches and interventions for implementation" (Weare & Nind,

2011, p. i30). Of the systematic review of 52 reviews included, 46 were universal, targeting all children in school, and 14 of these also included interventions on targeted or indicated populations. The remaining six reviews focused exclusively on targeted or indicated groups of children showing signs of mental health problems, violence, and aggression or emotional and behavioral problems. Most of the reviews came out of the US (27) and the UK (13). Nineteen reviews addressed internalizing mental health problems and disorders of depression and anxiety as main outcome variables, and all reported positive effect sizes in the small to moderate range.

The authors claim that even if intervention effects are small to moderate in the statistical sense, they may represent real-world effects that are relatively large and important (see also Durlak et al., 2011). Based on these findings, Weare and Nind (2011) strongly recommended that work on mental health promotion and problem prevention in schools is endorsed, continued, and expanded. A short overview of their overall findings across the included studies can be summed up as follows:

- Interventions have greater and longer-lasting impact when mental health issues are integrated into the general classroom curriculum rather than when implemented in isolation.
- CBT is a particularly effective approach when addressing a wide range of both externalizing and internalizing problems.
- The best-informed approach is to integrate universal and targeted initiatives.
- Start with the youngest students and develop generic social and emotional skills over several years and then turn to specific problems such as bullying and violence when they appear.
- Different professionals have different roles to play within interventions. Clinically trained staff are important at the start of the implementation process, whereas teachers and other staff are essential for sustaining and integrating interventions into regular school practice.
- Skills training is paramount.
- Behavioral strategies alone are unlikely to be effective, as are information-only strategies.
- Active teaching methods applying interactive techniques such as games, simulations, and small group work are recommended over didactic teaching methods.
- For optimal impact, skills training should be integrated into a whole-school multimodal approach that includes efforts to improve school ethos (or culture), teacher education, liaison with parents, parenting education, community involvement, and collaboration with outside agencies.

Taking a whole-school approach is compatible with several European initiatives of large-scale, agency-led, school-wide programs. But even if these school-wide programs are broadly disseminated, they have not been designed or evaluated in such a way that they may be included in systematic reviews. None of the high-profile European programs has met the evaluation requirements needed to be included in systematic reviews. The advice from Weare and Nind (2011) is that in order to ensure consistent implementation of evidence-based interventions, initiatives should build on what is known, consolidate and formalize the guidance and include clear procedures, and provide clarity and direction for future initiatives. On a more modest level, they also advise schools to only undertake interventions that fit their context and that they can easily implement with fidelity and rigor. In addition to this broad presentation of mental health services in schools and their outcomes, we have chosen to highlight a selection of research-based interventions that have been found to prevent mental health problems and promote competence and well-being in schools through controlled research.

Evidence-based mental health interventions in schools

Even though the literature on the development, validation, and promotion of evidence-based practices in schools is growing, the impact of this work on standard practice has been limited (Paternite, 2005). Part of the explanation may be that research-based mental health interventions have been developed largely in isolation from schools (Hoagwood & Johnson, 2003). Successful implementation in school systems is dependent on effective communication of program goals to school staff, the provision of feedback to staff about program effects, and consultation and support to teachers, including refresher training sessions, classroom observation, and small group discussions (Gottfredson, Gottfredson, & Hybl, 1993). Among the promising service models in schools, we take a closer look at the English Social and Emotional Aspects of Learning (SEAL) and the Targeted Mental Health in Schools (TaMHS) projects, and the School-Wide Positive Behavior Support (SWPBS) model. Also, among the research-based interventions to promote a safe and orderly learning environment are anti-bullying interventions and teacher–classroom management models. Another promising approach, social skills training, is covered more extensively in Chapter 6.

The Social and Emotional Aspects of Learning project

The Social and Emotional Aspects of Learning (SEAL) project was established as a national school-based program in England to promote social and emotional skills in pupils and staff. The aim was to increase effective learning, positive behavior, regular attendance, staff effectiveness, and emotional health and well-being of both those who learn and those who work in schools (Humphrey, Lendrum, & Wigelsworth, 2013). The SEAL components were: (1) the use of a whole-school approach to create a positive school climate and ethos, (2) direct teaching of social and emotional skills in whole-class contexts, (3) the use of teaching and learning approaches that support the learning of such skills, and (4) continuing professional development of school staff (Department for Children, Schools and Families, 2007). This might seem to be an overly ambitious project with a comprehensive list of potential outcomes. The project differed from those developed in the US by recommending a loose enabling framework for school improvement rather than a structured "package" to be applied in schools. Schools, and particularly secondary schools, were encouraged to explore different approaches to implementation rather than to follow a single model. The flexibility was intended to promote local ownership and sustainability and was initially met with enthusiasm by staff in the participating schools who felt that it encouraged their professional autonomy (Humphrey, Lendrum, & Wigelsworth, 2010). Later on, however, research findings consistently indicated that schools did not implement programs with fidelity (Lendrum & Humphrey, 2012). In fact, one third of the schools made little or no progress in implementation over a 2-year period. A consistent trend in the various evaluations of SEAL was the failure to use research findings to inform the development and refinement of the program.

Altogether, a summary of the research showed that the SEAL program failed to meet its intended objectives. Research evidence was not used to ensure high-quality interventions and proper piloting was not carried out before the project was scaled up nationally. An assessment of the implementation quality would have been helpful to determine "critical components" that should be delivered with fidelity. But allowing more locally driven approaches resulted in a somewhat confusing array of approaches being implemented, many of which were not supported by evidence. The evaluations also indicated that not all schools and/or teachers are receptive to SEL, particularly in secondary schools. Secondary school tends to be subject focused rather than youth centered, and several of their teachers were resistant to non-academic interventions. Some ambivalence and even some resistance was registered toward the promotion of student emotional health and well-being. They neither had the time, knowledge, nor skills to deliver such interventions and needed more information and training in SEL interventions. The SEAL evaluation clearly demonstrated that the teachers failed to implement the program as intended by the program designers. Clearer guidelines about how often an intervention should be delivered (dosage) were needed, as was information about the elements essential for change and how to implement them with adherence.

The Targeted Mental Health in Schools project

The aim of the Targeted Mental Health in Schools (TaMHS) project was to build on existing school-wide interventions (like SEAL) and develop innovative, locally crafted models to provide early intervention and targeted support for children aged 5–13 years at risk of developing, or already experiencing, mental health problems, and their families (Wolpert, Humphrey, Belsky, and Deighton, 2013). The funding was £60 million over a 3-year period in selected schools in every local authority across England and between 2500 and 3000 schools were involved in delivering TaMHS projects. According to the prevention model, effective school-based prevention should not focus on single risk factors or outcomes, but instead combine universal, school-wide approaches with targeted and indicated interventions for special groups of students (Domitrovich et al., 2010). The waves model of prevention and intervention for SEAL/TaMHS included:

Wave 1. *Effective whole-school frameworks* for promoting emotional well-being and mental health; quality teaching of social and emotional skills to all children through SEAL program and related work with families.

Wave 2. *Skills-focused interventions*: small group SEAL for students who needed help to develop social and emotional skills.

Wave 3. *Therapeutic interventions*: individual and small group interventions complementary to SEAL.

The two national guiding principles were that the selection of interventions should be informed by the evidence regarding "what works" and that the program should support strategic integration across agencies involved in the delivery of child and adolescent mental health services. The differences in organizational and professional cultures, lack of communication, differences in service priorities, and attitudes among professionals in both service groups together represent a barrier to the joint workings between schools and child and adolescent mental health services.

Child-focused support: consisted of individual psychological therapy, small group work, creative and physical activity to support well-being, information and advice giving, peer support techniques, behavior for learning and structural support for pupils and universal social and emotional learning approaches (e.g., SEAL).

Parent-focused support: included provision of information about available services, support to manage parental stress and other emotional reactions, and training to improve skills and confidence in relation to parenting.

Staff-focused support: included supervision and consultation, staff training, counseling, and support for stress and other emotional adversities.

Schools reported different combinations of these approaches and mental health support for students was generally provided by teachers and teaching assistants. The TaMHS initiative was a major effort to improve the psychological well-being and mental health of students and their families. Rather than using a prescriptive and manualized "program for every problem" (Jones & Bouffard, 2012) the approach embraced an integrated model (Domitrovich et al., 2010) as a robust framework for action. It was acknowledged that the "fidelity at all costs" emphasis in the research literature may create challenges in relation to local ownership and the professional autonomy of teachers.

The national evaluation of the project applied a mixed methods design with a longitudinal observational study of 20,000 students in 350 schools and an RCT with 30,000 students in 550 schools. Moreover, an interview study of TaMHS stakeholders and in-depth cases studies were carried out. Even if the evaluation outcome study demonstrated an increase in the use of evidence-based practices in certain contexts (e.g., primary schools), on the whole, schools did not engage in this effort as fully as was hoped. Outcome studies reported that no schools implemented interventions that followed a rigorous protocol or manual. The norm could be described as practice-based evidence rather than evidence-based practice. The most frequent category was "based on a plan, but open to adaption." In other words, the optimal delivery model balanced between prescriptiveness and flexibility. Factors that promoted success were integration of mental health support activities into the school setting, interventions building on previous successful initiatives, and interventions that were sensitive to the existing context. Findings from the randomized trial indicated that TaMHS benefited children with behavioral difficulties in primary schools, but not in secondary school or for older age groups, and not for emotional problems in students in primary school. TaMHS turned out to be more effective dealing with behavioral than with emotional difficulties in primary schools. The impact was also more pronounced in students of primary than in secondary school. Secondary schools are usually larger with more organizational and managerial challenges when it comes to implementing mental health promotion. In sum, the national evaluation of TaMHS provided a somewhat mixed picture of the success of the model. On the one hand, some of the main findings were very positive and demonstrated the impact of the approach on children's mental health. Staff, students, and parents were all positive about the experience of embedding mental health in schools. However, several analyses showed no benefit, suggesting areas for improvement and refinement.

The School-Wide Positive Behavior Support model

The School-Wide Positive Behavior Support (SWPBS) model has several forerunners, and common to them all is a continuum of research-based strategies that promote positive behavior: "Schoolwide systems provide the processes, structures, and routines to prevent problem behavior; they promote early intervention at the first signs of problem behavior; and they use comprehensive individual support plans" (Lewis, Newcomer, Trussell, & Richter, 2006, p. 844). One of the widely disseminated versions of the model was developed by Sprague and Walker (2005) with the aim of helping schools communicate to students the rules and expectations about what they are expected to do rather than what they should *not* do. This is achieved by the systematic use of positive feedback and predictable consequences. The model involves all students and the entire staff and emphasizes that monitoring and interventions should target all arenas of the school. What goes on at the classroom level should reflect values and standards at the school level. The approach stresses the importance of consistency in the communication of norms and common rules. Norms and expectations are filtered down the school organization from leadership to individual students. All students are taught positively formulated rules and norms for expected behavior and these are backed up with the use of consistent, frequent, and instant positive feedback to both the students, their teachers and, occasionally, their caregivers.

The general idea is to replace reactive and punishing approaches to problem behavior with proactive strategies that influence students through teaching and learning activities, generous support for positive behavior, and quality of the learning environment. Students with problem behaviors often experience academic failure and they tend to be rejected by their peers and confronted by their teachers. Rejection and failure undermine their "social bond" to the school. They easily turn to students with similar problems for contact and support and they may start reinforcing each other's negative behaviors. Moreover, cognitive deficits, attention problems in combination with a dysfunctional context, are likely to cause both academic and social and behavioral problems in school. Consequently, both academic deficits and social skills deficits are targeted in an overall intervention strategy with problem students. Multimodal interventions are implemented at the individual level, the classroom or group level, the school level, and at the system (school-wide) level. Interventions may target students directly or indirectly through the staff. Interventions are tailored to the students' risk level and organized at the universal, targeted, and indicated level. The main objective of the model is to establish a positive school climate for all students and at the same time promote long-term changes in the behavior of higher-risk students.

The universal interventions: Tier 1

Universal prevention at Tier 1 addresses the whole school population with particular emphasis on reaching the 80–90 percent of students with few or no behavior problems (Muscott, Mann, & LeBrun, 2008). Most students are well behaved, but they nonetheless deserve a reasonable amount of praise, encouragement, and rewards for complying with school rules, norms, and expectations. Interventions for all students might include: (1) school-wide rules and procedures for encouragement of positive student behavior; (2) predictable consequences for problem behavior; and (3) proactive classroom management, academic support, and good directions. Students are taught behavioral expectations the same way they are taught academics (Darch & Kame'enui, 2004). Consequently, behavioral expectations are defined, taught, monitored, and rewarded across all arenas of the school. Additionally, a clearly defined and consistently implemented continuum of consequences for problem behaviors is established. The monitoring of the students' social behavior is used for planning and implementing changes in routines.

The targeted group interventions: Tier 2

Approximately 5–10 percent of the student body have difficulties in coping with normal expectations from teachers and peers. The students who barely respond to the universal interventions may receive additional social skills training, individually or in small groups, and additional academic support as individual or small group instruction. The teachers learn proactive classroom management skills, how to teach emotional regulation techniques, and effective problem-solving skills. At this level, increased home–school cooperation is also established (Muscott et al., 2008). Intervention modules included at the selected level are intensive social skills teaching and support, self-management programs, school-based adult mentors, increased academic support and practice, and alternatives to school suspension (Smith, 2005a).

The intensive individual interventions: Tier 3

Intervention modules at this level addresses the remaining 3–5 percent of the students who are likely to be at high risk. Interventions at this level include: (1) individual and multisystemic support plans based on functional behavior assessment (FBA), (2) intensive social skills training, (3) parent training, and (4) behavior management training for teachers. Increased family or community collaboration aims at preventing the emergence or continuation of more serious problem behavior. Functional behavioral assessment is part of a problem-solving approach to manage behavior problems in schools and should result in a behavior support plan (Crone & Horner, 2003). The plan contains the following steps: (1) problem identification, (2) functional behavioral assessment, (3) designing a support plan, and (4) implementation of the plan.

Typically, the SWPBS model is implemented in a school over a period of 3 years. The first year is a "planning-year" in which universal school-wide and classroom planning occurs and the school staff receives training. The school staff is responsible for establishing systems and procedures that promote positive change in student behavior (Bradshaw, Mitchell, & Leaf, 2010). During the second year, the staff combines universal interventions targeting all students with selected interventions for at-risk students. In the third year, the school staff continues the implementation at the individual and group levels and adds to the program FBA and interventions targeting the high-risk students.

Research on the SWPBS model

The School-Wide Positive Behavior Support model has been extensively evaluated (Horner et al., 2009), and most evaluations have focused on the primary prevention tier (Tier 1). Promising results have been documented, although mostly in non-randomized studies. An exception is a study by Bradshaw et al. (2010) who conducted a 5-year longitudinal randomized controlled effectiveness trial in 37 elementary schools in the US. The school-level analyses indicated a significant reduction in student suspensions and office discipline referrals (ODRs) in the schools trained in SWPBS compared to schools not trained in the model. In another study by Bradshaw, Reinke, Brown, Bevans, and Leaf (2008), 21 schools were randomly assigned to receive training in SWPBS, and 16 were untrained control schools. The non-trained schools showed some improvements but lagged behind trained schools on most assessments of outcomes. In a later study, Bradshaw, Waasdorp, and Leaf (2015) explored the extent to which the effects of SWPBS varied as a function of the students' baseline pattern of social–emotional and behavioral risk. In this group-randomized effectiveness study, data were collected across five time points over four school years from 12,334 children in 37 public elementary schools.

Four subgroups were identified based on the teachers' baseline ratings of student problem behavior, concentration problems, social–emotional functioning, and pro-social behavior. Significant group differences in the outcomes were found: children in the "at-risk" and "high-risk" classes demonstrated the greatest benefits relative to their counterparts in the control schools. Horner, Sugai, and Anderson (2010) concluded in their review of research that the SWPBS model could be classified as evidence based, arguing that the experimental support for the model was sufficient. Using a more sophisticated approach, Chitiyo, May, and Chitiyo (2012) reviewed most of the same research but came to a different conclusion. They were critical to studies using only one outcome variable, predominately the ODR, and found that only two of ten experimental studies published in 34 articles had satisfactory implementation quality. They recommended more studies with rigorous research designs, measures of implementation integrity, and the use of more valid and reliable student outcome measures.

The Norwegian adapted model of SWPBIS: N-PALS

An adapted version of the SWPBS model was introduced to Norwegian primary schools in 2002, and 2 years after the introduction of the model, an evaluation study showed reduced student problem behavior and increased social competence compared to the schools without the model (Sørlie & Ogden, 2007). The N-PALS model is a system-wide, structured, and evidence-based framework to support schools in preventing problem behavior and establish safe and positive learning conditions for all students. This model actively promotes pro-social behavior, academic engagement, and motivation to cope with developmental challenges. Comprehensive preventive strategies are combined with more intensive and individually tailored interventions for students struggling with serious behavior problems. The general idea behind N-PALS is to replace reactive and punishing approaches to problem behavior with proactive strategies that influence students through teaching and learning activities, generous positive support, and through the quality of the learning environment. The approach also stresses the importance of consistency in the communication of norms and common rules both at home and at school (Horner et al., 2009). One of the key elements is that the students' social behavior is directly influenced by how teachers and other staff members model behavior, how they express positive expectations, how they teach and enforce discipline, and how they support social skills. In line with recent research findings, school-wide interventions are expected to influence all staff and all students more effectively than those that address only a limited group of teachers or classes. A representative leadership team is established in each school to lead the implementation of N-PALS. The leadership team plans, initiates, and implements databased interventions at their school. In addition, they assess and monitor implementation progress and student outcomes, introduce N-PALS to parents, train their colleagues in the core features of N-PALS, and organize school-wide assessment of risk and protective factors. The teams are trained by a local N-PALS coach. The N-PALS coach ensures a safe communication climate and motivates the team members to achieve the N-PALS goals and desired outcomes. Optimal outcomes are dependent on strong leadership, effective systems and processes at all levels in the school, and ongoing support that helps the school to be more effective and efficient in their work with N-PALS.

The Preventing Problem Behavior in School (PPBS; Sørlie, Ogden, & Olseth, 2015) intervention is based on the same principles as the N-PALS model, but the abbreviated PPBS intervention focuses solely on the universal level. The key features are: (1) a school-wide approach, (2) systematic positive reinforcement of expected pro-social behavior, (3) corrections (mild consequences) following problem behavior, (4) good directions, and (5) establishing a functional support system. The PPBS includes a 4-day, 30-hour in-service training program for school staff and is locally organized with up to seven schools per site. The entire school staff participates in the training program, which is provided free of charge. The participants are also provided with an intervention manual, and all of the training materials can be downloaded from the Internet. The training sessions are composed of a combination of lectures, demonstrations, training, coaching and "homework."

Norwegian research outcomes

Results from a more comprehensive evaluation study of the three-tiered School-Wide Positive Behavior Support model in Norway (SWPBS, called N-PALS) used a strengthened non-randomized design (Sørlie & Ogden, 2014). Data were collected from more than 1200 teachers and 7640 students at four measure points over 4 school years in 28 Norwegian intervention schools and 20 control schools. Multilevel analyses revealed significant positive main and differential intervention effects on student problem behavior and classroom learning climate (Sørlie & Ogden, 2015). Moreover, the number of segregated students (in special education classes) decreased in the intervention group, but increased in the control group. Implementation quality predicted more positive outcomes. In a second study from the same project, longitudinal multilevel analyses indicated positive 3-year main effects of the N-PALS model for staff-reported collective efficacy, self-efficacy, and positive behavior support practices (Sørlie, Ogden, & Olseth, 2016). The effects on student perceptions of teachers' behavior management strategies were, however, not consistent with the positive staff ratings. That is, the students' reports did not confirm teacher assessments on improved teacher management strategies.

PPBS was developed and piloted as an abbreviated version of the Norwegian N-PALS model. This model included a 4-day in-service training program for a school's entire staff. Seventeen primary schools (first through seventh grade) implementing PPBS and 20 control schools engaging in "practice as usual" were compared using a three-wave measurement design (Sørlie et al., 2015). PPBS schools reported substantial reductions in negative behavior incidents occurring *outside* the classroom context. Intervention effects were evident both for less severe and for more severe problem behaviors such as theft, vandalism, and physical attacks. Analyses of moderating effects indicated greater decreases in student conduct problems in small and medium schools compared to larger schools (a "large" primary being one with more than 300 students). The moderation analyses indicated that schools that implemented the intervention with high fidelity, schools with a larger number of untrained staff members, and small- to medium-sized schools had better staff-reported outcomes on classroom climate. Moreover, a more positive development in perceived collective efficacy in the intervention group indicated that the staff in the PPBS schools, compared with their colleagues in the control schools, perceived greater confidence in their mutual ability to motivate and support student learning, to reach difficult students, and to prevent and manage problem behavior.

A CASE DESCRIPTION OF HOME–SCHOOL COLLABORATION

Karen is a "problem student." When she is not truant, she is passive during lessons and does not do any homework. The school situation is difficult, partly because she skips school several days a week and partly because she has not been doing any schoolwork for the last 6 months. She is not disruptive, but very passive in class. Still, she is good in mathematics and artwork, and she enjoys working with data. The teachers and the headmaster care about Karen, and they are willing to cooperate with the parents to get her to go to school every day and to be more active during classes. She affiliates with some peers who also stay away from school. Besides being passive during lessons, Karen lacks strategies and energy to tackle problems. There are several other students with behavior problems in the same class and there is also a conflict between the parents and the school about the school arrangement. The home–school relationship is strained, and there is a mutual communication problem. Therefore, a meeting is scheduled to plan common goals and routines for cooperation. Both parents are willing to do something about the situation and the school staff is convinced that the parents want to help improving the school situation for Karen.

At the meeting, the headmaster and the school counselor present the school's perspective on Karen's situation and describe what they have tried to do to improve Karen's school situation. The parents and the school present and discuss possible risk factors that may have contributed to the development of Karen's problems. Based on an analysis of the risk factors, they agree on a home–school contract and decide on interventions to be tried. Karen also agrees to sign a contract in which she commits herself to attend school on a regular basis, improve her academic efforts, do homework, and behave more appropriately in school. The parents commit themselves to follow up on Karen's schoolwork by communicating clear expectations, and administering rewards and consequences in relation to schoolwork, school behavior, and attendance. On a daily basis, the school informs the parents whether or not rules are followed so that they can effectuate agreed-upon rewards or negative consequences. The parents also make an agreement with Karen that she will present her schoolwork to them every day, and also do her homework. The parents also keep updated on homework and tests and generally hold a positive focus on schooling. After a few weeks, Karen and her parents work well with the contract at home and the school reports that Karen has started to change in a positive direction. The school and the parents then discuss Karen's expectations in different subjects. The mother contacted a homework mentor for a first appointment and a new meeting was set up with the school to adjust the contract between home and school.

Anti-bullying interventions in school

Unfortunately, bullying is quite common in most schools. Many resources have been invested in research on the phenomenon, and in the development of interventions to prevent, reduce, and put an end to bullying. Olweus (1993) defines bullying as the recurring exposure, over time, to negative actions by others. A more elaborate definition is suggested by Smith (2005b):

> the apparent intent to physically, socially, or mentally harm the target victim(s) and may include (1) physical and/or verbal threats or assaults, (2) offensive and/or threatening gestures and facial expressions, (3) verbal, physical, or social intimidation, and (4) social exclusion from groups and friends.
>
> *(p. 81–82)*

It is difficult to tackle bullying in schools because it is often covert and therefore difficult to detect by others. Compared to other forms of antisocial behavior, bullying tends to occur in settings that are not easily accessible to adult monitoring. Prevalence numbers vary depending on both country and school context, and on the age and gender of the students. Estimates from European studies indicate that 7–9 percent of students in grades one to nine had bullied other students, and that about 5 percent were involved in serious bullying at least once a week (Olweus, 1996). Due to the social stigma attached to reporting bullying, these figures may be an underestimation of the actual prevalence of such behavior. Smith (2005a) argues that based on US studies, the prevalence may be even higher in North American schools.

Several programs have been developed to prevent and reduce bullying in schools, but the majority of these have yielded non-significant outcomes. In a meta-analysis by Merrell, Gueldner, Ross, & Isava (2008), 16 studies were included and the overall conclusion was that meaningful and clinically important positive effects were found for about one third of the variables. The authors concluded that school bullying interventions produced modest positive outcomes and that they influenced knowledge, attitudes, and self-perceptions relating to bullying, more than actual bullying behavior. The student variables that were positively affected by the anti-bullying efforts were social competence, self-esteem, and peer acceptance. Teachers enhanced their knowledge of effective practices and how to respond to incidents of bullying at school, and they increased their sense of efficacy regarding intervening skills. The interventions reduced student participation in bully and victim roles to a lesser extent. One program, however, showed significant decreases in victimization and bullying behavior: the internationally disseminated Olweus anti-bullying program (1993; 1997). The aim of the program is to prevent, reduce, or stop bullying both inside and outside the school context. The implementation requires the school staff and the parents of the students to be aware of the magnitude of the problem in their school and that they make serious attempts at changing the situation. The school staff should take responsibility for reducing bullying behavior and communicate a clear and unwavering position against such behavior. The program includes measures at the school level, the classroom level, and the individual level (Olweus, 1993). Interventions at the school level include: (1) assessment of the problem through surveys and questionnaires; (2) arranging school conferences on bully/victim issues with staff, students, and parents; (3) increasing adult supervision in unstructured, high-census common areas like playgrounds; (4) improving common area infrastructures; (5) problem-solving efforts with staff, students, and parents; and (6) establishing a school-based pro-social improvement team dedicated to school culture and climate issues (Olweus, 1993; Smith, 2005c). At the classroom level, activities include: (1) creating rules prohibiting bullying; (2) establishing positive reinforcement (praise) for appropriate behavior and negative consequences for inappropriate behavior; (3) engagement in role-playing, cooperative learning groups, and positive classroom activities; (4) regular class meetings addressing the problem of bullying; and (5) meetings with teachers, students, and parents (Olweus, 1993; Smith, 2005c).

Intervention modules at the individual level are: (1) one-on-one talks of a serious nature with both bully and victim, (2) separate debriefings with the participating students and their parents, (3) joint talks between the bully and his or her parents and the victim and his or her parent, (4) provision of social and behavioral support resources for parents of participants, (5) discussion groups for parents and perpetrators, and (6) change in placement of bully/victim (classroom or school) if required (Olweus, 1993; Smith, 2005c).

The Olweus anti-bullying program has been disseminated and evaluated in Norway, as well as in other countries including England, Germany, and the US. The first evaluation of the Olweus program showed a reduction in bullying by 50 percent or more in grades four to nine, 2 years after implementation. The effectiveness of the program was stronger in the second year of implementation than in the first. A significant reduction was also found for antisocial behavior in general. Moreover, the program also influenced the social climate in a positive way

(Olweus, 1993; 1994). Replication studies have shown reduction of the prevalence of bullying in the range of 20–30 percent in the intervention schools, compared to the control schools in which the bullying actually increased over time (Olweus, 1994; 1996). Summing up the research evidence, Smith (2005b) emphasizes that bullying has multiple determinants and is subject to a range of risk factors, and that effective interventions should target the school context as well as victims and bullies, individually.

Teacher–classroom management

In order for teachers to address the mental health needs of students, they must first acknowledge that they are important persons in their students' lives. It is important to identify the kinds of classroom practices teachers need to strive for in order to help all students learn, whilst at the same time supporting and caring for those who have social, emotional, and behavioral difficulties. Classroom management is one of the most important universal strategies for creating a social climate in which students are offered good working conditions and learning opportunities. Teachers' effective management skills promote and protect learning activities and they influence the behavior of the students and their academic achievement in a positive manner. Successful classroom management increases the proportion of active learning time compared to time spent establishing order or dealing with disruptions. Positive student–teacher relations and positive attitudes toward learning among students are also important factors. Early research on classroom management consisted of observational studies of how effective teachers organize and manage their classrooms and of experimental studies that examined components of classroom management (Oliver, Wehby, & Reschly 2011). In a meta-analysis of 100 studies of classroom management, Marzano, Waters, and McNulty (2003) found good student–teacher relations to be the most important condition for the prevention of problem behavior; without good relations, the student would often protest against rules and routines. The other important predictors of effective classroom management were rules and procedures that communicated the general expectations for positive behavior, disciplinary interventions that adequately balanced positive and negative consequences for student behavior, and teachers' emotional objectivity in difficult situations. Simonsen, Fairbanks, Briesch, Myers, & Sugai (2008), who examined 81 studies in a "best-evidence" systematic review, reached similar conclusions. They recommended a few broad categories of classroom management for teachers: (1) maximize structure and predictability; (2) post, teach, review, and provide feedback on expectations; (3) actively engage students in observable ways; and (4) use a continuum of strategies to acknowledge appropriate behavior and respond to inappropriate behavior. In an overview of the development of research on classroom management, Brophy (2006) describes a change of perspective from general teacher characteristics to defined models and principles of leadership, and from interaction with individual students to the management of the class as a group. Brophy also describes a change in teacher focus from reactive discipline to proactive implementation of good procedures and routines, from behavior to learning activities, and from isolated "tricks" to long-term socialization. At the same time, the students' responsibility and self-regulation have been emphasized to a greater extent. In sum, current studies of classroom management emphasize organization and leadership with a focus on the planning and implementation of learning activities. From this perspective, teachers are like leaders of an activity system, and classroom activities become more important than teaching. Increased interest in and focus on the context of the education has resulted in a greater exploration of the mutual influences of students and teachers in a defined classroom.

Controversial issues: collaboration between school staff and mental health staff

Schools today are systems with multiple and often competing pressures. Mental health interventions may be regarded as an additional burden to school staff, unless they are integrated into the regular school setting and part of everyday activities. Schools are not primarily concerned about student mental health, and many teachers argue that activities that promote mental health are taking focus and resources away from their primary mission, which is to teach and educate. The *non-academic* interests of mental health providers and the *academic* interests of educators have often led to a mismatch, a lack of cooperation, and absence of effort coordination. Tensions between school personnel and mental health professionals may be due to differences in philosophies, poor communication, scheduling conflicts, limited resources, and poor knowledge by mental health staff of school regulations and procedures (Waxman, Weist, & Benson, 1999). From a critical point of view, mental health practices in school pay too little attention to characteristics of the school context that might influence service delivery. It may be argued that mental health practitioners tend to be disinterested in outcomes of relevance to schools such as academic achievement. School-relevant outcomes of mental health intervention have not been examined properly by its proponents. Ringeisen et al. (2003) concluded that developers of "evidence-based" mental health practices have paid insufficient attention to features of the school context that might secure effective service delivery. One challenge is the monitoring of the implementation process to ensure that the intervention is conducted with fidelity. Generally, important implementation components seem to have been ignored in many school efforts. These components include the support of school-leaders and staff, negotiating pragmatic issues such as time and space in the school day, and providing training, technical assistance, and support to practitioners who are responsible for the intervention (Paternite, 2005). Implementation is generally a major obstacle when new programs are introduced in secondary schools (Elias & Schwab, 2006; Gottfredson & Gottfredson, 2002). Macklem (2011) states:

> In order to successfully implement a program and sustain it in school, the program must be implemented consistently; parents, teachers and students

must be included and involved; multiple intervention modalities must be included; the content of the program must be integrated into the general classroom; and program components must be developmentally appropriate.

(p. 12)

A quality assurance system should therefore be in place at the local level to ensure that the program is implemented as intended and that the interventions are carried out with integrity.

Teachers who appear resistant or uncooperative to mental health programs or interventions in their school may in fact be reacting to interventions that are too complex for their current level of training or too far removed from the educational practice with which they are familiar. School staff operate within a system of multiple, and sometimes competing, demands, and they rarely have opportunities to receive training and support for dealing with student mental health problems. The importance of examining provider-level variables such as teacher stress, "burnout," or professional training has often been overlooked in mental health intervention research (Ringeisen et al., 2003). Teachers who give their students opportunities for academic and social success probably have a facilitative or protective role. Nevertheless, we need to know more about how teachers perceive the mental health of their students and how such perceptions influence how they act in the classroom.

Concluding comments

From a mental health perspective, adolescence is a developmental stage characterized by both vulnerability to risk and opportunities for good adjustment. Entering secondary school, adolescents are faced with an increased workload and greater demands to achieve. They also have to cope with social challenges including peer relations, peer pressure, bullying, and victimization. That the relationship between mental health and academic achievement is complex and multifaceted is evident from the research reviewed in this chapter. There is a mutual interdependence and overlap between the students' academic functioning and their mental health, and the school environment may influence both, as well as their interaction. Most scholars in the field of adolescent mental health stress the importance of multilevel interventions, either at the individual, group, and school level or by matching interventions to student risk (i.e., universal, selected, or indicated). The importance of school-wide interventions aiming at improving both the learning climate and the students' sense of safety and well-being should also be stressed. The school environment influences students in formal as well as informal ways; the school context matters. Students who struggle to cope with the academic and social demands of school may react with either internalizing and externalizing problems, or both, or these problems may escalate when facing such demands.

Children and youths spend much of their day at school, and their social bonds to school as well as their relationships to peers and teachers are important for their intellectual, social, and emotional development. Even if schools cannot and should not be held responsible for meeting every need of every student, they should take responsibility for identifying students who struggle. First, emotional and behavioral problems are serious barriers to learning, and second, by having access to virtually all children and youths, schools ought to address their educational, emotional, and behavioral needs (Paternite, 2005). Schools are in a unique position to prevent and reduce mental health problems, yet most schools lack both the resources and competence to take on this task. Some schools are also indifferent or resistant to dealing with topics of mental health and to delivering school-based mental health services (Weist et al., 2005). This may be partly due to the increased focus on achievement and grades over the last years fueled by current OECD comparative studies, and partly due to the fact that mental health programs are considered to be "add-ons" with little relevance to the academic mission of the schools. Strategies that may increase the level of academic achievement only, may lead to increased stress and anxiety, particularly in secondary school. Whilst schools may function as norming institutions for many children and youths, schools may amplify problems for others. One of the most important ways for schools to prevent mental health problems is to ensure that adolescents experience success in school, that they experience a sense of mastery and opportunities for developing a positive self-image. Equally important is that all students feel safe in school, that they are socially accepted, feel belongingness, and are able to make friends. Friendship, acceptance, and a sense of mastery are probably the closest we can get to a universal vaccine against mental health problems, and what better place than a school can provide this?

8

IMPLEMENTATION

Linking research and practice

Implementation involves activities needed to make decisions, plans, or interventions work in practice. It is targeted and systematic work that translates interventions with known characteristics into ordinary practice (Fixsen et al., 2005). The implementation process is both complex and non-linear as commented on by Greenhalgh, Macfarlane, Bate, and Kyriakidou (2004): "[…] a messy, stop-start, and difficult to research process of implementation." Their widely cited strategies for the spread of innovations in service organizations contrast active and passive forms of dissemination: (1) *"Let it happen"* refers to the diffusion of innovations, a process by which a growing body of information about an intervention is initially absorbed and acted upon by a small body of highly motivated recipients; (2) *"Help it happen"* refers to dissemination, which is the targeted distribution of information and intervention materials to a specific audience; and (3) *"Make it happen,"* which is the active use of strategies to adopt and integrate evidence-based interventions and change practice patterns within specific settings.

Chapter overview

This chapter starts with an analysis of the construct of implementation and how it links research and practice. Next, we present central dimensions of implementation that may be of interest to both researchers and practitioners. We discuss the dimensional structure laid out by several authors (Dane & Schneider, 1998; Durlak & DuPre, 2008; and Humphrey et al., 2016). Furthermore, implementation strategies are presented, emphasizing different approaches to the process of transferring research into practice. Research can make important contributions to identifying facilitators and challenges in the implementation process, and here we summarize some of the most documented implementation drivers and obstacles (Fixsen et al., 2005; Sørlie, Ogden, Solholm, & Olseth, 2010). A selection of implementation research is examined, some of which is based on conceptual models or implementation frameworks. We end the chapter by discussing the challenges of large-scale implementation and sustainability, exemplified by developments in Norway (Ogden et al., 2017). The core topics of this chapter are the "what," "how," and "who" of implementation. That is, "what" should be implemented, "how" should implementation be conducted to ensure success, and "who" should "make it happen" (Ogden & Fixsen, 2014)?

Even if implementation may have relevance for a wider spectrum of plans and models, we are particularly concerned about the implementation of evidence-based practices and programs that we have presented in the other chapters of this book. Evidence-based practices may be simple research-based procedures with relevance for any individual practitioner. Programs, on the other hand, are structured and standardized packages of practices involving whole teams of professionals or agencies. Both practices and programs represent several common challenges and requirements when it comes to implementation (Kessler & Glasgow, 2011). They have to be used in the way they were designed, qualified practitioners should have sufficient training and coaching, there should be support and buy-in from stakeholders at all levels, inclusion criteria should be appropriate, and fidelity and outcomes ought to be monitored. "How" evidence-based programs and practices should be implemented is an empirical question with no firm answers, but several ideas may be derived from research on facilitators and obstacles and from research on conceptual models or implementation frameworks. And last but not least, the "who" are competent facilitators such as implementation teams who can "make it happen" in efforts to transfer research knowledge into practice.

Dimensions of implementation

One of the first attempts to establish implementation as a multidimensional construct was made by Dane and Schneider (1998). In the following section, the dimensional approach is elaborated on and exemplified. Construct dimensions include: (1) adaptations; (2) fidelity, competent adherence, and "flexibility within fidelity"; (3) dosage; (4) quality of delivery and participant responsiveness; (5) reach; and (6) program differentiation.

Adaptation

When implementing programs in new places or with new target groups, there is a natural tension between the need for a high degree of fidelity and the need for adaptation to the local site. Adaptation describes the extent to which change agents add or modify the content and processes described in the manual, and is to some extent addressed under the headings of "fidelity" and "quality." Most interventions need to be adapted or modified to fit the host setting within which they will be implemented. The important question is how much practitioners may deviate from the manual without compromising the intervention. Some recommend significant adaptations to local conditions to avoid resistance to change (Castro, Barrera, & Martinez, 2004), but others warn against making adjustments to the original program to the extent that "the zone of drastic mutation" is entered (Ferrer-Wreder, Stattin, Lorente, Tubman, & Adamson, 2004).

Mihalic and Irwin (2003) found that, in most cases, they found few examples of local adaptations. Some authors argue in favor of adapting interventions to cultural or local conditions up front (Sundell, Beelmann, Hasson, & Schwartz, 2016), but most warn against such practice (Gardner, Montgomery, & Knerr, 2015; Ogden, Amlund Hagen, Askeland, & Christensen, 2009). We conclude that implementers are well advised not to evaluate interventions or further modify them before they are implemented with sufficient fidelity; too much modification of the original program can lead to reduced benefits for the client or user (Elliott & Mihalic, 2004; Schoenwald, Sheidow, & Letourneau, 2004). Durlak and DuPre (2008) argue that, rather than framing the debate in an either/or, the focus should be on finding the right mix of fidelity and adaptation so as to reliably achieve intended outcomes. Adaptations may also refer to the development of shorter versions of a program, or modifications made to adapt the program to new target groups (Institute of Medicine, 2014). Rotheram-Borus, Swendeman, and Chorpita (2012) claimed that many of the existing intervention programs may "overserve" the majority of users and that users' essential needs could be met by alternatives that are both less time-consuming and less expensive.

Fidelity, competent adherence, and "flexibility within fidelity"

Fidelity is a combination of measures of context, compliance, and competence (Fixsen et al., 2005). Context "refers to the prerequisites that must be in place for a program or practice to operate" (e.g., the number of practitioners, the practitioner–consumer ratio, the supervisor–practitioner ratio, prior training, and/or technical and practical requirements). Compliance or adherence "[…] refers to the extent to which the practitioners use the core intervention components as prescribed." Competence "refers to the level of skill shown by the therapist in using the core intervention components as prescribed whilst delivering the treatment to a consumer" (p. 48). High fidelity scores have been associated with good outcomes in several studies (Henggeler, Melton, Brondino, Scherer, & Hanley, 1997; Schoenwald, Halliday-Boykins, & Henggeler, 2003; Washington State Institute for Public Policy, 2002). Interventions may vary in their degree of prescriptiveness, but most programs do not recommend rigid adherence to the protocol, as this would imply a too-inflexible approach. The expressions "competent adherence" (Forgatch, Patterson, & DeGarmo, 2005) or "flexibility within fidelity" (Hamilton, Kendall, Gosch, Furr, & Sood, 2008) are used to emphasize that some diversion of flexibility is expected from the practitioners. *Competent adherence* highlights that the ideal is not to follow the manual blindly, but rather to be sensitive to variations among clients and their environments. Measuring competent adherence is complicated, and ratings ought to be made by skilled practitioners whose assessments should in turn be tested for inter-rater reliability (Forgatch & DeGarmo, 2011).

In other words, strict adherence to protocols may not be necessary, or even desirable, for therapists who have a deep understanding of the underlying theory and principles and who can make adjustments that do not interfere with the mechanisms of change (Forgatch & DeGarmo, 2011). Competence may be demonstrated as a clear and enthusiastic presentation of the program content, but also as *interactive teaching skills* that promote dialogue and openness and engage participants in the learning process. Moreover, *clinical process skills* may be demonstrated as reflective listening, summaries, and other efforts to create a safe and supportive environment that encourage participation and promote learning.

There may be both negative and positive additions to a manualized program or structured intervention. Negative additions may lead to less effective delivery, for instance if the practitioner adds components from a completely different intervention because he or she thinks it is appropriate for the audience. On the other hand, positive additions may occur when practitioners use their cultural competence and interpersonal skills to achieve a better result. They may use their interpersonal skills and take into consideration the local or cultural context when they choose stories or examples to increase the participants' involvement or responsiveness. Indications of positive contributions may be registered as increased client attendance, activity, and commitment, thus increasing their benefit from the intervention. It is important, however, that such adaptations match the program's theory and objectives. Kendall et al. (2008) claim that critics may overestimate the rigidity of manuals, and that creativity and clinical skill play a major role in the proper implementation of a manual-based treatment. "Flexibility within fidelity" implies that therapists are encouraged to be flexible within the context of a positive alliance with clients. A collaborative approach is associated with a favorable therapeutic relationship, and when manuals are properly implemented, they act as a guide. Therapists may take into consideration the client's needs and address the client's concerns whilst using the therapeutic goals of the treatment to guide the process. In order to check whether adaptations venture beyond "flexibility within fidelity" and into non-adherence, the authors recommend considering whether the stated goals of each session are being met, whether they conceptualize the client's difficulties within the relevant theoretical perspective (e.g., social learning theory or the social interaction and learning model [SIL]), and confirm that the treatment is action oriented rather than passive (Kendall et al., 2008).

To assess fidelity, innovations need to have specific standards such as core components or a specified curriculum and these standards form the basis for what will be measured (Meyers, Katz, Chien, Wandersman, Scaccia, & Wright 2012). Quantitative ratings of fidelity may include surveys or structured observations, preferably supplemented by interviews with implementers to explore their reasons for any lack of adherence, challenges to fidelity, and the extent to which fidelity is feasible (Humphrey et al. 2016). In addition to fidelity measures like a priori checklists, rating scales, and record reviews, qualitative methods may also be applied, such as semi-structured interviews.

Dosage: how much and for how long?

Dosage, or duration, is a measure of how much of the innovation was actually delivered to patients or clients. A frequently used way of measuring dosage is to tally up the number of sessions conducted and compare that number to the total number of sessions prescribed by the protocol. But even if the prescribed number of sessions is delivered, that does not necessarily mean that participants have received them. If some of the participants have been absent or inattentive at some of the sessions, they may not have been exposed to the prescribed dosage of the intervention. Dosage can also be measured by time (weeks or months) in treatment, or as the frequency of sessions implemented (Meyers et al., 2012). Interview data may help shed light on variations in dosage among recipients (Humphrey et al., 2016). Some deviations from the prescribed number or length of sessions may be acceptable as clients' needs usually differ. Moreover, it is not always the case that more sessions or longer treatment periods are related to better outcomes. For example, Shirk, Gudmundsen, Kaplinski, and McMakin (2008) found that depressed adolescents who received CBT showed significant improvement after treatment and that this positive change in scores was unrelated to the number of sessions delivered.

Quality of delivery and participant responsiveness

Quality of implementation describes how an intervention should be delivered to meet the standards necessary to achieve the desired outcomes. Implementation quality has been shown to be associated with program results (e.g., Domitrovich & Greenberg, 2000). Quality ratings may include assessment of how interested and enthusiastic the *implementers* appear, how prepared they are, and their effectiveness and responsiveness during sessions. The practitioner's engagement and interactive skills may increase the participants' responsiveness and, consequently, their benefit. On the other hand, if interventions are delivered with a high degree of fidelity, but the participants do not show up or are inattentive and passive in the sessions, no results will be achieved.

Quality is therefore also dependent on the *participants'* involvement, that is, their attentiveness, their degree of participation and motivation (Dane & Schneider, 1998). Behavioral change does not depend on the intervention delivery alone, but on the actual uptake of the content by the participants (Meyers et al., 2012). Their responsiveness may be influenced by a range of characteristics like age, gender, socioeconomic and cultural background, education, previous treatment experiences, and attitudes toward the intervention offered. These background characteristics may impact responsiveness that, again, may impact the quality of delivery and practitioner fidelity. Indicators include the number of sessions they attend, their active participation in the sessions, how satisfied they are, and whether they perform home assignments. If clients react negatively, the implementers or practitioners may opt for discontinuation of the intervention. Participant obstacles may also include low motivation, not showing up, low cognitive level, and co-occurring health problems (Egeland, Hauge, Ruud, Ogden, & Heiervang, 2017).

Assessments of quality may include interviews with participants (Tighe, Pistrang, Casdagli, Baruch, & Butler, 2012) or external support personnel (e.g., coaches; Humphrey et al., 2016). Participant responsiveness may be assessed through focus group interviews with recipients and/or implementers and by measuring whether participants engage particularly well or poorly with certain aspects of the intervention, and the reasons for this. Participants may also rate their engagement and interest in the intervention materials and activities (Humphrey et al., 2016).

Reach: the scaling-up of interventions

Reach refers to the proportion and representativeness of the target participants. An index of program reach may be the actual number of individuals in the target group reached divided by the total number of individuals in the target population (Glasgow Vogt, & Boles, 1999; Glasgow, Lichtenstein & Marcus, 2003). But of course, estimating the size of the target population may be difficult. Glasgow and Boles argue that standardized behavioral interventions should appeal to a broadly defined target group, not just those who are self-recruited. In order to reach a broadly defined target audience, the intervention should be suitable for use in several organizations or agencies such as schools and health institutions and practiced by staff with different degrees of training and expertise. Even effective interventions have limited public health value if they only reach a few individuals. Interventions will gradually yield less benefit if only a limited number of people know about them, if only a few are motivated to try them out, or if they are difficult to implement.

The "reach" of programs may depend on characteristics of the programs as well (i.e., how expensive they are and how much expertise is needed), on how well the programs match the political conditions and cultural framework, and on how well they are adapted to the current practice in the organizations. And some interventions are only effective as long as they receive additional funding and attention. Measuring "reach" may include gauging the characteristics and size of the target group, and then estimating how many of these the intervention reaches. Moreover, the number and proportion of participants present in each session may be registered and interviews with implementers may explain why some intended recipients may not be present for the intervention (Humphrey et al., 2016). The adoption rate also clarifies how many of the current practice organizations will use a new intervention and how representative these organizations are for those that are eligible for the new initiative.

Program differentiation

Program differentiation, also called program uniqueness, refers to the extent to which the selected intervention differs from other interventions in the organization or community (Meyers et al., 2012). It is important to consider how distinctive the theory, activities, and practices of the intervention are when comparing them to those already in use in current practices. Intervention activities that can be distinguished from existing activities may provide information about important change mechanisms (Humphrey et al. 2016).

Implementation strategies

The implementation of new practices can be described in terms of implementation strategies or implementation frameworks. *Frameworks* are more theoretical and usually have a broader view on implementation than do strategies. Implementation frameworks will be addressed later in the chapter. *Implementation strategies* are more hands-on and describe practical approaches to the implementation of programs (Walsh, Reutz, & Williams, 2015). Implementation strategies may be considered as interventions in their own right, and should therefore be described accordingly, that is, as methods used to enhance the adoption, implementation, and sustainability of interventions. Strategies may be categorized as "bottom-up," "top-down," or a combination of these.

The *bottom-up* strategy is a decentralized approach to the development of new practice, where local services or individual practitioners, based on their own needs, choose programs or practices. This strategy maintains the principles of professional autonomy and freedom of method choice. The advantage is that the practitioners develop a local ownership of the interventions, which may increase their motivation and degree of commitment. On the downside, it is difficult to achieve stable funding and support from the policy or service level, and it may be challenging to maintain the intervention with sufficient fidelity, dosage, intensity, and quality over time. Employee turnover and lack of funding due to shifting priorities may lead to a change of approach, or that the quality of the intervention declines over time. Local initiatives may not always be based on current research, and outcomes are typically not systematically measured.

The *top-down strategy* is a centralized developmental strategy where decisions made at the central level are communicated to the local level for transfer into practice. The advantage of this strategy is that resources and efforts can be coordinated, thus offering local services high-quality training, guidance, and practical support. The disadvantage is that this strategy may trigger resistance at the local level, especially if priorities do not match local needs or if practitioners feel that their professional autonomy is threatened. A third implementation strategy can be described as a hybrid strategy that combines bottom-up and top-down strategies (Ferrer-Wreder et al. 2004; Ogden, Hagen, Askeland, & Christensen, 2009). The goal of this strategy is to secure sustained funding and to develop a self-sustaining infrastructure with ongoing training and intervention delivery with fidelity (Forgatch et al., 2013).

Implementation theory and frameworks

There is no unified implementation theory, but different conceptual frameworks organize a set of coherent ideas or concepts in a manner that makes them easy to communicate. They provide an overview of ideas and practices that characterizes the implementation process and encourages researchers and practitioners to use ideas from others who have implemented similar projects (Fixsen, 2017). More generally, frameworks provide guidance for purposeful and effective action in complex human service environments (Fixsen, 2017).

Diffusion of innovation

Diffusion of innovation was coined by Rogers (1995) to describe a process in which a growing amount of information about an intervention is first captured and then used by a small group of highly motivated practitioners. Good ideas can be spread informally as a grassroots movement. Rogers (1995) highlights what promotes the spread of innovative practices or new ideas: there must be a new and effective intervention that can be communicated at a favorable time through functional communication channels to receptive practice environments that have the motivation and other prerequisites for implementing the innovation. Rogers (1995) attaches great importance to the individual openness to innovative practices. He distinguishes between "early adopters" who are quick to try out new ideas or methods, "late adopters" who take on a wait-and-see approach and only use the innovation after it has become recognized and when many others have adopted it, and "refusers" who under no circumstances will use the innovation, although many others have done it. In line with Rogers' emphasis on individual openness to change, much of the research on implementation focuses on individual characteristics of the practitioners who implement the innovations. Greenhalgh et al. (2004) disagree and caution that this approach has produced varied and difficult-to-generalize results. They highlight the importance of contextual factors and how individual and organizational factors interact with the intervention characteristics (Wandersman et al., 2008).

The Active Implementation Framework

The Active Implementation Framework was introduced by Fixsen et al. (2005), is based on a systematic review of implementation research, and includes the following core components or "implementation drivers" (Fixsen et al., 2005; 2009):

- *Recruitment and selection of practitioners.* When an innovation is introduced, new practitioners must be hired to work with clients or users according to the method. The component covers routines for selecting suitable practitioners, but the criteria may vary depending on whether new practitioners are hired to work with the intervention or whether the recruitment takes place internally.
- *Training.* Innovations involve new ways of working and often require practitioners and their colleagues to acquire new knowledge, skills, and attitudes.
- *Guidance/consultation/coaching.* This may include personal observation, instruction, feedback, emotional support, job training, and debriefing. Included are decisions about where and how frequently the guidance should be given and about the content.

- *Evaluation of practice.* This addresses the quality and quantity of work. This component covers measurement of treatment fidelity, as well as decisions about who should evaluate practice and how often.
- *Data systems as decision support.* Data systems provide information about how the intervention is practiced in the organization and that can be used to make decisions that enhance quality. The component describes how systematic data collection can provide feedback to interest groups, therapists, supervisors, and executives internal and external to the organization.
- *Facilitative administration.* This is about how leaders of implementation in the host organization introduce new structures and procedures to support and encourage the use of the intervention.
- *Leadership.* The organization has managers at different levels who make decisions that affect how the employees deliver the intervention to the participants. This component covers how the management in the host organization provides systematic support and clear communication with the practitioners, as well as how they provide feedback, make decisions, and commit themselves to making the implementation work. Even if there seems to be consensus among scholars that leadership is essential for successful implementation, it has rarely been empirically examined (Aarons, Ehrhart, & Farahnak, 2014). A review of relevant research, however, indicated that leaders of change are able to break with the past, operate outside of existing paradigms, challenge prevailing values and norms, and find solutions that are emergent, unbounded, and complex (Marzano et al., 2003).

In response to the lack of research, Aarons et al. (2014) developed a brief measure of implementation leadership with the following sub-scales: (1) proactive leadership with clear standards, a plan to facilitate, and the removal of obstacles to the implementation of EBPs; (2) knowledgeable leadership that signals that the leader knows what he/she is talking about, is knowledgeable and able to answer questions about EBP; (3) supportive leadership toward employees in their efforts to learn or practice EBP; and (4) perseverant leadership through the ups and downs of implementing, coping with challenges, and reacting to critical issues regarding the implementation of EBP (Aarons et al., 2014). Fixsen (2017) recommends that leaders start the change process with those who are willing and able and then continue to create readiness among the rest. Leaders should assure that they have the ability to use the innovation and to create an implementation team to initiate and manage supportive organizational changes.

- *System change.* This describes the extent to which the organization is working to influence external systems in the region or country to develop better support for the use of innovation (e.g., referrals of cases, recruitment of practitioners, new collaboration and contact routines, operating structures, and funding).

The implementation drivers or components are integrated and interdependent and, to some extent, can compensate for each other. Good training and supervision can compensate for weaknesses in the employment procedures. The "implementation drivers" are grouped into competency drivers (recruitment, training, coaching, and evaluation of practice) and organizational drivers (data-supported decisions, facilitative administration, system change), whilst "leadership" is singled out as the critical component that keeps it all together.

Implementation climate. Fixsen et al. (2005) draw attention to the importance of the implementation climate and explain that organizations have a "personality." This personality is reflected in day-to-day operations and characterizes the way employees perceive work and their colleagues as well as management and workplace. An organization's implementation climate is the practitioners' overall perception of the extent to which a particular intervention is rewarded, supported, and perceived within the organization (Klein & Sorra, 1996). Still, the implementation climate does not necessarily regulate the individual practitioner's commitment to the intervention. Commitment is related to the implicit or common values the employees have. The climate concept moves the focus away from single components and toward the cumulative impact of all the implementation components.

The Quality Implementation Framework

The Quality Implementation Framework (QIF), introduced by Meyers, Durlak, and Wandersman in 2012 was the result of their synthesizing information from 25 implementation frameworks that led to the identification of 14 common dimensions, grouped into six areas: (1) assessment strategies, conducting assessments of needs and resources, fit assessment and capacity/readiness assessment; (2) decisions about adaptations and possibility for adaptation; (3) capacity-building strategies, including explicit buy-in from critical stakeholders and promoting a supportive climate in the community or the organization, building general capacity in the organization, recruitment and maintenance of staff and effective staff training; (4) creating a structure for implementation with implementation teams and an implementation plan; (5) ongoing implementation support strategies, including technical assistance/coaching/supervision, process evaluation, and supportive feedback loops; and (6) improving future applications by learning from experience. Based on this synthesis of frameworks, a practical tool for implementation quality improvement was developed as the Quality Implementation Tool (Meyers et al., 2012). The tool has a worksheet format that pairs each step with a quality implementation component. The steps are:

Establish an overall implementation team and leadership. The first component is establishment of an overall implementation team that should plan and monitor the whole implementation process from idea to practice. Sometimes such a team may also be called a *steering committee* or *advisory board*. The members should have in-depth knowledge of the intervention and be able to problem-solve and provide assistance when challenges appear. They can be area specialists or community members who can help ensure that the team has adequate capacity and knowledge to tailor the implementation to the local context. Having local representation on the team may also promote local buy-in. Team members may have roles that qualify them for a variety of tasks, including training, technical assistance, advocating for the innovation, monitoring and evaluation, logistical support, and developing strategies to overcome implementation barriers. The roles and responsibilities of each implementation team member ought to be documented. The next step is to appoint an implementation team leader or a leadership group who can facilitate group decision-making and problem-solving in the implementation resource team. The leader should have experience with the innovation and know how to implement innovations effectively.

The change organization and its staff deliver or implement the intervention (external/internal change agents). They may be identical to the overall implementation team but may also be private contractors or other external deliverers of the intervention. Among the most important characteristics of this organization is the capacity for training and supervision. In other words, effective interventions with no capacity for competent training and supervision are of little value. Important staff characteristics are good leadership, commitment, competent and credible implementers, and the use of an interactive dissemination style (Meyers et al., 2012). Good implementers are also described as knowledgeable, experienced, friendly, available as good listeners, and effective problem-solvers (Mihalic & Irwin, 2003). Fixsen et al. (2009) attach great importance to establishing implementation teams that may implement evidence-based programs with a high degree of integrity and good effect. Purveyors are implementation teams or individuals with high competence in relation to the intervention and have in-depth knowledge of implementation. As intermediaries, they can accumulate knowledge over time such that they can anticipate potential problems that will arise when implementing a new program and proactively plan how difficulties can be solved.

Foster a supportive climate and conditions in the organization or in the community. The next component includes the identification and fostering of a relationship with a champion for the innovation. A program champion may know the local system well and will have the ability to mobilize and encourage potential users. It is useful to identify candidate champions early on as part of overall planning for implementation. Whilst the role of the implementation team leader is to manage the implementation, the champion's role is to foster buy-in and support for the innovation and its proper use. But even if enthusiasts or champions play an important role when new ideas are introduced into organizations, their key role may have been related to a particular innovation rather than to interventions in general (Greenhalgh et al., 2004).

The implementation efforts will hardly be successful if the local employees have doubts about whether the innovation is even needed or if the innovation will provide value above current practice.

Resistance to change may be handled by providing opportunities for local stakeholder participation and creating a sense of ownership in the innovation, for instance by including them in decisions about the implementation process. Formal collaborative communication, open feedback and review, and clear communication of mission and goals all contribute to "effective implementation." And last but not least, the implementation team should ensure that the innovation has adequate administrative support.

Develop an implementation plan. The next action step is to develop an implementation plan. This plan should list specific tasks required for implementation, establish a timeline for implementation tasks, and assign those tasks to specific stakeholders. The plan should communicate "who" does "what" and "when."

Training and technical assistance (TA). Technical support and assistance include training programs, guidance, monitoring of fidelity, and manuals. In more detail, technical support includes the structure, content, timing, and quality of training and regular supervision or coaching in the implementation of programs. Training materials should be culturally sensitive, of high quality, user-friendly, and adapted to the target audience in other ways (Durlak & DuPre, 2008; Greenberg, Greenberg, Domitrovich, Graczyk, & Zins, 2005; Mihalic & Irwin, 2003). Those responsible for the technical assistance may be members of the implementation team, those delivering the training, or other resource persons qualified to deliver support on the job (Durlak & DuPre 2008). Moreover, trainer(s) and TA providers should be well informed about the organization or community's needs and resources, as well as its goals and objectives. They should also be sufficiently knowledgeable about the end user who will implement the innovation. A failure to clearly communicate goals and objectives to trainers and TA providers can deter implementation and weaken quality. Studying the implementation of programs for prevention and treatment of youth violence (Blueprints for Violence Prevention Initiative), Mihalic and Irwin (2003) found that the quality of technical support, ideal program features, low turnover in staff, and local community support were among the most significant factors. Among these, technical support seemed to be the most important ingredient.

Practitioner–developer collaboration in implementation. The first action step here is to collaborate with expert developers (e.g., researchers) about factors that may impact the quality of implementation in the organization or the community and engage them in problem-solving.

When problems arise within the implementation process, the support system can assist the community in identifying strategies to work through these difficulties. The support system comprises resource persons like the implementation team and internal or external consultants or coaches who assist in the implementation process. They are the "middlemen" between the practitioners and the program developers and should be available during the whole implementation.

Implementation research

The growing amount of empirical findings showing that variations in implementation quality affect intervention outcomes may help explain the increasing interest in and focus on implementation research. Disappointing or unexpected outcomes may be due to the fact that delivery of the interventions was inadequate or failed, rather than because the intervention was ineffective. If implementation quality is not measured, it is virtually impossible to know the reasons for the failed results. There is little evidence confirming that passive dissemination of ideas, information, and guidelines changes practice on its own (Fixsen et al., 2005). Rather, dissemination ought to be supplemented or replaced by active implementation strategies that continuously ensure feedback from practice. Fixsen (2017) concludes that when used alone, the following methods do not result in use of innovations as intended: (1) diffusion or dissemination of information; (2) training without measuring how well the intervention is conducted; (3) passing laws, mandates, or regulations; (4) providing funding and incentives; and (5) changing organizational structures. On the positive side, long-term multilevel approaches to implementation seem to be most beneficial for the consumers. The strongest evidence was found for skill-based training, coaching, and assessment of practitioners' fidelity. There was also good research support for the importance of practitioner selection. Less empirical support was found for organizational components like program evaluation, facilitative administrative support, and system intervention methods (Ogden & Fixsen, 2014).

There is still little evidence showing how implementation quality and evidence-based interventions are linked or are affected by each other. In other words, there is little evidence for the implementation of evidence-based interventions. Therefore, it is a challenge to uncover which components are both necessary and sufficient for a successful implementation.

Implementation outcomes. Implementation outcomes are different from intervention efficacy or effectiveness outcomes. Perhaps the most important overall evaluation criterion for both kinds of research is higher well-being and quality of life among clients or users (Proctor et al., 2009). In addition, implementation implies outcomes that are conceptually and empirically different from those used to measure effectiveness of the interventions. These may include how well the intervention is integrated into the practice organization, how broad the acceptance among different stakeholder groups is, how available it is and how easy it is to use, and how well it can be sustained in the service system.

Successful implementation may cause the intervention to gradually penetrate the host organization. In other words, the intervention is increasingly accepted and adopted within the organization, it becomes easier to use for those who need it, and it is maintained in the service system over time (Proctor et al., 2009). Outcomes at the client level include satisfaction with treatment, clients' functional improvements, and/or fewer symptoms. Results can also be measured at the practice level, such as how many practitioners have learned how to use the method, how many use the method after training, and changes in the level of knowledge and competence of the practitioners (Guldbrandsson, 2007). Several studies have tried to identify critical components of successful implementation, but it turns out that single components interact in complex, unpredictable, and non-generalizable ways (Greenhalgh et al., 2004). Therefore, some scholars warn against the search for critical components for effective implementation and recommend that one should rather try to document the cumulative effect of all components (Klein & Sorra, 1996).

Facilitators and obstacles

Most of the knowledge about implementation barriers and facilitators comes from observational studies and from theoretical reflections (Grol & Wensing, 2004), although today there is an increasing amount of knowledge that comes from systematic reviews of research with advanced designs (Fixsen et al., 2005). The identification of facilitators and obstacles has been a major aim of most implementation studies, and relevant findings are summarized below. These findings overlap with some of the other sections in this chapter. Whilst not always the case, facilitators and obstacles are often opposites, that is, a lack of facilitators may be an obstacle, and the removal of an obstacles may constitute a facilitator.

Facilitators. Facilitators of evidence-based practice include characteristics of the intervention, the change agents, the practice environments and context, and the implementation process itself. The timing of the introduction of a new intervention and how well it matches the needs, attitudes, and values of the practice environment are also important factors that can help promote the implementation of a new intervention. Additional facilitators include high problem awareness (i.e., a sense of urgency), the motivation for change, and a general perception that the intervention is more effective than that which is currently offered. Durlak and DuPre (2008) identified the following key elements in the process of transferring effective programs to ordinary practice, based on a systematic review of approximately 500 studies (see also Greenberg et al., 2005):

Contextual or local factors include policy and system support, financial resources, and *readiness for change*. Even the best or most effective program will not succeed without an adequate support system (Greenberg et al., 2005). Several facilitators operate at the policy level, such as support from the political and administrative level, consensus about aims and priorities, sanctions for practices that are not evidence based, long-term perspectives on service and competence development, and sufficient resources and stable funding (Goldman et al., 2001). Most often, however, these supportive ingredients are scarce but in demand, as is often the case in fragmented service systems. High problem awareness and readiness for change are indicators of the demand or support for new practices by local managers, practitioners, and users. But research also shows that readiness may be less important than the quality of the training and supervision, adequate recruitment procedures, and management support (Fixsen et al., 2005).

Organizational factors related to the local implementation site include organizational structure and culture, such as effective leadership, staff loyalty, and unity. Several organizational characteristics have been linked to successful implementation: (1) leadership; (2) program goals/vision; (3) commitment; (4) size; (5) skills for planning, implementation, and evaluation; (6) climate; (7) structure; and (8) capacity building (Wandersman et al., 2008). New practice needs support not only from the local communities, but also from management and employees in the service delivery system. Conducive leadership is probably the most important predictor of change, particularly when leaders have clear strategic visions (Greenhalgh et al., 2004). Large, experienced, differentiated, and specialized organizations seem to be more open to change than small ones.

Characteristics of the staff include several factors like educational level and the theoretical orientation, competence level, and experience with evidence-based interventions. Moreover, openness to change and evidence-based practice, self-efficacy, and implementation skills are found to be important (Aarons et al. 2012). Greenhalgh et al. (2004) emphasize that individual practitioners are not passive recipients of new interventions; rather, they evaluate it, express opinions and attitudes toward it, challenge it, complain about it, and try to improve it. In other words, they interact with new and complex interventions in a targeted and creative manner. Still, the introduction of new practices is influenced by decisions and attitudes in the workplace. Most evidence-based interventions seem to undergo an extended period of negotiation with potential users, during which their goals and intentions may be discussed, challenged, and reformulated in the implementation process (Greenhalgh et al., 2004). Also of importance is the perception among users that the intervention is appealing, acceptable, and relevant to users' needs. This is a prerequisite for practitioners to volunteer to learn how to work according to principles and guidelines in handbooks or practice protocols.

Five characteristics of the intervention that affect the likelihood of innovations being adopted were identified by Rogers (1995) and Dearing (2009): (1) *relative benefits*: how effective the innovation is in relation to existing practice; (2) *compatibility*: how credible the intervention is, how well it is adapted to the existing system, and how well it matches the values, norms, and needs of the recipients; (3) *complexity*: how complex the innovation is and how easy it is to use; (4) *testability*: whether innovation can be tested on a small scale; and (5) *observability*: whether it is possible to observe others who use the innovation. To these characteristics, Greenhalgh et al. (2004) added the *relevance* of the innovation to the tasks at hand and the *transferability* of the implementation knowledge from one context to another. No less important are the *costs* of the intervention, its *research base* and *core components*.

Obstacles. Time pressure and competition from other high-priority tasks are among the most important obstacles when new practices are implemented alongside current practice (Goldman et al., 2001). It may also prove difficult to integrate new and old practices if these are based on different assumptions, concepts, and methods (Fixsen et al., 2005). Turnover or changes in management and/or practitioners is a threat to any implementation endeavor. New executives and employees may not feel committed to earlier agreements to the same extent and, consequently, may not be as motivated for the new intervention. Another problem arises if the trainees receive less training than required, or if there is limited follow-up from the support system. A third problem is referred to as *assimilation* and occurs when practitioners argue that the innovation does not represent anything new, but actually is something they have been doing all along.

Large-scale implementation and intervention sustainability

Sustainability can be discussed at individual, organizational, and system levels. At the environmental or system level, focus is on whether the program itself is maintained and whether the practitioners continue to provide services or perform at a high level of fidelity (Kellam & Langevin, 2003). Although an intervention has been implemented with a high degree of fidelity, one cannot assume that it will continue to work just as well over time.

Kellam and Langevin (2003) point to the importance of having social and political support for large-scale implementation so that programs can be maintained with a high degree of implementation quality. They focus in particular on the need for continual training, guidance, practical program support, and monitoring. Whilst the number of efficacy studies has steadily increased, there has been less research on large-scale implementation at the national or regional level. Recently, this picture has changed somewhat and a few large-scale implementation projects have now been undertaken.

We end this chapter with a presentation of the large-scale implementation of family- and community-based programs for the prevention and intervention of mental health problems among children and youth with serious behavior problems in Norway (Ogden et al., 2009).

Large-scale implementation of family programs in Norway

A governmental initiative was introduced in Norway in 1998 to improve the competence of Norwegian practitioners delivering treatment designed to reduce antisocial or delinquent behavior among Norwegian children and youth. By strengthening the clinical competence of Norwegian practitioners, new and evidence-based initiatives aimed at increasing the capacity of the service system to address these challenges were introduced. Another goal was to decrease placements out of home due to serious behavior problems among adolescents. Family and community intervention programs with documented effects were selected based on recommendations from both international researchers and a Norwegian expert group (Zeiner, 1998).

The Oregon model of Parent Management Training was the program of choice to strengthen early intervention and prevention of aggressive behavior in children (Ogden et al., 2005). MST was selected as the most promising treatment program targeting violent and criminal behavior and drug abuse among adolescents (Ogden et al., 2008). Currently, these two programs have been implemented in Norway for a period of 17 years, and they are still active. Among the 430 PMTO® therapists trained and certified in Norway, 350 were still active in 2015. Today, 23 MST teams are operating in all regions of Norway and have become a standard part of the specialized state Child Welfare Services agency (Ogden et al., 2017). The effectiveness of both programs has been successfully tested in a Norwegian context (Ogden & Halliday-Boykins, 2004; Ogden & Hagen, 2006, 2008).

In 2009, a case study of the national implementation strategy in Norway indicated that both programs had been implemented with a high degree of sustainability over a period of 10 years (Ogden et al., 2009). Among the factors that assumed to have contributed to their long-term sustainability and effectiveness are: (1) at the political and administrative level, a genuine interest in and commitment to supporting and funding national implementation; (2) interest among practitioners for conducting evidence-based practice; (3) establishment of a self-sustaining national center for implementation and research; (4) support from the program developers in the process of implementing and testing the programs; and (5) positive feedback from families and media. The Norwegian Center for Child Behavioral Development (NCCBD) was established to create a strong infrastructure when testing and implementing selected intervention programs. The center has separate departments for child and adolescent development, each responsible for the recruitment, training, supervision, and ongoing support of local sites for these age groups. A third department, for research, assesses the outcomes and processes of the interventions, and conducts longitudinal studies on child development in general. According to Forgatch et al. (2013), large-scale implementation requires strong leadership that combines social and political capital, leadership skills, access to resources, and commitment to see the project through. The wide-scale implementation of PMTO® in Norway was supported by government funds to ensure sustained practice throughout the country. Although developed in the US, these intervention programs (MST and PMTO®) seemed to work reasonably well in Norwegian contexts with modest but robust and encouraging results obtained in clinical outcome studies. The core intervention components were successfully transferred across geographical and language borders, and only surface changes were made to adapt the programs to the new cultural context. Transatlantic collaboration requires time, however, along with money and energy, as reported by a panel of European implementers who were interviewed by Ferrer-Wreder et al. (2004).

Next, we describe the implementation stages of the national implementation of evidence-based parenting programs in Norway, using PMTO® as an example.

Exploration and preparation stage. Exploration involves the identification of a problem that needs to be addressed in a more effective way and, in this case, it was clear from the outset that serious conduct problems in children and youth should be emphasized. Decisions were made in two ministries to adopt and recommend the scaling-up of PMTO® (and MST). The Norwegian implementation process accelerated with a strong touch of top-down implementation. This phase also involved establishment of an implementation group, the National Implementation Team, and an implementation strategy. The national strategy included a plan for local implementations at the county and municipal levels, a comprehensive therapist recruitment, training and maintenance program, and a network for collaboration, supervision, and monitoring program fidelity.

The early adoption and installation stage. At this stage, the focus was on tasks that had to be accomplished before the first client or user was even treated. The initial implementation phase could be described as "awkward" because resistance to change and forces to keep status quo were mobilized. Fear of change, inertia, and an investment in status quo occurred at a time when a program was struggling to get a foothold, and the implementation organization was inexperienced and vulnerable (Fixsen et al., 2005). Initially, the Norwegian practitioners were less than enthusiastic to meet the requirements of the new program to be implemented. The implementation team had to engage agencies and trainees, ensure referrals, provide training context and resources, and complete training. The contribution from the program developer and purveyors included practitioner training, materials and technology, adaptation of the program, evaluation of fidelity, and provision of technical assistance. The role of the implementation team changed, placing more emphasis on problem-solving and quick responses to challenges encountered. The team had to prepare for common barriers to implementation like changes in leadership, staff turnover, and changes in policies and funding.

Implementation stage. At this stage, the program delivery started and important tasks were to monitor fidelity to the program (e.g., self-reports and observations), and evaluate feasibility (e.g., client, practitioner, and stakeholder satisfaction) and process outcomes (e.g., the number of clients referred and the number of sessions completed). It is important that these are done from the start to ensure that they are considered part of standard practice (Walsh, Reutz, & Williams, 2015).

Sustainment stage. After the programs had been running for a while, the time came for adaptations and refinements to fit the needs of different target groups and adopting communities. One example is the adaptations made to PMTO® to make it more accessible and user-friendly when transferred from specialized mental health outpatient clinics and child welfare specialist services to municipal child services. The adapted program Interventions for Children at Risk used PMTO® principles for further development and had the same intake criteria as the original version. The intervention was delivered in five modules, and employees in the municipalities were trained and supervised by two certified PMTO® therapists to deliver these interventions to children and families. The therapists were also trained and responsible for the delivery of the parent group intervention. The modules were Assessment (Solholm et al., 2013), Brief Parent Training (Kjøbli & Ogden, 2012), Social Skills Training (Kjøbli and Ogden, 2014), PMTO® parent groups (Kjøbli, Hukkelberg, & Ogden, 2013), and School Consultation (Tømmerås et al. forthcoming), and all were tested in RCTs. Positive outcomes were achieved for all except the Social Skills Training, which preferably should be delivered in combination with Brief Parent Training.

At this stage, the challenges of large-scale implementation of programs had to be dealt with.

Is there a scale-up penalty?

Welsh, Sullivan, and Olds (2010) found that when preventive programs evaluated in small efficacy studies were scaled up and evaluated in normal practice, their effect was reduced due to "drift" and dilution. After the expansion, not only do these programs serve children and families who are at greater risk but also those with fewer risk factors who are less likely to develop severe problems. Moreover, the infrastructure may not be able to handle the expansion of programs, given there will be greater variations between practice sites and practitioners. Participating agencies will vary from competent organizations that support their staff to organizations undermining the work morale and quality of services. There will also be greater variation among implementers in terms of education and experience, their social and clinical skills, and the quality of the training they have received (Welsh et al., 2010). Fixsen et al. (2005) also expect that the scaling-up of programs will inevitably lead to reduced integrity and less efficiency over time.

According to the implementation experiences of PMTO® in Norway, the challenges of large-scale implementation should be addressed through strengthening and enhancing implementation infrastructure by establishing good quality assurance and integrity-measurement procedures. Additionally, a permanent and self-sustaining infrastructure should supply continual training and guidance. In Norway, a permanent center was established to monitor program and practice fidelity and outcomes on a regular basis. Also, the center provides training and supervision of practitioners to sustain program fidelity. The center is also responsible for the testing of new interventions in controlled trials and for conducting implementation studies.

One of the studies from the NCCBD investigated how large-scale implementation influenced the composition of the target group and the service providers (Tømmerås & Ogden, 2015). Even if a larger heterogeneity of the service providers and the target group were observed, no reduction in treatment fidelity was detected (based on independent coding by trained therapists). Fidelity was measured by the Fidelity of Implementation Rating System (FIMP; Knutson, Forgatch, Rains, & Sigmarsdottir, 2009), which is a rating system that evaluates therapists' competent adherence of PMTO® during treatment. The measurement of fidelity scores across six generations of therapists who completed training from 1999 to 2014 was also reassuring; the ratings of 402 therapists showed no drop in fidelity with an overall mean score of 6.8 (range 6.34–6.94) on a scale from 1 to 9. In other words, when the nationwide implementation and sustainability of an evidence-based parenting program was supported by a permanent center, a stable infrastructure was created that maintained levels of fidelity even as new generations of therapists were trained and certified.

Final comments

In summary, implementation is a process rather than a one-time event, and describes how practitioners are becoming increasingly skilled, more consistent, and committed in their use of new practices (Klein & Sorra, 1996). The process may be described with emphasis on the different *phases* or *stages of implementation* like the exploration and adoption phase, early adoption and installation phase, full implementation stage, innovation stage, and sustainability phase (Fixsen et al, 2005; Forgatch et al., 2013). Others emphasize that implementation is carried out at *different levels of change*, including: (1) the environment or the larger system in which legal and regulatory policies are key; (2) the organizational level where structure and strategy are key; (3) the group or team level in which cooperation, coordination, and shared knowledge are key; and (4) the individual level where knowledge, skill, and expertise are key (Shortell, 2004).

A third way of presenting implementation is by emphasizing the *dimensions* upon which it is based. Based on their examination of prevention programs from 1980 to 1990, this is precisely what Dane and Schneider (1998) did in identifying the following dimensions: (1) fidelity, which is the extent to which program components are disseminated, combining measures of adherence with measures of context and competence; (2) dosage, which represents how often and how long a program is disseminated; (3) quality, meaning the quality of program communication, including content and affective qualities; (4) participant responsiveness, including involvement and engagement; and (5) program differentiation, which is the difference between the current intervention and other interventions.

The implementation process may also be described as *approaches* or *strategies* (e.g., top-down and bottom-up), or framed in theoretical models as implementation frameworks like the Active Implementation Framework (Fixsen et al., 2005) or the Quality Implementation Framework (Meyers, Durlak, & Wandersman, 2012). And last but not least, implementation research has produced knowledge about *facilitators* and *obstacles* of implementation. Important contributions from implementation science are empirically based actions that have proved to facilitate or hinder the successful implementation of new practices. Facilitators may be implementation drivers that in Fixsen et al.'s model are linked to recruitment, training, coaching, and regular practice assessment to improve practitioner performance. On the organizational side, the drivers are identified as program evaluation, facilitative administrative support, leadership, and systems interventions.

In a number of problem areas, we are better now at identifying effective interventions than we are at persuading practitioners to use them in a systematic and binding way. Furthermore, we know more about characterizing people who are open to new ideas (see early adopters) than we do about realizing change in organizations or practice communities.

REFERENCES

Aarons, G., Ehrhart, M., & Farahnak, L. (2014). The implementation leadership scale (ILS): Development and a brief measure of unit level implementation leadership. *Implementation Science*, 9, 45.

Aarons, G., Green, A., Palinkas, L., Self-Brown, S., Whitaker, D., Lutzker, J., ... Chafinn, M. (2012). Dynamic adaptation process to implement an evidence-based child maltreatment intervention. *Implementation Science*, 7, 32.

Adelman, H. & Taylor, L. (1999). Mental health in schools and system restructuring. *Clinical Psychology Review*, 19, 137–163.

Alexander, J. & Parsons, B. (1973). Short-term behavioral intervention with delinquent families: Impact on family processes and recidivism. *Journal of Abnormal Psychology*, 81, 219–225.

Alexander, J. & Parsons, B. (1982). *Functional family therapy: Principles and procedures*. Carmel, CA: Brooks & Cole.

Algozzine, B., Duanic, A., & Smith, S. (2010). *Preventing problem behaviors. Schoolwide programs and classroom practices* (2nd ed.). Thousand Oaks, CA: Corwin.

American Psychiatric Association. (1994). *Diagnostic and statistical manual of mental disorders* (4th ed.) (DSM-IV-TR). Washington, DC: American Psychiatric Association, 75, 78–85.

American Psychiatric Association. (2013). *Diagnostic and statistical manual of mental disorders* (5th ed.) (DSM-V). Washington, DC: American Psychiatric Association.

Amlund Hagen, K. & Christensen, B. (2010). Atferdsproblemer hos ungdom. Utvikling, riskofaktorer og behandling [Behavior problems in adolescents. Development, risk factors and treatment]. In: E. Befring, I. Frønes, & M.-A. Sørlie (Eds.), *Sårbare unge. Nye perspektiver og tilnærminger*. Oslo: Gyldendal Akademisk forlag.

Amlund Hagen, K., Olseth, A., Laland, H., Rognstad, K., Apeland, A., Askeland, E., ... Weisz, J. (2018). *Evaluating Modular Approach to Therapy for Children with Anxiety, Depression, Trauma and Conduct Problems (MATCH-ADCT) in Norwegian child and adolescent outpatient clinics: Study protocol for a randomized controlled trial*. [Manuscript under consideration for trials.]

Amlund Hagen, K. & Ogden, T. (2016). Predictors of changes in child behaviour following parent management training: Child, context, and therapy factors. *International Journal of Psychology*, 52, 106–115.

Amlund Hagen, K., Ogden, T., & Bjørnebekk, G. (2011). Treatment outcomes and mediators of parent management training: A one-year follow-up of children with conduct problems. *Journal of Child and Adolescent Psychology*, 40, 165–178.

Ang, R. & Hughes, J. (2001). Differential benefits of skills training with antisocial youth based on group composition: A meta-analytic investigation. *School Psychology Review*, 31, 164–185.

Angold, A. & Costello, E. (2006). Puberty and depression. *Child and Adolescent Psychiatric Clinics of North America*, 15, 919–937.

APA Task Force on Evidence Based Practice (2006). Report of the 2005 presidential task force on evidence-based practice. *American Psychologist*, 61, 271–285.

Arbelle, S., Benjamin, J., Golin, M., Kremer, I., Belmaker, R., & Ebstein, R. (2003). Relation of shyness in grade school children to the genotype for the long form of the serotonin transporter promoter region polymorphism. *American Journal of Psychiatry*, 160, 671–676.

Arnold, M. & Hughes, J. (1999). First do no harm: Adverse effects of grouping deviant youth for skills training. *Journal of School Psychology*, 37, 99–115.

Asher, S. (1990). Recent advances in the study of peer rejection. In: S. Asher & J. Coie (Eds.), *Peer rejection in childhood*. Cambridge: Cambridge University Press (referred from Beauchamp & Anderson, 2010).

Asher, S. & Renshaw, P. (1981). Children without friends: social knowledge and social skill training. In: S. Asher & J. Gottman (Eds.), *The development of children's friendships*. Cambridge: Cambridge University Press.

Asher, S. & Wheeler, V. (1985). Children's loneliness: A comparison of rejected and neglected peer status. *Journal of Consulting and Clinical Psychology*, 53(4), 500.

Aslund, C., Leppert, J., Comasco, E., Nordquist, N., Oreland, L., & Nilsson, K. (2009). Impact of the interaction between the 5HTTLPR polymorphism and maltreatment on adolescent depression. A population-based study. *Behavior Genetics*, 39, 524–531.

Asscher, J., Deković, M., van der Laan, P., Prins, P., & Arum, S. (2007). Implementing randomized experiments in criminal justice settings: An evaluation of multisystemic therapy (MST) in the Netherlands. *Journal of Experimental Criminology*, 3, 113–129.

Au, A., Lau, S., & Lee, M. (2009). Suicide ideation and depression: The moderation effects of family cohesion and social self-concept. *Adolescence*, 44, 851–868.

Austin, A., Macgowan, M., & Wagner, E. (2005). Effective family-based interventions for adolescents with substance use problems: A systemic review. *Research on Social Work Practice*, 15, 67–83.

Aviles, A., Anderson, T., & Davila, E. (2006). Child and adolescent social–emotional development within the context of school. *Child and Adolescent Mental Health*, 11, 32–39.

Azrin, N. (1976). Improvements in the community-reinforcement approach to alcoholism. *Behaviour Research and Therapy*, 14(5), 339–348.

Azrin, N., Donohue, B., Teichner, G., Crum, T., Howell, J., & DeCato, L. (2001). A controlled evaluation and description of individual-cognitive problem solving and family behavior therapies in dually diagnosed conduct-disordered and substance-dependent youth. *Journal of Child and Adolescent Substance Abuse*, 11, 1–43.

Bandelow, B., Tichauer, G., Spath, C., Broocks, A., Hajak, G., Bleich, S., & Ruther, E. (2001). Separation anxiety and actual separation experiences during childhood in patients with panic disorder. *The Canadian Journal of Psychiatry/La Revue Canadienne de Psychiatrie*, 46, 948–952.

Bandura, A. (1986). *Social foundations of thought and action. A social cognition theory*. Englewood Cliffs, NJ: Prentice Hall.

Bank, L., Marlowe, J., Reid, J., Patterson, G., & Weinrott, M. (1991). A comparative evaluation of parent training for families of chronic delinquents. *Journal of Abnormal Child Psychology*, 19, 15–33.

Barnes, J. (2010). From evidence-base to practice: Implementation of the Nurse Family Partnership programme in England. *Journal of Children's Services*, 5, 4–17.

Barnoski, R. (2002). *Washington State's implementation of functional family therapy for juvenile offenders: Preliminary findings.* Retrieved November 2012 from www.swipp.wa.gov

Barrett, P., Farrell, L., Ollendick, T., & Dadds, M. (2006). Long-term outcomes of an Australian universal prevention trial of anxiety and depression symptoms in children and youth: An evaluation of the friends program. *Journal of Clinical Child and Adolescent Psychology*, 35, 403–411.

Barrett, P., Lock, S., & Farrell, L. (2005). Developmental differences in universal preventive intervention for child anxiety. *Clinical Child Psychology and Psychiatry*, 10, 539–555.

Barth, R. & Liggett-Creel, K. (2014). Common components of parenting programs for children birth to eight years of age involved in child welfare services. *Children and Youth Services Review*, 40, 6–12.

Baumeister, R. & Tierny, F. (2011). *Willpower. Rediscovering the greatest human strength.* London: Penguin Books.

Bean, R., Barber, B., & Crane, D. (2006). Parental support, behavioral control, and psychological control among African American youth: The relationships to academic grades, delinquency, and depression. *Journal of Family Issues*, 27, 1335–1355.

Beauchamp, M. & Anderson, V. (2010). SOCIAL: An integrative framework for the development of social skills. *Psychological Bulletin*, 136, 39–64.

Becker, S. & Curry, J. (2008). Outpatient interventions for adolescent substance abuse: A quality of evidence review. *Journal of Consulting and Clinical Psychology*, 76, 531–543.

Bedell, J. & Lennox, S. (1997). *Handbook for communication and problem-solving skills training: A cognitive–behavioral approach.* New York: Wiley.

Beeland, K. (1991). *Second step. A violence prevention program.* Seattle, WA: Committee for Children.

Beelmann, A. & Lösel, F. (2006). Child social skills training in developmental crime prevention: Effects on anti-social behaviour and social competence. *Psiothema*, 18, 603–610.

Beelmann, A., Pfingsten, U., & Lösel, F. (1994). Effects of training social competence in children: A meta-analysis of recent evaluation studies. *Journal of Clinical Child Psychology*, 23, 260–271.

Beidas, R., Benjamin, C., Puleo, C., Edmunds, J., & Kendall, P. (2010). Flexible applications of the Coping Cat Program for Anxious Youth. *Cognitive Behavioral Practice*, 17, 142–153.

Belsky, J., Steinberg, L., & Draper, P. (1991). Childhood experience, interpersonal development, and reproductive strategy: An evolutionary theory of socialization. *Child Development*, 62, 647–670.

Bender, H., Allen, J., McElhaney, K., Antonishak, J., Moore, C., Kelly, H., & Davis, S. (2007). Use of harsh physical discipline and developmental outcomes in adolescence. *Development and Psychopathology*, 19, 227–242.

Berger, A. (2011). *Self regulation. Brain, cognition and development.* Washington: American Psychiatric Association.

Beyers, W. & Goossens, L. (2008). Dynamics of perceived parenting and identity formation in late adolescence. *Journal of Adolescence*, 31(2), 165–184.

Bierman, K. (2004). *Peer rejection, developmental processes and intervention strategies.* New York: Guilford Press.

Biglan, A., Brennan, P., Foster, S., & Holder, H. (2004). *Helping adolescents at risk: prevention of multiple problem behaviors.* New York: Guilford.

Biglan, T. & Ogden, T. (2008). The evolution of the evidence based movement. *European Journal of Behavior Analysis*, 9, 81–95.

Bjørknes, R. & Manger, T. (2013). Can parent training alter parent practice and reduce conduct problems in ethnic minority children?: A randomized controlled trial. *Prevention Science*, 14, 52–63.

Bjørnebekk, G., & Kjøbli, J. (2017). Observed callousness as a predictor of treatment outcomes in parent management training. *Clinical child psychology and psychiatry*, 22(1), 59–73.

Bjørnebekk, G., Kjøbli, J., & Ogden, T. (2015). Children with conduct problems and co-occurring ADHD: Behavioral improvements following Parent Management Training. *Child & Family Behavior Therapy*, 37, 1–19.

Blair, R. (2005). Responding to the emotions of others: Dissociating forms of empathy through the study of typical and atypical populations. *Consciousness and Cognition*, 14, 698–718.

Blakemore, S-J. & Choudhury, S. (2006). Development of the adolescent brain: Implications for executive functions and social cognition. *Journal of Child Psychology and Psychiatry*, 47, 296–312.

Bloom, M. & Gullotta, T. (2003). Evolving definitions of primary prevention. In: T. Gullotta & M. Bloom (Eds.), *Encyclopedia of primary prevention and health promotion*. New York: Kluwer Academic Plenum.

Bloom, M. & Gullotta, T. (2009). Primary prevention in adolescent substance abuse. In: C. Leukefeld, T. Gullotta, & M. Staton-Tindall (Eds.), *Adolescent substance abuse. Evidence-based approaches to prevention and treatment*. New York: Springer.

Bongers, I., Koot, H., van der Ende, J., & Verhulst, F. (2004). Developmental trajectories of externalizing behaviors in childhood and adolescence. *Child Development*, 75, 1523–1537.

Borduin, C., Mann, B., Cone, L., Henggeler, S., Fucci, B., Blaske, D., & Williams, R. (1995). Multisystemic treatment of serious juvenile offenders: Long-term prevention of criminality and violence. *Journal of Consulting and Clinical Psychology*, 63, 569–578.

Borntrager, C., Chorpita, B., Higa-McMillan, C., & Weisz, J. (2009). Provider attitudes toward evidence-based practices: Are the concerns with the evidence or with the manuals? *Psychiatric Services*, 5, 677–681.

Botvin, G. (1990). Substance abuse prevention: theory, practice and effectiveness. In: M. Tonry & J. Wilson (Eds.), *Drugs and crime* (pp. 461–519). Chicago: University of Chicago Press.

Botvin, G. & Griffin, K. (2004). Life skills training: Empirical findings and future directions. *The Journal of Primary Prevention*, 25, 211–232.

Botvin, G., Griffin, K., Diaz, T., & Ifill-Williams, M. (2001). Drug abuse prevention among minority adolescents: One year follow-up of a school-based preventive intervention. *Prevention Science*, 2, 1–13.

Bowlby, J. (1969). *Attachment and loss. 1. Attachment*. New York: Basic Books.

Boxer, P., Goldstein, S., Musher-Eizenman, D., Dubow, E., & Heretick, D. (2005). Developmental issues in school-based aggression prevention from a social-cognitive perspective. *Journal of Primary Prevention*, 26, 383–400.

Bradshaw, C., Mitchell, M., & Leaf, P. (2010). Examining the effects of schoolwide positive behavioural interventions and supports on student outcomes. Results from a randomized controlled effectiveness trial in elementary schools. *Journal of Positive Behaviour Interventions*, 12, 133–148.

Bradshaw, C., Reinke, W., Brown, L., Bevans, K., & Leaf, P. (2008). Implementation of school-wide positive behaviour interventions and supports (PBIS) in elementary schools: Observations from a randomized trial. *Education and Treatment of Children*, 31, 1–26.

Bradshaw, C., Waasdorp, T., & Leaf, P. (2015). Examining variation in the impact of school-wide positive behavioral interventions and supports: Findings from a randomized controlled effectiveness trial. *Journal of Educational Psychology*, 107(2), 546.

Brady, E. & Kendall, P. (1992). Comorbidity of anxiety and depression in children and adolescents. *Psychological Bulletin*, 111, 244–255.

Brannigan, B., Schackman, M., Falco, M., & Millman, R. (2004). The quality of highly regarded adolescent substance abuse treatment programs: Results of an in-depth national survey. *Archives of Pediatrics and Adolescent Medicine*, 158, 904–909.

Brendgen, M., Bukowski, W., Wanner, B., Vitaro, F., & Tremblay, R. (2007). Verbal-abuse by the teacher during childhood and academic, behavioral, and emotional adjustment in young adulthood. *Journal of Educational Psychology*, 99, 26–38.

Bronfenbrenner, U. (1979). *The ecology of human development: Experiment by nature and design.* Cambridge, MA: Harvard University Press.

Bronfenbrenner, U. & Morris, P. (1998). *The ecology of developmental processes.*

Brophy, J. (2006). History of research on classroom management. In: C. Evertson & C. Weinstein (Eds.), *Handbook of classroom management. Research, practice and contemporary issues.* New York: Lawrence Erlbaum.

Brophy-Herb, H., Lee, R., Nievar, M., & Stollak, G. (2007). Preschoolers' social competence: Relations to family characteristics, teacher behaviors and classroom climate. *Journal of Applied Developmental Psychology*, 28, 134–148.

van der Bruggen, C., Stams, G., & Bogels, S. (2008). Research review: The relation between child and parent anxiety and parental control: A meta-analytic review. *Journal of Child Psychology and Psychiatry*, 49, 1257–1269.

Bry, B. (1988). Family-based approaches to reducing adolescent substance use: theories, techniques and findings. In: E. Rahdert & J. Grabowski (Eds.), *Adolescent drug abuse: Analyses of treatment research.* NIDA research monograph 77, 1988.

Buehler, C. & Gerard, J. (2004). Cumulative environmental risk and youth maladjustment: The role of youth attributes. *Child Development*, 75, 1832–1849.

Bullock, R. (1992). A framework for making international comparisons of services for adolescents. In: R. Bullock (Ed.), *Problem adolescents. An international view.* London: Whiting and Birch Ltd.

Burt, K., Obradovic, J., Long, J., & Masten, A. (2008). The interplay of social competence and psychopathology over 20 years: Testing transactional and cascade models. *Child Development*, 79, 359–374.

Butler, S., Baruch, G., Hickley, N., & Fonagy, P. (2011). A randomized controlled trial of multisystemic therapy and a statutory therapeutic intervention for young offenders. *Journal of the American Academy of Child & Adolescent Psychiatry*, 12, 1220–1235.

Calix, S. & Fine, M. (2009). Evidence-based family treatment of adolescent substance abuse and dependence. In: C. Leukefeld, T. Gullotta, & M. Staton-Tindall (Eds.), *Adolescent substance abuse. Evidence-based approaches to prevention and treatment.* New York: Springer.

Cartledge, G. & Milburn, J.-A. (1995). *Teaching social skills to children and youth. Innovative approaches* (3rd ed.). Boston: Allyn & Bacon.

Caspi, A. & Moffitt, T. (1991). Individual differences are accentuated during periods of social change: The sample case of girls at puberty. *Journal of Personality and Social Psychology*, 61, 157–168.

Caspi, A., Moffitt, T., Newman, D., & Silva, P. (1996). Behavioral observations at age 3 years predict adult psychiatric disorders. Longitudinal evidence from a birth cohort. *Archives of General Psychiatry*, 53, 1033–1039.

Caspi, A., Sugden, K., Moffitt, T., Taylor, A., Craig, I., Harrington, H., … Poulton, R. (2003). Influence of life stress on depression: Moderation by a polymorphism in the 5-HTT gene. *Science*, 301, 386–389.

Castro, F., Barrera, M., & Martinez, C. (2004). The cultural adaptation of prevention interventions: Resolving tensions between fidelity and fit. *Prevention Science*, 5, 41–45.

Catalano, R., Berglund, M., Ryan, J., Lonczaak, H., & Hawkins, J. (2002). Positive youth development in the United States: Research findings on evaluations of positive youth development programs. *Prevention and Treatment*, 5, Article 15.

Chamberlain, P. (1994). *Family connections: A treatment foster care model for adolescence with delinquency.* Eugene, OR: Northwest Media.

Chamberlain, P. (1998). Treatment foster care. *Family Strengthening Series.* Washington, DC: U.S. Department of Justice. (OJJDP Bulletin NCJ 1734211).

Chamberlain, P. & Reid, J. (1998). Comparison of two community alternatives to incarceration for chronic juvenile offenders. *Journal of Consulting and Clinical Psychology,* 66(4), 624–633.

Chamberlain, P., Leve, L., & DeGarmo, D. (2007). Multidimensional treatment foster care for girls in the juvenile justice system: 2-year follow-up of a randomized clinical trial. *Journal of Consulting and Clinical Psychology,* 75, 187–193.

Chambless, D. & Ollendick, T. (2001). Empirically supported psychological interventions: Controversies and evidence. *Annual Review of Psychology,* 52, 685–716.

Chassin, L., Ritter, J., Trim, R., & King, K. (2006). Adolescent substance use disorders. In: E. Mash & R. Barkley (Eds.), *Child psychopathology* (2nd ed.). New York: Guilford Press.

Chen, X. & Lie, B. (2000). Depressed mood in Chinese children: Development significance for social and school adjustment. *International Journal of Behavioral Development,* 24, 472–479.

Chitiyo, M., May, M., & Chitiyo, G. (2012). An assessment of the evidence base for school-wide positive behavior support. *Education and Treatment of Children,* 35(1), 1–24.

Chorpita, B., Weisz, J., Daleiden, E., Schoenwald, S., Palinkas, L., Miranda, J., ... Ward, A. (2013). Long-term outcomes for the Child STEPs randomized effectiveness trial: A comparison of modular and standard treatment designs with usual care. *Journal of Consulting and Clinical Psychology,* 81, 999.

Chronis-Tuscano, A., Degnan, K., Pine, D., Perez-Edgar, K., Henderson, H., Diaz, Y., ... Fox, N. (2009). Stable early maternal report of behavioral inhibition predicts lifetime social anxiety disorder in adolescence. *Journal of the American Academy of Child & Adolescent Psychiatry,* 48(9), 928–935.

Clark, L., Watson, D., & Mineka, S. (1994). Temperament, personality, and the mood and anxiety disorders. *Journal of Abnormal Psychology,* 103, 103–116.

Clarke, G., Lewinsohn, P., & Hops, H. (1990). *Adolescent coping with depression course.* Eugene, OR: Castalia Publishing.

Cohn, J., Campbell, S., Matias, R., & Hopkins, J. (1990). Developmental psychology, face-to-face interactions of postpartum depressed and nondepressed mother-infant pairs at 2 months. *Developmental Psychology,* 26, 15–23.

Coie, J. & Dodge, K. (1998). Aggression and antisocial behavior. In: W. Damon & N. Eisenberg (Eds.), *Handbook of child psychology (5th ed.). Social, emotional and personality development* (Vol. 3). Hoboken, NJ: John Wiley & Sons.

Cole, D. (1991). Preliminary support for a competency-based model of depression in children. *Journal of Abnormal Psychology,* 100, 181–190.

Collins, W. & Steinberg, L. (2006). Adolescent development in interpersonal context. In: W. Damon & R. Lerner (Eds.), *Child and adolescent development. An advanced course.* New York: John Wiley & Sons.

Commission on Chronic Illness. (1957). *Chronic illness in the United States* (Vol. 1). Cambridge, MA: Harvard University Press.

Connell, A., Dishion, T., Yasui, M., & Kavanagh, K. (2007). An adaptive approach to family intervention: Linking engagement in family-centered intervention to reductions in adolescent problem behavior. *Journal of Consulting and Clinical Psychology,* 75(4), 568.

Conradt, J. & Essau, C. (2003). Feasibility and efficacy of the FRIENDS program for the prevention of anxiety in children. Paper presented at the 24th International Conference. Lisbon: Stress and Anxiety Research Society.

Cornelius-White, J. (2007). Learner-centered teacher–student relationships are effective: A meta-analysis. *Review of Educational Research,* 77, 113–143.

Costello, E., Angold, A., Burns, B., Stangl, D., Tweed, D., Erkanli, A., & Worthman, C. (1996). The Great Smoky Mountains Study of Youth: Goals, design, methods, and the prevalence of DSM-III-R disorders. *Archives of General Psychiatry*, 53, 1129–1136.

CPPRG (Conduct Problems Prevention Research Group). (2010a). The difficulty of maintaining positive intervention effects: A look at disruptive behavior, deviant peer relations, and social skills during the middle school years. *The Journal of Early Adolescence*, 30, 593–624.

CPPRG (Conduct Problems Prevention Research Group). (2010b). The fast track project: preventing severe conduct problems in school-age youth. In: R. Murrihy, A. Kidman, & T. Ollendick (Eds.), *Clinical handbook of assessing and treating conduct problems in youth*. New York: Springer.

Crick, N. & Dodge, K. (1994). A review and reformulation of social information-processing mechanisms in children's social adjustment. *Psychological Bulletin*, 115, 74–101.

Crone, D. & Horner, R. (2003). *Building positive behavior support systems in schools. Functional behavioral assessment*. New York: Guilford Press.

CSPSC (The Consortium on the School-based Promotion of Social Competence). (1994). Theory, research, practice, and policy: The consortium on the school-based promotion of social competence. In: R. Haggerty, L. Sherrod, N. Garmezy, & M. Rutter (Eds.), *Stress, risk and resilience in children and adolescents: Processes, mechanisms and interventions* (pp. 268–316). Cambridge: Cambridge University Press.

Cunningham, P., Donohue, B., Randall, J., Swenson, C., Rowland, M., Henggeler, S., & Schoenwald, S. (2003). *Integrating contingency management into multisystemic therapy*. Charleston, SC: Medical University of South Carolina.

Cunningham, P. & Henggeler, S. (1999). Engaging multiproblem families in treatment: Lessons learned throughout the development of multisystemic therapy. *Family Process*, 38(3), 265–281.

Curtis, N., Ronan, K., & Borduin, C. (2004). Multisystemic treatment: A meta-analysis of outcome studies. *Journal of Family Psychology*, 18, 411–419.

Curtis, N., Ronan, K., Heiblum, N., & Crellin, K. (2009). Dissemination and effectiveness of multisystemic treatment in New Zealand: A benchmarking study. *Journal of Family Psychology*, 23, 119–129.

Dane, A. & Schneider, B. (1998). Program integrity in primary and early secondary intervention: Are implementation effects out of control? *Clinical Psychology Review*, 18, 23–45.

Daniel, S., Walsh, A., Goldston, D., Arnold, E., Reboussin, B., & Wood, F. (2006). Suicidality, school dropout, and reading problems among adolescents. *Journal of Learning Disabilities*, 39, 507–514.

Darch, C. & Kame'enui, E. (2004). *Instructional classroom management: A proactive approach to behaviour management* (2nd ed.). Upper Saddle River, NJ: Pearson-Merrill Prentice Hall.

Dearing, J. (2009). Applying diffusion of innovation theory to intervention development. *Research on Social Work Practice*, 19, 503–518.

Delligatti, N., Akin-Little, A., & Little, S. (2003). Conduct disorder in girls: Diagnostic and intervention issues. *Psychology in the Schools*, 40, 183–192.

Dennis, M. & Scott, C. (2007). Managing addiction as a chronic condition. *Addiction Science & Clinical Practice*, 4(1), 45.

Dembo, R. & Muck, R. (2009). Adolescent outpatient treatment. In: C. Leukefeld, T. Gullotta, & M. Staton-Tindall (Eds.), *Adolescent substance abuse. Evidence-based approaches to prevention and treatment*. New York: Springer.

Denham, S. & Almeida, M. (1987). Children's social problem solving skills, behavioural adjustment, and interventions: A meta-analysis evaluating theory and practice. *Journal of Applied Developmental Psychology*, 8, 391–409.

Department for Children Schools and Families. (2007). Social and Emotional Aspects of Learning (SEAL) Programme: Guidance for Secondary Schools. Nottingham: DCSF Publications.

Diamond, G., Mensinger, J., Kaminer, Y., & Wintersteen, M. (2006). Adolescent and therapist perception of barriers to outpatient substance abuse treatment. *The American Journal of Addiction*, 15, 16–25.

Dishion, T. & Loeber, R. (1985). Male adolescent marijuana and alcohol use: The role of parents and peers revisited. *American Journal of Drug and Alcohol Abuse*, 11, 11–25.

Dishion, T. & Patterson, G. (2006). The development and ecology of antisocial behavior in children and adolescents. In: D. Cicchetti & D. Cohen (Eds.), *Developmental psychopathology. Risk disorder and adaptation* (Vol. 3). New York: Wiley.

Dishion, T. & Stormshak, E. (2007). *Intervening in children's lives: An ecological family-centered approach to mental health care.* Washington, DC: The American Psychological Association.

Dishion, T., Nelson, S., & Kavanagh, K. (2003). The family check-up with high-risk young adolescents: Preventing early-onset substance use by parent monitoring. *Behavior Therapy*, 34(4), 553–571.

Dobbs, D. (2011). Teenage brains. *National Geographic*, 220, 36–59.

Dodge, K. (2008). Framing public policy and prevention of chronic violence in American youths. *American Psychologist*, 63, 573–590.

Dodge, K., Dishion, T., & Lansford, J. (2006). Deviant peer influences in intervention and public policy for youth. *Social Policy Report.* Vol. XX, 1–19.

Domitrovich, C. & Greenberg, M. (2000). The study of implementation: Current findings from effective programs that prevent mental disorders in school-aged children. *Journal of Educational and Psychological Consultation*, 11, 193–221.

Domitrovich, C., Bradshaw, C., Greenberg, M., Embry, D., Poduska, J., & Ialongo, N. (2010). Integrated models of school-based prevention: Logic and theory. *Psychology in the Schools*, 47(1), 71–88.

Donohue, B. & Azrin, N. (2001). Family behavior therapy. *Innovations in Adolescent Substance Abuse Interventions*, 205–227.

Donovan, K. & Brassard, M. (2011). Trajectories of maternal verbal aggression across the middle school years: Associations with negative view of self and social problems. *Child Abuse & Neglect*, 35, 814–830.

Doss, A. & Weisz, J. (2006). Syndrome co-occurrence and treatment outcomes in youth mental health clinics. *Journal of Consulting and Clinical Psychology*, 74(3), 416.

DuBois, D., Holloway, B., Valentine, J., & Cooper, H. (2002). Effectiveness of mentoring programs for youth: A meta-analytic review. *American Journal of Community Psychology*, 30, 157–198.

Duckworth, A., Quinn, P., & Tsukayama, E. (2012). What no child left behind leaves behind: The roles of IQ and self-control in predicting standardized achievement test scores and report card grades. *Journal of Educational Psychology*, 104, 39.

Duckworth, A. & Seligman, M. (2005). Self-discipline outdoes IQ in predicting academic performance of adolescents. *Psychological Science*, 16(12), 939–944.

Duncan, B. & Miller, S. (2005). Treatment manuals do not improve outcomes. In: J. Norcross, R. Levant & L. Beutler (Eds.), *Evidence-based practices in mental health: Debate and dialogue on the fundamental questions.* Washington, DC: American Psychological Association Press.

Durlak, J. (2003). Effective prevention and health promotion programming. In: M. Bloom & T. Gullotta (Eds.), *Encyclopedia of primary prevention and health promotion* (pp. 61–69). Boston, MA: Springer.

Durlak, J. & DuPre, E. (2008). Implementation matters: A review of research on the influence of implementation on program outcomes and the factors affecting implementation. *American Journal of Community Psychology*, 41, 327–350.

Durlak, J. & Wells, A. (1997). Primary prevention mental health programs for children and adolescents: A meta-analytic review. *American Journal of Community Psychology*, 25, 115–152.

Durlak, J., Weissberg, R., Dymnicki, A., Taylor, R., & Schellinger, K. (2011). The impact of enhancing students' social and emotional learning: A meta-analysis of school-based universal interventions. *Child Development*, 82, 405–432.

Eccles, J., Midgley, C., Wigfield, A., Buchanan, C., Reuman, D., Flanagan, C., & Iver, D. (1993). Development during adolescence. The impact of stage-environment fit on young adolescents' experiences in schools and in families. *American Psychologist*, 48, 90–101.

Eddy, J. & Chamberlain, P. (2000). Family management and deviant peer association as mediators of the impact of treatment condition on youth antisocial behavior. *Journal of Consulting and Clinical Psychology*, 68, 857–863.

Egeland, K., Hauge, M-I., Ruud, T., Ogden, T. & Heiervang, K. (2017). *Leaders as key for mental health practitioners' sustained use of new practices.* (submitted).

Eisenberg, N., Fabes, R., Shepard, S., Murphy, B., Guthrie, I., Jones, S., ... Maszk, P. (1997). Contemporaneous and longitudinal prediction of children's social functioning from regulation and emotionality. *Child Development*, 68, 642–664.

Eisner, M. & Malti, T. (2015). Aggressive and violent behavior. In: R. Lerner & M. Lamb (Eds.), *Handbook of child psychology and developmental science. Vol 3. Socioemotional processes.* Wiley online library.

Elias, M. & Schwab, Y. (2006). From compliance to responsibility: social and emotional learning and classroom management. In: C. Evertson & C. Weinstein (Eds.), *Handbook of classroom management. Research, practice and contemporary issues.* Mahwah, NJ: Lawrence Erlbaum.

Elias, M., Zins, J., Weissberg, R., Frey, K., Greenberg, M., Haynes, N., ... Shriver, T. (1997). *Promoting social and emotional learning: Guidelines for educators.* Alexandria, VA: Association for Supervision and Curriculum Development.

Elliott, D. (1997). *Blueprints for violence prevention: Books 1–11.* Boulder, CO: University of Colorado, Institute of Behavioral Science, Center for the Study and Prevention of Violence.

Elliott, D. (1998). *Blueprints for violence prevention.* Boulder, CO: University of Colorado, Center for the Study and Prevention of Violence. Blueprints Publications.

Elliott, D., Huizinga, D., & Ageton, S. (1985). *Explaining delinquency and drug use.* Beverly Hills, CA: Sage.

Elliott, D. & Mihalic, S. (2004). Issues in disseminating and replicating effective prevention programs. *Prevention Science*, 5, 47–53.

Elliott, S. & Gresham, F. (1991). *Social skills intervention guide.* Circle Pines, MN: American Guidance Service, Inc.

Ellis, B., Shirtcliff, E., Boyce, W., Deardorff, J., & Essex, M. (2011). Quality of early family relationships and the timing and tempo of puberty: Effects depend on biological sensitivity to context. *Development and Psychopathology*, 23, 85–99.

Embry, D. & Biglan, A. (2008). Evidence-based kernels: Fundamental units of behavioral influence. *Clinical Child and Family Psychology Review*, 11(3), 75–113.

Emslie, G. (2008). Pediatric anxiety: Unrecognized and untreated. *The New England Journal of Medicine*, 359, 2835–2836.

Englund, M., Levy, A., Hyson, D., & Sroufe, L. (2000). Adolescent social competence: Effectiveness in a group setting. *Child Development*, 71, 1049–1060.

Ennett, S., Foshee, V., Bauman, K., Hussong, A., Cai, L., McNaughton Reyes, H., … DuRant, R. (2008). The social ecology of adolescent alcohol misuse. *Child Development*, 79, 1777–1791.

Ennett, S., Ringwalt, C., Thorne, J., Rohrbach, L., Vincus, A., Simons-Rudolph, A., & Jones, S. (2003). A comparison of current practice in school-based substance use prevention programs with meta-analysis findings. *Prevention Science*, 4(1), 1–14.

Evans, D., Foa, E., Gur, R., Hendin, H., O'Brien, C., Seligman, M., & Walsh, B. (2005). *Treating and preventing adolescent mental health disorders: What we know and what we don't know. A research agenda for improving the mental health of our youth.* Oxford: Oxford University Press.

Eyberg, S., Nelson, M., & Boggs, S. (2008). Evidence-based psychosocial treatments for children and adolescents with disruptive behavior. *Journal of Clinical Child and Adolescent Psychology*, 37, 215–237.

Fabiano, E. & Porporino, F. (1997). *Reasoning and re-acting. A handbook for teaching cognitive skills.* Ottowa, ON: T3 Associates.

Fals-Stewart, W., Lam, W., & Kelley, M. (2009). Learning sobriety together: Behavioral couples therapy for alcoholism and drug abuse. *Journal of Family Therapy*, 31, 115–125.

Ferrer-Wreder, L., Stattin, H., Lorente, C., Tubman, J., & Adamson, L. (2004) *Successful prevention and youth development programs: Across borders.* New York: Plenum Publisher.

Fixsen, D. (2017). From public policy to public impact. Presentation at Rambøll Management, Oslo, October 27.

Fixsen, D., Blase, K., Naoom, S., & Wallace, F. (2009). Core implementation components. *Research on Social Work Practice*, 19, 531–540.

Fixsen, D., Naoom, S., Blase, K., Friedman, R., & Wallace, F. (2005). *Implementation research: A synthesis of the literature.* University of South Florida, Louis de la Parte Florida Mental Health Institute, The National Implementation Research Network (FMHI Publication #231). Retrieved March 2006 from http://nirn.fmhi.usf.edu/resources/publications/Monograph/index.cfm

Fluckiger, C., Del Re, A., Wampold, B., Symonds, D., & Horvath, A. (2012). How central is the alliance in psychotherapy? A multilevel longitudinal meta-analysis. *Journal of Counseling Psychology*, 59, 10–17.

Foa, E., Costello, E., Franklin, M., Kagan, J., Kendall, P., Klein, R., … Spear, L. (2005). In: D. Evans et al., *Treating and preventing adolescent mental health disorders: What we know and what we don't know. A research agenda for improving the mental health of our youth* (pp. 161–182). New York: Oxford University Press.

Fontaine, R. & Dodge, K. (2009). Social information processing and aggressive behavior: a transactional perspective. In: A. Sameroff (Ed.), *The transactional model of development: How children and contexts shape each other.* Washington, DC: American Psychological Association.

Fontaine, R., Yang, C., Dodge, K., Pettit, G., & Bates, J. (2009). Development of response evaluation and decision (RED) and antisocial behavior in childhood and adolescence. *Developmental Psychology*, 45, 447–459.

Forgatch, M. (1994). *Parenting through change: A programmed intervention curriculum for groups of single mothers.* Eugene, OR: Oregon Social Learning Center.

Forgatch, M. & DeGarmo, D. (1999). Parenting through change: An effective prevention program for single mothers. *Journal of Consulting and Clinical Psychology*, 67, 711–724.

Forgatch, M. & DeGarmo, D. (2011). Sustaining fidelity following the nationwide PMTO™ implementation in Norway. *Prevention Science*, 12, 235–246.

Forgatch, M., Patterson, G., & DeGarmo, D. (2005). Evaluating fidelity: Predictive validity for a measure of competent adherence to the Oregon model of parent management training. *Behavior Therapy*, 36, 3–13.

Forgatch, M., Patterson, G., & Gewirtz, A. (2013). Looking forward: The promise of widespread implementation of parent training programs. *Perspectives on Psychological Science*, 8(6), 682–694.

Fraser, M., Galinsky, M., Smokowski, P., Day, S., Terzian, M., Rose, R., & Guo, S. (2005). Social information-processing skills training to promote social competence and prevent aggressive behavior in the third grade. *Journal of Consulting and Clinical Psychology*, 73, 1045–1055.

Fraser, M., Richman, J., Galinsky, M., & Day, S. (2009). *Intervention research. Developing social programs*. Oxford; New York: Oxford University Press.

Frick, P. (1998). Conduct disorders. In: T. Ollendick & M. Hersen (Eds.), *Handbook of child psychopathology* (3rd ed.). New York: Plenum Press.

Frick, P. & Viding, E. (2009). Antisocial behavior from a developmental psychopathology perspective. *Development and Psychopathology*, 21, 1111–1131.

Frick, P. & White, S. (2008). Research review: The importance of callous-unemotional traits for developmental models of aggressive and antisocial behavior. *Journal of Child Psychology and Psychiatry*, 49, 359–375.

Frith, C. & Frith, U. (2005). Theory of mind. *Current Biology*, 15, 644–645.

Frydenberg, E. (2008). *Adolescent coping: Advances in theory, research and practice*. London; New York: Routledge.

Fuller, F. (2008). *Drug use, smoking and drinking among young people in England in 2007*. London: National Center for Social Research and National Foundation for Educational Research.

Garbarino, J. (1985). *Adolescent development. An ecological perspective* (Ch. 2: Human ecology and competence in adolescence). Columbus, OH: Charles Merrill Publishing Company.

Garbarino, J. (2005a). Lost boys: Why our sons turn violent and how we can save them. (adapted by Robert Haslam) *Paediatric Child Health*, 10, 447–450.

Garbarino, J. (2005b). Children in a violent world: A metaphysical perspective. *Family Court Review*, 36, 360–367.

Gardner, F., Burton, J., & Klimes, I. (2006). Randomized controlled trial of a parenting intervention in the voluntary sector for reducing child conduct problems: Outcomes and mechanisms of change. *Journal of Child Psychology and Psychiatry*, 47, 1123–1132.

Gardner, F., Hutchings, J., Bywater, T., & Whitaker, C. (2010). Who benefits and how does it work? Moderators and mediators of outcome in an effectiveness trial of parenting intervention. *Journal of Clinical Child and Adolescent Psychology*, 39, 568–580.

Gardner, F., Montgomery, P., & Knerr, W. (2015). Transporting evidence-based parenting programs for child problem behaviour (age 3–10) between countries: Systematic review and meta-analysis. *Journal of Clinical Child and Adolescent Psychology*. [online] www.tandfonline.com/doi/full/10.1080/15374416.2015.1015134?scroll=top&needAccess=true

Garmezy, N. (1989). The role of competence in the study of children and adolescents under stress. In: B. Schneider, G. Attili, J. Nadel, & R. Weissberg (Eds.), *Social competence in developmental perspective*. Dordrecht, Holland: Kluwer Academic.

Gibbs, L. & Gambrill, E. (2002). Evidence-based practice: Counterarguments to objections. *Research on Social Work Practice*, 12, 452–476.

Gillham, J., Shatte, A., & Freres, D. (2000). Preventing depression: A review of cognitive-behavioral and family interventions. *Applied & Preventive Psychology*, 9, 63–88.

Gjerde, P. (1995). Alternative pathways to chronic depressive symptoms in young adults: Gender differences in developmental trajectories. *Child Development*, 66(5), 1277–1300.

Gladstone, T., Beardslee, W., & O'Connor, R. (2010). The prevention of adolescent depression. *Psychiatric Clinics of North America*, 34, 35–52.

Glasgow, R., Lichtenstein, E., & Marcus, A. (2003). Why don't we see more translation of health promotion research to practice? Rethinking the efficacy-to-effectiveness transition. *American Journal of Public Health*, 93(8), 1261–1267.

Glasgow, R., Vogt, T., & Boles, S. (1999). Evaluating the public health impact of health promotion interventions: The RE-AIM framework. *American Journal of Public Health*, 89, 1322–1327.

Goldman, H., Ganju, V., Drake, R., Gorman, P., Hogan, M., Hyde, P., & Morgan, O. (2001). Policy implications for implementing evidence-based practices. *Psychiatric Services*, 52(12), 1591–1597.

Goldstein, A. (1999). *The Prepare Curriculum: revised edition. Teaching prosocial competencies.* Champaign, IL: Research Press.

Goldstein, A., Glick, B., & Gibbs, J. (1998). *Aggression replacement training. A comprehensive intervention for aggressive youth* (Revised ed.). Champaign, IL: Research Press.

Goldston, D., Walsh, A., Arnold, E., Reboussin, B., Daniels, S., Erkanli, A., ... Wood, F. (2007). Reading problems, psychiatric disorders, and functional impairment from mid- to late adolescence. *Journal of the American Academy of Child and Adolescent Psychiatry*, 46, 25–32.

Goleman, D. (2007). *Social intelligence, the new science of human relationships.* London: Arrow Books.

Gordon, D., Graves, K., & Arbuthnot, J. (1995). The effect of functional family therapy for delinquents on adult criminal behavior. *Criminal Justice and Behavior*, 22, 60–73.

Gordon, R. (1987). An operational classification of disease prevention, In: J. Steinberg & M. Silverman (Eds.), *Preventing mental disorders.* Rockville, MD: US Department of Health and Human Services.

Gorman, D. (2003). Prevention programs and scientific nonsense. *Policy Review*, 117, 65–75.

Gottfredson, D. & Gottfredson, G. (2002). Quality of school-based prevention programs: Results from a national survey. *Journal of Research in Crime and Delinquency*, 39, 3–35.

Gottfredson, D. & Wilson, D. (2003). Characteristics of effective school-based substance abuse prevention. *Prevention Science*, 4, 27–38.

Gottfredson, D., Gottfredson, G., & Hybl, L. (1993). Managing adolescent behavior: A multiyear, multischool study. *American Educational Research Journal*, 30, 179–215.

Gottfredson, M. & Hirschi, T. (1990). *A general theory of crime.* Stanford University Press.

Greenberg, M., Domitrovich, C., Graczyk, P., & Zins, J. (2005). *The study of implementation in school-based preventive interventions: Theory, research and practice*, bind 3. Rockville, MD: Center for Mental Health Services, Substance Abuse and Mental Health Services Administration.

Greenberg, M., Weissberg, R., O'Brien, M., Zins, J., Fredericks, L., Resnik, H., & Elias, M. (2003). Enhancing social and emotional learning school-based prevention and youth development through coordinated social, emotional, and academic learning. *American Psychologist*, 58, 466–474.

Greenhalgh, T., Macfarlane, R., Bate, P., & Kyriakidou, O. (2004). Diffusion of innovations in service organizations: Systematic literature review and recommendations for future research. *The Milbank Quarterly*, 82, 581–629.

Gresham, F. (1986). Conceptual issues in the assessment of social competence in children. In: P. Strain, M. Guralnick, & H. Walker (Eds.), *Children's social behavior: Development, assessment and modification* (pp. 145–146). New York: Academic Press.

Gresham, F. & Elliott, S. (1984). Advances in the assessment of children's social skills. *School Psychology Review*, 13, 292–301.

Gresham, F. & Elliott, S. (1990). *Social skills rating system.* Circle Pines, MN: American Guidance Service.

Gresham, F. & Elliott, S. (2008). *Social skills improvement system (SSIS) rating scales.* Bloomington, MN: Pearson Assessments.

Gresham, F., Elliott, S., & Black, F. (1987). Teacher-rated social skills of mainstreamed mildly handicapped and nonhandicapped children. *School Psychology Review,* 16, 8–88.

Grohl, R. & Wensing, M. (2004). What drives change? Barriers to and incentives for achieving evidence-based practice. *The Medical Journal of Australia,* 180, 57–60.

Guldbrandsson, K. (2007). *Från nyhet till vardagsnytta. Om implementeringens mödosamma konst.* [From news to everyday use. On the art of implementation. A research review] Stockholm: Statens Folkhälsoinstitut.

Gustafsson, J.-E., Allodi, M., Alin Åkerman, B., Eriksson, C., Eriksson, L. Fischbein, S., … Persson, R. (2010). *School learning and mental health. A systematic review.* Report. Stockholm: The Health Committee, The Royal Swedish Academy of Sciences.

Haley, J. (1976). *Problem solving therapy.* San Francisco, CA: Jossey-Bass.

Hamdan-Mansour, A., Puskar, K., & Bandak, A. (2009). Effectiveness of cognitive-behavioral therapy on depressive symptomatology, stress and coping strategies among Jordanian university students. *Issues in Mental Health Nursing,* 30, 188–196.

Hamilton, J., Kendall, P., Gosch, E., Furr, J., & Sood, E. (2008). Flexibility within fidelity. *Journal of the American Academy of Child & Adolescent Psychiatry,* 47(9), 987–993.

Hamm, J. (2000). Do birds of a feather flock together? The variable bases for African American, Asian American, and European American adolescents' selection of similar friends. *Developmental Psychology,* 36, 209–219.

Harden, A., Rees, R., Sheperd, J., Brunton, G., Oliver, S., & Oakley, A. (2001). *Young people and mental health: A systematic review on research on barriers and facilitators.* Report, London Institute of Education, EPPI Centre.

Hartnett, D., Carr, A., Hamilton, E., & O'Reilly, G. (2017). The effectiveness of functional family therapy for adolescent behavioral and substance misuse problems: A meta-analysis. *Family Process,* 56, 607–619.

Hattie, J. (2009). *Visible learning. A synthesis of over 800 meta-analyses relating to achievement.* London: Routledge.

Hawkins, J., Catalano, R., & Miller, J. (1992). Risk and protective factors for alcohol and other drug problems in adolescence and early adulthood: Implications for substance abuse prevention. *Psychological Bulletin,* 112, 64–105.

Hawkins, J., Catalano, R., Kosterman, R., Abbott, R., & Hill, K. (1999). Preventing adolescent health-risk behaviors by strengthening protection during childhood. *Archives of Pediatric Adolescent Medicine,* 153, 226–234.

Heckman, J. (2008). The case for investing in disadvantaged young children. CESifo DICE Report, 6(2), 3–8.

Heckman, J. & Mosso, S. (2014). The economics of human development and social mobility. *Annual Review of Economics,* 6(1), 689–733.

Heiervang, E., Goodman, A., & Goodman, R. (2008). The Nordic advantage in child mental health: Separating health differences from reporting style in a cross-cultural comparison of psychopathology. *Journal of Child Psychology and Psychiatry,* 49(6), 678–685.

Heiervang, E., Stormark, K., Lundervold, A., Heiman, M., Goodman, R., Posserud, M., … Gilleberg, C. (2007). Psychiatric disorders in Norwegian 8-to-10-year-olds: An epidemiological survey of prevalence, risk factors, and service use. *Journal of the American Academy of Child and Adolescent Psychiatry,* 46, 438–447.

Henderson, C., Rowe, C., Dakof, G., Hawes, S., & Liddle, H. (2009). Parenting practices as mediators of treatment effects in an early intervention trial of Multidimensional Family Therapy. *The American Journal of Drug and Alcohol Abuse,* 35, 220–226.

Henggeler, S., Melton, G., & Smith, L. (1992). Family preservation using multisystemic therapy: An effective alternative to incarcerating serious juvenile offenders. *Journal of Consulting & Clinical Psychology*, 60, 953–961.

Henggeler, S., Melton, G., Brondino, M., Scherer, D., & Hanley, J. (1997). Multisystemic Therapy with violent and chronic juvenile offenders and their families: The role of treatment fidelity in successful dissemination. *Journal of Consulting and Clinical Psychology*, 65, 821–833.

Henggeler, S., Pickrel, S., & Brondino, M. (1999). Multisystemic treatment of substance abusing and dependent delinquents: Outcomes, treatment fidelity, and transportability. *Mental Health Services Research*, 1, 171–184.

Henggeler, S., Clingempeel, W., Brondino, M., & Pickrel, S. (2002). Four-year follow-up of multisystemic therapy with substance-abusing and substance-dependent juvenile offenders. *Journal of the American Academy of Child and Adolescent Psychiatry*, 41, 868–874.

Henggeler, S., Halliday-Boykins, C., Cunningham, P., Randall, J., Shapiro, S., & Chapman, J. (2006). Juvenile drug court: Enhancing outcomes by integrating evidence based treatments. *Journal of Consulting and Clinical Psychology*, 74, 42–54.

Henggeler, S., Schoenwald, S., Borduin, C., Rowland, M., & Cunningham, P. (2009). *Multisystemic treatment of antisocial behaviour in children and adolescents* (2nd ed.). New York: Guilford Press.

Hill, J. (2002). Biological, psychological and social processes in the conduct disorders. *Journal of Child Psychology and Psychiatry*, 43, 133–165.

Hinshaw, S. (1992). Externalizing behavior problems and academic under-achievement in childhood and adolescence: Causal relationships and underlying mechanisms. *Psychological Bulletin*, 111, 127–155.

Hirschi, T. (1969). *Causes of delinquency*. Berkeley, CA: University of California Press.

Hoagwood, K. & Johnson, J. (2003). School psychology: A public health framework I. From evidence-based practices to evidence-based policies. *Journal of School Psychology*, 41, 3–21.

Hoffman, D. (2009). Reflecting on social-emotional learning: A critical perspective on trends in the United States. *Review of Educational Research*, 79, 533–566.

Hogue, A., Dauber, S., Faw, L, Cecero, J., & Liddle, H. (2006). Early therapeutic alliance and treatment outcome in individual and family therapy for adolescent behavior problems. *Journal of Consulting and Clinical Psychology*, 74, 121–129.

Hogue, A., Henderson, C., Ozechowski, T., & Robbins, M. (2014). Evidence base on out-patient behavioral treatments for adolescent substance use: Updates and recommendations 2007–2013. *Journal of Clinical Child & Adolescent Psychology*, 43, 695–720.

Hogue, A. & Liddle, H. (2009). Family-based treatment for adolescent substance abuse: Controlled trials and new horizons in services research. *Journal of Family Therapy*, 31, 126–154.

Holmbeck, G., Paikoff, R., & Brooks-Gunn, J. (1995). Parenting adolescents. In: M. Bornstein (Ed.), *Handbook of parenting* (pp. 91–118). Hillsdale, NJ: Lawrence Erlbaum.

Holth, P., Torsheim, T., Sheidow, A., Ogden, T., & Henggeler, S. (2011). Intensive quality assurance of therapist adherence to behavioral interventions for adolescent substance use problems. *The Journal of Child and Adolescent Substance Abuse*, 20, 289–313.

Horner, R., Sugai, G., & Anderson, C. (2010). Examining the evidence base for school-wide positive behavior support. *Focus on Exceptional Children*, 42(8), 1.

Horner, R., Sugai, G., Smolkowski, K., Eber, L., Nakasato, J., Todd, A., & Esperanza, J. (2009). A randomized wait-list controlled effectiveness trial assessing school-wide positive behaviour support in elementary schools. *Journal of Positive Behaviour Interventions*, 11, 133–144.

Horowitz, J. & Garber, J. (2006). The prevention of depressive symptoms in children and adolescents: A meta-analytic review. *Journal of Consulting and Clinical Psychology*, 74, 401–415.

Huey, S. Jr., Henggeler, S., Brondino, M., & Pickrel, S. (2000). Mechanisms of change in multisystemic therapy: Reducing delinquent behavior through therapist adherence and improved family and peer functioning. *Journal of Consulting and Clinical Psychology*, 68, 451–467.

Humayun, S., Herlitz, L., Chesnokov, M., Doolan, M., Landau, S., & Scott, S. (2017). Randomized controlled trial of Functional Family Therapy for offending and antisocial behavior in UK youth. *Journal of Child Psychology and Psychiatry*.

Humphrey, N., Lendrum, A., & Wigelsworth, M. (2010). Social and emotional aspects of learning (SEAL) programme in secondary schools: National evaluation [Research Report DFE-RR049]. London: UK Government Department for Education.

Humphrey, N., Lendrum, A., & Wigelsworth, M. (2013). Making the most out of school-based prevention: Lessons from the social and emotional aspects of learning (SEAL) programme. *Emotional and Behavioural Difficulties*, 18, 248–260.

Humphrey, N., Lendrum, A., Ashworth, E., Frearson, K., Buck, R., & Kerr, K. (2016) *Implementation and process evaluation (IPE) for interventions in education settings: An introductory handbook*. Education Endowment Foundation, Manchester University.

Iarocci, G., Yager, J., & Elfers, T. (2007). What gene-environment interactions can tell us about social competence in typical and atypical populations. *Brain and Cognition*, 65, 112–127.

Institute of Medicine (IOM) and National Research Council (NRC) (2014). *Strategies for scaling effective family focused preventive interventions to promote children's cognitive, affective and behavioral health: Workshop summary*. Washington, DC: The National Academies Press.

Jaffee, S., Strait, L., & Odgers, C. (2012). From correlates to causes: Can quasi-experimental studies and statistical innovations bring us closer to identifying the causes of antisocial behavior? *Psychological Bulletin*, 138, 272–295.

Jennings, J. & DiPrete, T. (2010). Teacher effects on social and behavioral skills in early elementary school. *Sociology of Education*, 83, 135–159.

Jensen, F. (2015). *The teenage brain. A neuroscientist's survival guide to raising adolescents and young adults*. New York: Harper.

Jessor, R. & Jessor, S. (1977). *Problem behavior and psychosocial development: A longitudinal study of youth*. San Diego, CA: Academic Press.

Johnson, D. & Johnson, F. (2006). *Joining together. Group theory and group skills* (9th ed.). New York: Pearson.

Jones, S. & Bouffard, S. (2012). Social and emotional learning in schools. From programs to strategies. *Social Policy Report, Sharing Child and Youth Developmental Knowledge*. 26, 3–22.

Kagan, J. (1975). Resilience in cognitive development. *Ethos*, 3, 231–247.

Kaminer, Y. (2002) Adolescent substance abuse treatment: Evidence-based practice in outpatient services. *Current Psychiatry Reports*, 4, 397–401.

Karevold, E., Roysamb, E., Ystrom, E., & Mathiesen, K. (2009). Predictors and pathways from infancy to symptoms of anxiety and depression in early adolescence. *Developmental Psychology*, 45, 1051–1060.

Kaufman, E. (1985). Family systems and family therapy of substance abuse: An overview of two decades of research and clinical experience. *International Journal of Addiction*, 20, 897–916.

Kaufman, N., Rohde, P., Seeley, J., Clarke, G., & Stice, E. (2005). Potential mediators of cognitive-behavioral therapy for adolescents with comorbid major depression and conduct disorder. *Journal of Consulting and Clinical Psychology*, 73, 38–46.

Kazdin, A. (1993). Adolescent mental health. Prevention and treatment programs. *American Psychologist*, 48, 127–141.

Kazdin, A. (1995). Child, parent and family dysfunction as predictors of outcome in cognitive-behavioral treatment of antisocial children. *Behaviour Research and Therapy*, 33, 271–281.

Kazdin, A. (1997). Practitioner review: Psychosocial treatments for conduct disorder in children. *Journal of Child Psychology and Psychiatry*, 18, 161–178.

Kazdin, A. (2003). Problem-solving skills training and parent management training for conduct disorder. In: A. Kazdin & J. Weisz, (Eds.), *Evidence-based psychotherapies for children and adolescents*. New York: Guilford Press.

Kazdin, A. (2008). Evidence-based treatment and practice. New opportunities to bridge clinical research and practice, enhance the knowledge base, and improve patient care. *American Psychologist*, 63, 146–159.

Kazdin, A. & Weisz, J. (1998). Identifying and developing empirically supported child and adolescent treatments. *Journal of Consulting and Clinical Psychology*, 66, 19–36.

Kazdin, A. & Nock, M. (2003). Delineating mechanisms of change in child and adolescent therapy: Methodological issues and research recommendations. *Journal of Child Psychology and Psychiatry*, 44, 1116–1129.

Kazdin, A. & Whitley, M. (2006). Comorbidity, case complexity, and effects of evidence-based treatment for children referred for disruptive behavior. *Journal of Consulting and Clinical Psychology*, 74, 455–467.

Kazdin, A., Siegel, T., & Bass, D. (1992). Cognitive problem-solving skills training and parent management training in the treatment of antisocial behavior in children. *Journal of Consulting and Clinical Psychology*, 60, 733–747.

Kellam, S. & Langevin, D. (2003). A framework for understanding «evidence» in prevention research and programs. *Prevention Science*, 4, 137–153.

Kelly, B. (2012). Implementation science for psychology in education. In: B. Kelly & D. Perkins (Eds.), *Handbook of implementation science for psychology in education*. Cambridge: Cambridge University Press.

Kendall, P., Crawford, E., Kagan, E., Furr, J., & Podell, J. (2017). Child-focused treatment for anxiety. In: J. Weisz & A. Kazdin (Eds.), *Evidence-based psychotherapies for children and adolescents* (3rd ed.). New York: Guilford.

Kendall, P., Flannery-Schroeder, E., Panichelli-Mindel, S., Southam-Gerow, M., Henin, A., & Warman, M. (1997). Therapy for youths with anxiety disorders: A second randomized clinical trial. *Journal of Consulting and Clinical Psychology*, 65, 366–380.

Kendall, P. & Hedtke, K. (2006). *Cognitive-behavioral therapy for anxious children: Therapist manual*. Ardmore, PA: Workbook Publishing.

Kendall, P., Hudson, J., Gosch, E., Flannery-Schroeder, E., & Suveg, C. (2008). Cognitive-behavioral therapy for anxiety disordered youth: A randomized clinical trial evaluating child and family modalities. *Journal of Consulting and Clinical Psychology*, 76, 282–297.

Kendall, P. & Southam-Gerow, M. (1996). Long-term follow-up of a cognitive-behavioral therapy for anxiety-disordered youth. *Journal of Consulting and Clinical Psychology*, 64, 724–730.

Kendall, P. & Treadwell, K. (2007). The role of self-statements as a mediator in treatment for anxiety-disordered youth. *Journal of Consulting and Clinical Psychology*, 75, 380–389.

Kessler, R., Avenevoli, S., & Merikangas, K. (2001). Mood disorders in children and adolescents: An epidemiologic perspective. *Biological Psychiatry*, 49(12), 1002–1014.

Kessler R., Chiu W., Demler O., & Walters, E. (2005). Prevalence, severity, and comorbidity of twelve-month DSM-IV disorders in the National Comorbidity Survey Replication (NCS-R). *Archives of General Psychiatry*, 62, 617–627.

Kessler, R. & Glasgow, R. (2011). A proposal to speed translation of healthcare research into practice: Dramatic change is needed. *American Journal of Preventive Medicine*, 40(6), 637–644.

Kiuru, N., Aunola, K., Nurmi, J., Leskinen, E., & Salmela-Aro, K. (2008). Peer group influence and selection in adolescents' school burnout: A longitudinal study. *Merill-Palmer Quarterly*, 54, 23–55.

Kjøbli, J. & Bjørnebekk, G. (2013). A randomized effectiveness trial of brief parent training: Six-month follow-up. *Research on Social Work Practice*, 23(6), 603–612.

Kjøbli, J., Hukkelberg, S., & Ogden, T. (2013). A randomized trial of group parent training: Reducing child conduct problems in real-world settings. *Behaviour Research and Therapy*, 51(3), 113–121.

Kjøbli, J. & Ogden, T. (2012). A randomized effectiveness trial of brief parent training in primary care settings. *Prevention Science*, 13, 616–626.

Kjøbli, J. & Ogden, T. (2014). A randomized effectiveness trial of individual child social skills training: Six-month follow up. *Child and Adolescent Psychiatry and Mental Health*, 8, 31.

Kjøbli, J., Zachrisson, H. D., & Bjørnebekk, G. (2016). Three Randomized Effectiveness Trials—One Question: Can Callous-Unemotional Traits in Children Be Altered? *Journal of Clinical Child & Adolescent Psychology*, 1–8. DOI: 10.1080/15374416.2016.1178123

Kjøge, A., Turtumøygard, T., Berge, T., & Ogden, T. (2015). From training to practice: A survey study of clinical challenges in implementing cognitive behavioural therapy in Norway. *The Cognitive Behaviour Therapist*, 8, 1–16. doi:10.1017/S1754470X15000471

Klein, K. & Sorra, J. (1996). The challenge of innovation implementation. *Academy of Management Review*, 21, 1055–1080.

Knutson, N., Forgatch, M., Reins, L., & Sigmarsdottir, M. (2009). *Fidelity of Implementation Rating system (FIMP). The Manual for PMTO*. Eugene, OR: Implementation Sciences International. Inc.

Kosterman, R., Hawkins, J., Spoth, R., Haggerty, K., & Zhu, K. (1997). Effects of a preventive parent-training intervention on observed family interactions: Proximal outcomes from preparing for the drug free years. *Journal of Community Psychology*, 25, 337–352.

Koutakis, N., Stattin, H., & Kerr, M. (2008). Reducing youth alcohol drinking through a parent-targeted intervention. The Örebro prevention program. *Addiction*, 103, 1629–1637.

Kristoffersen, C., Holth, P., & Ogden, T. (2011). *Modeller i rusbehandling*. [Treatment models for drug abuse]. Report. Oslo: Norwegian Center for Child Behavioral Development.

Kutash, K., Duchnowski, A., & Lynn, N. (2006). *School-based mental health: An empirical guide for decision-makers*. Online Etymology Dictionary. Douglas Harper, Historian. May 5 2012. [online] Dictionary.com http://dictionary.reference.com/browse/empirical

Ladd, G. & Burgess, K. (2001). Do relational risk and protective factors moderate the linkage between childhood aggression and early psychological and school adjustment? *Child Development*, 72, 1579–1601.

La Greca, A., Silverman, W., & Lochman, J. (2009). Moving beyond efficacy and effectiveness in child and adolescent intervention research. *Journal of Consulting and Clinical Psychology*, 77, 373–382.

Lamb, J., Puskar, K., Sereika, S., & Corcoran, M. (1998). School-based intervention to promote coping in rural teens. *American Journal of Maternal Child Nursing*, 23, 187–194.

Latendresse, S., Bates, J., Goodnight, J., Lansford, J., Budde, J., Goate, A., … Dick, D. (2011). Differential susceptibility to adolescent externalizing trajectories: Examining the interplay between CHRM2 and peer group antisocial behavior. *Child Development*, 82, 1797–1814.

Layard, R. & Dunn, J. (2009). *A good childhood: Searching for values in a competitive age*. London: The Children's Society.

Lendrum, A. & Humphrey, N. (2012). The importance of studying the implementation of interventions in school settings. *Oxford Review of Education*, 38(5), 635–652.

Lengua, L. (2002). The contribution of emotionality and self regulation to the understanding of children's response to multiple risk. *Child Development*, 73, 144–161.

Levant, R. (2008). *Evidence-based practice in psychology*. Presentation at the CIEBP 2008 National Conference. See also: Norcross, J., Beutler, L., & Levant, R. (2006). *Evidence-based practices in mental health: Debate and dialogue on the fundamental questions*. American Psychological Association.

Levin, H. (2012). More than just test scores. *Prospects*, 42(3), 269–284.

Lewinsohn, P., Antonuccio, D., Steinmetz-Breckenridge, J., & Teri, L. (1984). *The coping with depression course: A psychoeducational intervention for unipolar depression*. Eugene, OR: Castalia Publishing Company.

Lewis, T., Newcomer, L., Trussell, R., & Richter, M. (2006). Schoolwide positive behavior support: building systems to develop and maintain appropriate social behavior. In: C. Evertson & C. Weinstein (Eds.), *Handbook of classroom management. Research, practice and contemporary issues*. New York: Lawrence Erlbaum.

Liber, J., McLeod, B., Van Widenfelt, B., Goedhart, A., van der Leeden, A., Utens, E., & Treffers, P. (2010). Examining the relation between the therapeutic alliance, treatment adherence, and outcome of cognitive behavioural therapy for children with anxiety disorders. *Behavior Therapy*, 41, 172–186.

Liddle, H. (2010). Treating adolescent substance abuse using multidimensional family therapy. In: J. Weisz & A. Kazdin (Eds.), *Evidence-based psychotherapies for children and adolescents*. New York: Guilford Press.

Liddle, H. & Dakof, G. (1995). Family based treatment for adolescent drug use: state of the science. In E. Rahdert & D. Czechowicz (Eds.), *Adolescent drug abuse: Clinical assessment and therapeutic interventions*. NIDA Research Monograph, 156.

Liddle, H., Dakof, G., Turner, R., Henderson, C., & Greenbaum, P. (2008). Treating adolescent drug abuse: A randomized trial comparing multidimensional family therapy and cognitive behavior therapy. *Addiction*, 103, 1660–1670.

Liddle, H., Rowe, C., Dakof, G., Henderson, C., & Greenbaum, P. (2009). Multidimensional Family Therapy for early adolescent substance abusers: Twelve month outcomes of a randomized controlled trial. *Journal of Consulting and Clinical Psychology*, 77, 12–25.

Lieberman, M. (2013). *Social. Why our brains are wired to connect*. New York: Crown Publishers.

Lipsey, M. (2009). The primary factors that characterize effective interventions with juvenile offenders: A meta-analytic overview. *Victims and Offenders*, 4, 124–147.

Lipsey, M. & Cullen, F. (2007). The effectiveness of correctional rehabilitation: A review of systematic reviews. *The Annual Review of Law and Social Science*, 3, 297–320.

Lochman, J. & Wells, K. (2004). The Coping Power program for preadolescent aggressive boys and their parents: Outcome effects at the 1-year follow-up. *Journal of Consulting and Clinical Psychology*, 72, 571–578.

Lösel, F. & Beelmann, A. (2003). Effects of child skills training in preventing antisocial behavior: A systematic review of randomized evaluations. *Annals of the American Academy of Political and Social Science*, 587, 84–109.

Lowry-Webster, H., Barrett, P., & Lock, S. (2003). A universal prevention trial of anxiety symptomatology during childhood: Results at one-year follow-up. *Behaviour Change*, 20(1), 25–43.

Luborsky, L., Singer, B., & Luborsky, L. (1975). Comparative studies of psychotherapies: Is it true that "everyone has won and all must have prices?" *Archives of General Psychiatry*, 32, 995–1008.

Macklem, G. (2011). *Evidence-based school mental health services. Affect education, emotion regulation training and cognitive behavioral therapy*. New York: Springer.

Markham, W. & Aveyard, P. (2003). A new theory of health promoting schools based on human functioning, school organisation and pedagogic practice. *Social Science and Medicine*, 56, 1209–1220.

Martinson, R. (1974). What works? Questions and answers about prison reform. *The Public Interest*, 35, 22–54.

Marzano, R., Marzano, J., & Pickering, D. (2003). *Classroom management that works. Research based strategies for every teacher.* Alexandria, VA: ASCD.

Marzano, R., Waters, T., & McNulty, B. (2003). Balanced leadership: What 30 years of research tells us about the effect of leadership on student achievement. A working paper. http://eric.ed.gov/ERICWebPortal/custom/portlets/recordDetails/detailmini.jsp?_nfpb=true&_&ERICExtSearch_SearchValue_0=ED481972&ERICExtSearch_SearchType_0=no&accno=ED481972

Mason, D. & Frick, P. (1994). The heritability of antisocial behavior: A meta-analysis of twin and adoption studies. *Journal of Psychopathology and Behavioral Assessment*, 16, 301–323.

Masten, A. & Coatsworth, J. (1998). The development of competence in favorable and unfavorable environments. *American Psychologist*, 53(2), 205–220.

Masten, A. & Powell, J. (2003). A resilience framework for research, policy and practice. In: S. Luthar (Ed.), *Resilience and vulnerability. Adaptation in the context of childhood adversities*. Cambridge: Cambridge University Press.

Masten, A., Coatsworth, J., Neemann, J., Gest, S., Tellegen, A., & Garmezy, N. (1995). The structure and coherence of competence from childhood trough adolescence. *Child Development*, 66, 1635–1659.

Mathew, A., Pettit, J., Lewinsohn, P., Seeley, J., & Roberts, R. (2011). Co-morbidity between major depressive disorder and anxiety disorders: Shared etiology or direct causation? *Psychological Medicine*, 41, 2023–2034.

Mayberry, M., Espelage, D., & Koenig, B. (2009). Multilevel modeling of direct effects and interactions of peers, parents, school and community influences on adolescent substance abuse. *Journal of Youth and Adolescence*, 38, 1038–1049.

McCarthy, C., Mason, W., Kosterman, R., Hawkins, J., Lengua, L., & McCauley, E. (2008). Adolescent school failure predicts later depression among girls. *Journal of Adolescent Health*, 43, 180–187.

McCart, M., Ogden, T., & Henggeler, S. (2014). *Youth who have broken the law.* In: A. Ben-Arieh, J. Cashmore, G. Goodman, J., Kampmann, & G. Melton (Eds.), *Handbook of Child Research.* London: Sage.

McCart, M. & Sheidow, A. (2016). Evidence-based psychosocial treatments for adolescents with disruptive behavior. *Journal of Clinical Child and Adolescent Psychology*, 45, 529–563.

McClure, E. & Pine, D. (2006). Social anxiety and emotion regulation: A model on developmental psychopathology perspective on anxiety disorders. In: D. Cicchetti & D. Cohen (Eds.), *Development psychopathology: Risk, disorders and adaption* (Vol. 3). Hoboken, NJ: John Wiley & Sons.

McCollum, J. & Ostrosky, M. (2008). Family roles in children's emerging peer-related social competence. In: W. Brown, S. Odom, & S. McConnell (Eds.), *Social competence of young children. Risk, disability and intervention.* London: Paul Brookes Publishing Company.

McCord, J. (1979). Some child-rearing antecedents of criminal behavior in adult men. *Journal of Personality and Social Psychology*, 37, 1477–1486.

McGee, R., Prior, M., Williams, S., Smart, D., & Sanson, A. (2002). The long term significance of teacher-rated hyperactivity and reading ability in childhood: Findings from two longitudinal studies. *Journal of Child Psychology and Psychiatry and Allied Disciplines*, 43, 1004–1017.

McLeod, J. & Fettes, D. (2007). Trajectories of failure: The educational careers of children with mental health problems. *American Journal of Sociology*, 113, 653–701.

McNeish, D., Newman, T., & Roberts, H. (2002). *What works for children?* Buckingham: Open University Press.

Mendle, J., Harden, K., Brooks-Gunn, J., & Graber, J. (2010). Development's tortoise and hare: Pubertal timing, pubertal tempo, and depressive symptoms in boys and girls. *Developmental Psychology*, 46, 1341–1353.

Merikangas, K., He, J., Burstein, M., Swanson, S., Avenevoli, S., Cui, L., … Swendsen, J. (2010). Lifetime prevalence of mental disorders in U.S. adolescents: Results from the National Comorbidity Survey Replication–Adolescent Supplement (NCS-A). *Journal of the American Academy of Children and Adolescent Psychiatry*, 49, 980–989.

Merrell, K. (2010). Linking prevention science and social and emotional learning: The Oregon Resiliency Project. *Psychology in the Schools*, 47, 55–70.

Merrell, K., Gueldner, B., Ross, S., & Isava, D. (2008). How effective are school bullying intervention programs? A meta-analysis of intervention research. *School Psychology Quarterly*, 23, 26–42.

Meyers, D., Katz, J., Chien, V., Wandersman, A., Scaccia, J., & Wright, A. (2012). Practical implementation science: Developing and piloting the Quality Implementation Tool. *American Journal of Community Psychology*, 50, 481–496.

Meyers, D., Durlak, J., & Wandersman, A. (2012). The quality implementation framework: A synthesis of critical steps in the implementation process. *American Journal of Community Psychology*, 50(3–4), 462–480.

Mihalic, S., Fagan, A., Irwin, K., Ballard, D., & Elliott, D. (2004). *Blueprints for violence prevention*. [online]. Retrieved June 2008 from www.ojp.usdoj.gov/ojjdp

Mihalic, S. & Irwin, K. (2003). Blueprints for violence prevention: From research to real world settings—factors influencing the successful replication of model programs. *Youth Violence and Juvenile Justice*, 1(4), 307–329.

Miller, T. (2015). Projected outcomes of nurse-family partnership home visitation during 1996–2013, USA. *Prevention Science*, 16, 765–777.

Miller, G., Brehm, K., & Whitehouse, S. (1998). Reconceptualizing school-based prevention for antisocial behavior within a resiliency framework. *School Psychology Review*, 27, 364–379.

Miller, W. & Rollnick, S. (2002). *Motivational interviewing: Preparing people for change* (2nd ed.). New York: Guilford Press.

Miner, J. & Clarke-Stewart, K. (2008). Trajectories of externalizing behavior from age 2 to age 9: Relations with gender, temperament, ethnicity, parenting and rater. *Developmental Psychology*, 44, 771–786.

Minuchin, S. (1974). *Families and family therapy*. Cambridge, MA: Harvard University Press.

Mischel, W. (1958). Preference for a delayed reinforcement. An experimental study of a cultural observation. *Journal of Abnormal and Social Psychology*, 56, 57–61.

Mitchell, P. (2011). Evidence-based practice in real-world services for young people with complex needs: New opportunities suggested by recent implementation science. *Children and Youth Services Review*, 33, 207–216.

Miyamoto, K., Huerta, M., & Kubacka, K. (2015) Fostering social and emotional skills for well-being and social progress. *European Journal of Education*. doi: 10.1111/ejed.12118

Mize, J. (1995). Coaching preschool children in social skills: A cognitive–social learning curriculum. In: G. Cartledge & J.-A. Milburn (Eds.), *Teaching social skills to children and youth*. Boston, MA: Allyn & Bacon.

Moffitt, T. (1993). Adolescence limited and life-course persistent antisocial behavior: A developmental taxonomy. *Psychological Review*, 100, 674–701.

Moffitt, T. (2006). Life-course-persistent versus adolescence-limited antisocial behavior. In D. Cicchetti & D. Cohen (Eds.), *Developmental psychopathology. Risk, disorder and adaptation* (Vol. 3). Hoboken, NJ: John Wiley & Sons.

Moffitt, T. & Caspi, A. (2001). Childhood predictors differentiate life-course persistent and adolescent limited antisocial pathways among males and females. *Development and Psychopathology*, 13, 355–375.

Moffitt, T., Caspi, A., Harrington, H., & Milne, B. (2002). Males on the life-course persistent and the adolescent limited antisocial pathways: Follow-up at 26 years. *Development and Psychopathology*, 14, 179–207.

Moffitt, T., Caspi, A., Rutter, M., & Silva, P. (2001). *Sex differences in antisocial behaviour.* Cambridge: Cambridge University Press.

Moffitt, T. & Scott, S. (2009). Conduct Disorders of Childhood and Adolescence In: M. Rutter (Ed.), *Child and adolescent psychiatry.* Blackwell Publishing Ltd. (pp. 543–564).

Monahan, K., Steinberg, L., & Cauffman, E. (2009). Affiliation with antisocial peers, susceptibility to peer influence, and antisocial behavior during the transition to adulthood. *Developmental Psychology*, 45, 1520–1530.

Moore, P., Whaley, S., & Sigman, M. (2004). Interactions between mothers and children: Impacts of maternal and child anxiety. *Journal of Abnormal Psychology*, 113, 471–476.

Mørkrid, D. & Christensen, B. (2007). Funksjonell familieterapi: En evidensbasert familieterapeutisk behandling for ungdom og familier med alvorlige atferdsvansker. [Functional family therapy: An evidence-based family therapeutic treatment of youth and families with serious behavior problems] *Norges Barnevern*, 84, 15–23.

Mrazek, P. & Haggerty, R. (1994). Illustrative preventive intervention research programs. In: P. Mrazek & R. Haggerty (Eds.), *Reducing risks for mental disorder: Frontiers for preventive intervention research.* Washington, DC: National Academy Press.

Muscott, H., Mann, E., & LeBrun, M. (2008). Positive behavioural interventions and supports in New Hampshire. Effects of large-scale implementation of schoolwide positive behaviour support on student discipline and academic achievement. *Journal of Positive Behaviour Interventions*, 10, 190–205.

Nærde, A., Ogden, T., Janson, H., & Zachrisson, H. (2014). Normative development of physical aggression from 8 to 26 months. *Developmental Psychology*, 50, 1710–1720.

Negriff, S. & Susman, E. (2011). Pubertal timing, depression and externalizing problems: A framework, review, and examination of gender difference. *Journal of Research on Adolescence*, 21, 717–746.

Nelson, E., Leibenluft, E., McClure, E., & Pine, D. (2005). The social re-orientation of adolescence: A neuroscience perspective on the process and its relation to psychopathology. *Psychological Medicine*, 35, 163–174.

NICHD Early Child Care Research Network. Trajectories from physical aggression from toddlerhood to middle childhood. *Monographs of the Society for Research in Child Development*. (2004), 69, 1–143.

Nihira, K., Mink, I. & Meyers, C. (1985). Home environment and development of slow-learning adolescents: Reciprocal relations. *Developmental Psychology*, 21(5), 784.

Nisbett, R., Aronson, J., Blair, C., Dickens, W., Flynn, J., Halpern, D., & Turkheimer, E. (2012). Intelligence. New findings and theoretical developments. *American Psychologist*, 67, 130–159.

Norcross, J., Beutler, L., & Levant, R. (2006). *Evidence-based practices in mental health.* Washington, DC: American Psychological Association.

Nutley, S., Walter, I., & Davies, H. (2007). *Using evidence: How research can inform public services.* Bristol: The Policy Press.

Odom, S., McConnell, S., & Brown, W. (2008). Social competence of young children. Conceptualization, assessment and influences. In: W. Brown, S. Odom, & S. McConnell (Eds.), *Social competence of young children. Risk disability and intervention.* London: Paul Brookes Publishing Company.

OECD. (2015). *Skills for the 21st century. The power of social and emotional skills.* Paris: OECD.

Ogden, T. (1995). *Kompetanse i kontekst: En studie av risiko og kompetanse hos 10- og 13- åringer.* [Competence in context: A study of risk and competence in 10- and 13-year-olds] Report 3. Oslo: Barnevernets Utviklingssenter.

Ogden, T. & Halliday-Boykins, C. (2004). Multisystemic treatment of antisocial adolescents in Norway: Replication of clinical outcomes outside of the U.S. *Child and Adolescent Mental Health,* 9, 77–83.

Ogden, T. & Amlund Hagen, K. (2006). Multisystemic therapy of serious behavior problems in youth: Sustainability of therapy effectiveness two years after intake. *Child and Adolescent Mental Health,* 11, 142–149.

Ogden, T. & Amlund Hagen, K. (2008). Treatment effectiveness of Parent Management Training in Norway: A randomized controlled trial of children with conduct problems. *Journal of Consulting and Clinical Psychology,* 76, 607–621.

Ogden, T., & Amlund Hagen, K. (2009). What works for whom? Gender differences in intake characteristics and treatment outcomes following multisystemic therapy. *Journal of Adolescence,* 32, 1425–1435.

Ogden, T. & Amlund Hagen, K. (2012). System oriented interventions in Europe. In: R. Loeber, M. Hoeve, N. Slot & P. van der Laan (Eds.), *Persisters and desisters in crime from adolescence into adulthood: Explanation, prevention and punishment.* Aldershot: Ashgate.

Ogden, T., Amlund Hagen, K., & Andersen, O. (2007). Clinical outcomes of the Norwegian MST program in the second year of operation. *Children's Services Review,* 2, 4–14.

Ogden, T., Amlund Hagen, K., Askeland, E., & Christensen, B. (2009). Implementing and evaluating evidence- based treatments of conduct problems in children and youth in Norway. *Research on Social Work Practice,* 19, 582–591.

Ogden, T., Askeland, E., Christensen, B., Christiansen, T., & Kjøbli, J. (2017). Crossing national, cultural, and language barriers: implementing and testing evidence-based practices in Norway. In: J. Weisz & A. Kazdin (Eds.), *Evidence based psychotherapies with children and adolescents.* New York: Guilford.

Ogden, T. & Fixsen, D. (2014). Implementation Science. A brief overview and a look ahead. *Zeitschrift für Psychologie,* 222, 4–11.

Ogden, T., Forgatch, M., Askeland, E., Patterson, G., & Bullock, B. (2005). Implementation of Parent Management Training at the national level: The case of Norway. *Journal of Social Work Practice,* 19, 317–329.

Ogden, T., Amlund-Hagen, K., Askeland, E., & Christensen, B. (2009). Implementing and evaluating evidence- based treatments of conduct problems in children and youth in Norway. *Research on Social Work Practice,* 19, 582–591.

Ogden, T., Bjørnebekk, G., Kjøbli, J., Patras, J., Christiansen, T., Taraldsen, K., & Tollefsen, N. (2012a). Measurement of implementation components ten years after a nationwide introduction of empirically supported programs: A pilot study. *Implementation Science* (pp. 1–11). Retrieved November 2012 from www.implementationscience.com/content/7/1/49

Ogden, T., Christensen, B., Sheidow, A., & Holth, P. (2008). Bridging the gap between science and practice: The effective nationwide transport of MST programs in Norway. *Journal of Children and Adolescent Substance Abuse,* 17, 93–109.

Ogden, T., Sørlie, M-A., Arnesen, A., & Meek-Hansen, W. (2012b). The PALS School-Wide Positive Behavior Support Model in Norwegian Primary Schools–implementation and evaluation. In: J. Visser (Ed.), *Transforming troubled lives: Strategies and interventions with children and young people with social emotional and behavioural difficulties.* London: Emerald Group Publishing.

Oliver, R., Wehby, J., & Reschly, D. (2011). *Teacher classroom management practices: Effects on disruptive or aggressive student behaviour.* Campbell systematic reviews, 2011:4, The Campbell Collaboration.

Olson, S., Sameroff, A., Lansford, J., Sexton, H., Davis-Kean, P., Bates, J., … Dodge, K. (2013). Deconstructing the externalizing spectrum: Growth patterns of overt aggression, covert aggression, oppositional behavior, impulsivity/inattention, and emotion dysregulation between school entry and early adolescence. *Developmental Psychopathology,* 25, (3), 817–842.

Olweus, D. (1993). *Bullying at school.* Cambridge, MA: Blackwell.

Olweus, D. (1994). Bullying at school: Basic facts and effects of a school-based intervention program. *Journal of Child Psychology and Psychiatry,* 35, 1171–1190.

Olweus, D. (1996). Bullying at school: Knowledge base and an effective intervention program. *Annals of the New York Academy of Sciences,* 794, 265.

Olweus, D. (1997). Bully/victim problems at school: Facts and intervention. *European Journal of Psychology of Education,* 12, 495–510.

Olweus, D. & Limber, S. (1999). *Bullying prevention program.* Blueprints for violence prevention. Book 9. Boulder, CO: Venture Publishing.

Paternite, C. (2005). School-based mental health programs and services: Overview and introduction to the special issue. *Journal of Abnormal Child Psychology,* 33, 657–663.

Patterson, G. (1982). *Coercive family process.* Eugene, OR: Castalia Books.

Patterson, G. (1986). Performance models for antisocial boys. *American Psychologist,* 41, 432–444.

Patterson, G. (2002). The early development of the coercive family process. In: J. Reid, G. Patterson & J. Snyder (Eds.), *Antisocial behavior in children and adolescents: A developmental analysis and a model for intervention.* Washington, DC: American Psychological Association.

Patterson, G. (2005). The next generation of PMTO models. *The Behavior Therapist,* 35, 27–33.

Patterson, G. & Forgatch, M. (2005). *Parents and adolescents living together: part 1. The basics.* Champaign, IL: Research Press.

Patterson, G., Debaryshe, B., & Ramsey, E. (1990). A developmental perspective on antisocial behavior. *American Psychologist,* 44, 329–335.

Patterson, G., Reid, J., & Dishion, T. (1992). *A social interactional approach: vol. 4. Antisocial boys.* Eugene, OR: Castalia.

Patterson, G. & Yoerger, K. (1997). A developmental model for late-onset delinquency. In: D. Osgood (Ed.), *Motivation and delinquency* (pp. 119–177). Lincoln, NE: University of Nebraska Press.

Perepletchikova, F. & Kazdin, A. (2005). Treatment integrity and therapeutic change: Issues and research recommendations. *Clinical Psychology: Science and Practice,* 12, 365–383.

Petraitis, J., Flay, B., & Miller, T. (1995). Reviewing theories of adolescent substance use: Organizing pieces in the puzzle. *Psychological Bulletin,* 117, 67–86.

Piquero, A., Farrington, D., Welsh, B., Tremblay, R., & Jennings, W. (2008). *Effects of early family/parent training programs on antisocial behavior and delinquency. A systematic review.* Report. Stockholm: Swedish National Council for Crime Prevention.

Plant, W. & Panzarella, P. (2009). Residential treatment of adolescent with substance use disorders: evidence-based approaches and best practice recommendations. In: C. Leukefeld, T. Gullotta & M. Staton-Tindall (Eds.), (2009). *Adolescent substance abuse. Evidence-based approaches to prevention and treatment.* New York: Springer.

Price, J. & Dodge, K. (1989). Reactive and proactive aggression in childhood. *Journal of Abnormal Child Psychology*, 17, 455–471.

Proctor, E., Landsverk, J, Aarons, G., Chambers, D., Glisson, C., & Mittman, B. (2009). Implementation research in mental health services: An emerging science with conceptual, methodological, and training challenges. *Administration and Policy of Mental Health*, 36(1), 24–34.

Puskar, K., Sereika, S., & Tusaie-Mumford, K. (2003). Effect of the Teaching Kids to Cope (TKC) program on outcomes of depression and coping among rural adolescents. *Journal of Child and Adolescent Psychiatric Nursing*, 16, 71–80.

Quintana, S. & Lapsley, D. (1990). Rapprochement in late adolescent separation-individuation: A structural equations approach. *Journal of Adolescence*, 13(4), 371–385.

Randall, J., Henggeler, S., Cunningham, P., Rowland, M., & Swenson, C. (2001). Adapting multisystemic therapy to treat adolescent substance abuse more effectively. *Cognitive & Behavioral Practice*, 8, 359–366.

Ravens-Sieberer, U., Wille, N., Erhart, M., Bettge, S., Wittchen, H., Rothenberger, A., … Döpfner, M., BELLA Study Group. (2008). Prevalence of mental health problems among children and adolescents in Germany: Results of the BELLA study within the National Health Interview and Examination Survey. *European Child & Adolescent Psychiatry (S1)*, 17, 22–33.

Reid, J., Patterson, G., & Snyder, J. (2002). *Antisocial behavior in children and adolescents: A developmental analysis and a model for intervention*. Washington, DC: American Psychological Association.

Reynolds, D. (2001). Beyond effectiveness and school improvement? In: A. Harris & N. Bennet (Eds.), *School effectiveness and school improvement: Alternative perspectives*. London: Continuum.

Rhee, S. & Waldman, I. (2002). Genetic and environmental influences on antisocial behavior: A meta-analysis of twin and adoption studies. *Psychological Bulletin*, 128, 490–529.

Ringeisen, H., Henderson, K., & Hoagwood, K. (2003). Context matters: School and the "research to practice gap" in children's mental health. *School Psychology Review*, 32, 153–168.

Robertson, E., David, S., & Rao, S. (2003). *Preventing drug use among children and adolescents. A research-based guide for parents, educators, and community leaders* (2nd ed.). *In Brief*. Bethesda, MD: Department of Health and Human Services, National Institutes of Health.

Robins, M., Liddle, H., Turner, C., Dakof, G., Alexander, J., & Kogan, S. (2006). Adolescent and parent therapeutic alliances as predictors of dropout in multidimensional family therapy. *Journal of Family Psychology*, 20, 108–116.

Rodney, L., Johnson, D., & Srivastava, R. (2005). The impact of culturally relevant violence prevention models on school-aged youth. *The Journal of Primary Prevention*, 26, 439–454.

Roeser, R., Eccles, J., & Strobel, K. (1998). Linking the study of schooling and mental health: Selected issues and empirical illustrations at the level of the individual. *Educational Psychologist*, 33, 153–176.

Roeser, R., Eccles, J., & Freedman-Doan, C. (1999). Academic functioning and mental health in adolescence: Patterns, progressions, and routes from childhood. *Journal of Adolescent Research*, 14, 135–174.

Rogers, E. (1995). *Diffusion of innovation* (4th ed.). New York: Free Press.

Rohde, P., Clarke, G., Mace, D., Jorgensen, J., & Seeley, J. (2004). An efficacy/effectiveness study of cognitive-behavioral treatment for adolescents with comorbid major depression and conduct disorder. *Journal of the American Academy of Child and Adolescent Psychiatry*, 43, 660–668.

Rones, M. & Hoagwood, K. (2000). School-based mental-health services: A research review. *Clinical Child and Family Psychology Review*, 3, 223–241.

Rønning, J., Haavisto, A., Nikolakaros, G., Helenius, H., Tamminen, T., Moilanen, I., … Sourander, A. (2011). Factors associated with reported childhood depressive symptoms at age 8 and later self-reported depressive symptoms among boys at age 18. *Social Psychiatry and Psychiatric Epidemiology*, 46(3), 207–218.

Rosenberg, E., Burt, K., Forehand, R., & Paysnick, A. (2016). Youth self-views, coping with stress, and behavioral/emotional problems: The role of incremental self-theory. *Journal of Child and Family Studies*, 25(6), 1713–1723.

Roth, A. & Fonagy, P. (2005). *What works for whom? A critical review of psychotherapy research* (2nd ed.). New York: Guilford Press.

Rotheram-Borus, M., Swendeman, D., & Chorpita, B. (2012). Disruptive innovations for designing and diffusing evidence-based interventions. *American Psychologist*, 67, 463–476.

Rowe, C. (2012). Family therapy for drug abuse: Review and updates 2003–2010. *Journal of Marital and Family Therapy*, 38, 59–81.

Rutter, M. (2005). Substance use and abuse: causal pathways considerations. In: M. Rutter & E. Taylor (Eds.), *Child and adolescent psychiatry* (4th ed.). Oxford: Blackwell Publishing.

Rutter, M. & Maughan, B. (2002). School effectiveness findings 1979–2002. *Journal of School Psychology*, 40, 451–475.

Rutter, M., Giller, H., & Hagell, A. (1998). *Antisocial behaviour by young people: The main messages from a major new review of the research.* Cambridge: Cambridge University Press.

Ryan, S., Jorm, A., Kelly, C., Hart, L., Morgan, A., & Lubman, D. (2011). Parenting strategies for reducing adolescent alcohol use: A Delphi consensus study. *BMC Public Health*, 11, 13.

Sackett, D., Richardson, W., Rosenberg, W., & Haynes, R. (1997). *Evidence-based medicine: How to practice and teach EBM.* Edinburgh: Churchill Livingstone.

Sanders, M. (2008). Triple P-Positive Parenting Program as a public health approach to strengthening parenting. *Journal of Family Psychology*, 22, 506–517.

Sanders, M., Markie-Dadds, C., Tully, L., & Bor, W. (2000). The Triple P-Positive Parenting Program: A comparison of enhanced, standard, and self-directed behavioral family intervention for parents of children with early onset conduct problems. *Journal of Consulting and Clinical Psychology*, 68(4), 624–640.

Santisteban, D., Muir, J., Mena, M., & Mitrani, V. (2003). Integrative borderline adolescent family therapy: Meeting the challenges of treating adolescents with borderline personality disorder. *Psychotherapy: Theory, Research, Practice and Training*, 40, 251–264.

Schaeffer, C. & Borduin, C. (2005). Long-term follow-up to a randomized clinical trial of multisystemic therapy with serious and violent juvenile offenders. *Journal of Consulting and Clinical Psychology*, 73, 445–453.

Schneider, B. (1993). *Children's social competence in context: The contributions of family, school and culture.* New York: Pergamon Press.

Schneider, B., Attili, G., Nadel, J., & Weissberg, R. (Eds.). (2012). Social competence in developmental perspective (Vol. 51). Berlin: Springer Science & Business Media.

Schoenwald, S., Halliday-Boykins, C., & Henggeler, S. (2003). Client-level predictors of adherence to MST in community service settings. *Family Process*, 42, 345–359.

Schoenwald, S., Sheidow, A., & Letourneau, E. (2004). Toward effective quality assurance in evidence-based practice: Links between expert consultation, therapist fidelity and child outcomes. *Journal of Clinical Child and Adolescent Psychology*, 33, 94–104.

Schrock, M. & Woodruff-Borden, J. (2010). Parent-child interactions in anxious families. *Child & Family Behavior Therapy*, 32, 291–310.

Schwartz, D., Gorman, A., Duong, M., & Nakamoto, J. (2008). Peer relationships and academic achievement as interacting predictors of depressive symptoms during middle childhood. *Journal of Abnormal Psychology*, 117, 289–299.

Scott, S. (2008). Parenting programs. In: M. Rutter, D. Bishop, D. Pine, S. Scott, J. Stevenson, E. Taylor, & A. Thapar (Eds.). *Rutter's child and adolescent psychiatry* (5th ed.). Oxford: Blackwell.

Scott, S. (2017). A national approach to improving child and adolescent mental health care: The children and young people's improving access to psychological therapies program in England. In: J. Weisz & A. Kazdin (Eds.), *Evidence-based psychotherapies for children and adolescents* (3rd ed.). New York: Guilford.

Seiffge-Krenke, I. & Stemmler, M. (2002). Factors contributing to gender differences in depressive symptoms: A test of three developmental models. *Journal of Youth and Adolescence*, 31(6), 405–417

Sexton, T. & Alexander, J. (2005). Functional family therapy for externalizing disorders in adolescents. In: J. Lebow (Ed.), *Handbook of clinical family therapy*. Hoboken, NJ: Wiley.

Sexton, T. & Turner, C. (2011). The effectiveness of functional family therapy for youth with behavioral problems in a community practice setting. *Couple and Family Psychology: Research and Practice*, 1, 3–15.

Shank, R. & Abelson, R. (1977). *Scripts. Plans, goals and understanding*. Hillsdale, NJ: Lawrence Erlbaum.

Sheidow, A. & Henggeler, S. (2008). Multisystemic therapy for alcohol and other drug abuse in delinquent adolescents. *Alcoholism Treatment Quarterly*, 26, 125–145.

Sher, K. (1991). *Children of alcoholics*. Chicago: University of Chicago Press.

Shields, A. & Cicchetti, D. (1998). Reactive aggression among maltreated children: The contributions of attention and emotion dysregulation. *Journal of Clinical Child Psychology*, 27, 381–395.

Shields, A., Cicchetti, D., & Ryan, R. (1994). The development of emotional and behavioral self-regulation and social competence among maltreated school-age children. *Development and Psychopathology*, 6, 57–75.

Shirk, S. & Karver, M. (2003). Prediction of treatment outcome from relationship variables in child and adolescent therapy: A meta-analytic review. *Journal of Consulting and Clinical Psychology*, 71, 452–464.

Shirk, S., Gudmundsen, G., Kaplinski, H., & McMakin, D. (2008). Alliance and Outcome in Cognitive-Behavioral Therapy for Adolescent Depression. *Journal of Clinical Child & Adolescent Psychology*, 37, 631–639.

Shortell, S. (2004). Increasing value: A research agenda for addressing the managerial and organizational challenges facing health care delivery in the United States. *Med. Care Res*, 61(3), 12S–30S. doi: 10.1177/1077558704266768

Simcha-Fagan, O., Langner, T., Gersten, J., & Eisenberg, J. (1975). Violent and antisocial behavior: A longitudinal study of urban youth. Unpublished report of the Office of Child Development, OCD-CB-480.

Simonsen, B., Fairbanks, S., Briesch, A., Myers, D., & Sugai, G. (2008). Evidence-based practices in classroom management: Considerations for research to practice. *Education and Treatment of Children*, 31, 351–380.

Skogen, J. & Torvik, F. (2013). *Atferdsforstyrrelser blant barn og unge i Norge. Beregnet forekomst og bruk av hjelpetiltak*. [Conduct disorders among children and adolescents in Norway. Estimated prevalence and the use of interventions] Report 2013/14. Oslo: Folkehelseinstituttet (the National Institute of Health).

Slade, E. (2003). The relationship between school characteristics and the availability of mental health and related health services in middle and high schools in the US. *The Journal of Behavioral Health Services & Research*, 30, 382–392.

Slesnick, N. & Prestopnik, J. (2009). Comparison of family therapy outcome with alcohol-abusing, runaway adolescents. *Journal of Marital and Family Therapy*, 35(3), 255–277.

Sloboda, Z. (2009). School prevention. In: C. Leukefeld, T. Gullotta, & M. Staton-Tindall (Eds.), *Adolescent substance abuse. Evidence-based approaches to prevention and treatment.* New York: Springer.

Sloboda, Z. & David, S. (1997). *Preventing drug use among children and adolescents. A research-based guide.* NIH Publication No. 97-4212.

Smith, S. (2005a). Developing a comprehensive school safety and prevention plan. In: J. Sprague & H. Walker (Eds.), *Safe and healthy schools. Practical prevention strategies.* New York: Guilford Press.

Smith, S. (2005b). Bullying and peer-based harassment in schools. In: J. Sprague & H. Walker (Eds.), *Safe and healthy schools. Practical prevention strategies.* New York: Guilford Press.

Smith, S. (2005c). Solutions for bullying and peer-harassment in the school setting. In: J. Sprague & H. Walker (Eds.), *Safe and healthy schools. Practical prevention strategies.* New York: Guilford Press.

Solholm, R., Kjøbli, J., & Christiansen, T. (2013). Early initiatives for children at risk—Development of a program for the prevention and treatment of behavior problems in primary services. *Prevention Science*, 14, 535–544.

Sørlie, M-A., Amlund Hagen, K., & Ogden, T. (2008). Social competence and antisocial behavior: Continuity and distinctiveness across early adolescence. *Journal of Research on Adolescence*, 18, 121–144.

Sørlie, M-A. & Ogden, T. (2007). Immediate impacts of PALS: A school-wide multilevel programme targeting behaviour problems in elementary school. *Scandinavian Journal of Educational Research*, 51, 471–492.

Sørlie, M-A. & Ogden, T. (2014) Reducing threats to validity by design in a nonrandomized experiment of a school-wide prevention model. *International Journal of School & Educational Psychology*, 2(4), 235–246. doi: 10.1080/21683603.2014.881309

Sørlie, M-A. & Ogden, T. (2015): School-wide positive behavior support – Norway: Impacts on problem behavior and classroom climate, *International Journal of School & Educational Psychology*. doi: 10.1080/21683603.2015.1060912

Sørlie, M-A., Ogden, T., & Olseth, A. (2015). Examining teacher outcomes of the school-wide positive behavior support model in Norway: Perceived efficacy and behavior management. *SAGE Open*, (2016), 6, 1–13. Online. doi: 10.1177/2158244016651914

Sørlie, M., Ogden, T., & Olseth, A. (2016). Examining teacher outcomes of the school-wide positive behavior support model in Norway: Perceived efficacy and behavior management. *SAGE Open*, 6(2). doi: 10.1177/2158244016651914

Sørlie, M-A., Ogden, T., Solholm, R., & Olseth, R. (2010). Implementeringskvalitet – om hvordan få tiltak til å virke [Implementation quality – how to make interventions work]. *Tidsskrift for Norsk psykologforening*, 47, 315–321.

Spence, S. (1995). *Social skills training: enhancing social competence with children and adolescents. Users guide.* Windsor: NFER-Nelson.

Spence, S. (2003). Social skills training with children and young people: Theory, evidence and practice. *Child and Adolescent Mental Health*, 8, 84–96.

Spivack, G., Platt, J., & Shure, M. (1976). *The problem solving approach to adjustment.* San Francisco, CA: Jossey-Bass.

Spivack, G. & Shure, M. (1974). *Social adjustment of young children: A cognitive approach to solving real-life problems.* Washington: Jossey-Bass.

Sprague, J. & Walker, H. (2005). *Safe and healthy schools. Practical prevention strategies.* New York: Guilford Press.

Sprenkle, D. & Blow, A. (2004). Common factors and our sacred models. *Journal of Marital and Family Therapy*, 30, 113–129.

Stanton, M. & Todd, T. (Eds.). (1982). *The family therapy of drug abuse and addiction*. New York: Guilford Press.

Stattin, H. & Magnusson, D. (1990). *Pubertal maturation in female development*. Vol. 2 in the series Paths Through Life (D. Magnusson, Ed.). Hillsdale, NJ: Erlbaum.

Stewart, E., Ceranoglu, T., O'Hanley, T., & Geller, D. (2005). Performance of clinician versus self-report measures to identify obsessive-compulsive disorder in children and adolescents. *Journal of Child and Adolescent Psychopharmacology*, 15, 956–963.

Sundell, K., Beelmann, A., Hasson, H., & Schwartz, E. (2016). Novel programs, international adoptions, or contextual adaptations? Meta-Analytical results from German and Swedish intervention research. *Journal of Clinical Child and Adolescent Psychology*, 45, 784–796.

Sundell, K., Hansson, K., Löfholm, C., Olsson, T., Gustle, L., & Kadesjö, C. (2008). The transportability of multisystemic therapy to Sweden: Short-term results from a randomized trial of conduct-disordered youths. *Journal of Family Psychology*, 22, 550–560.

Szapocznik, J. & Williams, R. (2000). Brief strategic family therapy: Twenty-five years of interplay among theory, research and practice in adolescent behavior problems and drug abuse. *Clinical Child and Family Psychology Review*, 3, 117–134.

Szapocznik, J., Hervis, O., & Schwartz, S. (2003). *Brief strategic family therapy for adolescent drug abuse (NIDA Therapy manuals for drug addiction series)* Rockville, MD: NIDA.

Tanner-Smith, E., Wilson, S., & Lipsey, M. (2013). The comparative effectiveness of outpatient treatment for adolescent substance abuse: A meta-analysis. *Journal of Substance Abuse Treatment*, 44, 145–158.

Thompson, E., Eggert, L., Randell, B., & Pike, K. (2001). Evaluation of indicated suicide risk prevention approaches for potential high school dropouts. *American Journal of Public Health*, 91, 742–752.

Tighe, A., Pistrang, N., Casdagli, L., Baruch, G., & Butler, S. (2012). Multisystemic therapy for young offenders; Families experience of therapeutic processes and outcomes. *Journal of Family Psychology*. doi: 10.1037/a0027120

Tobler, N., Roona, M., Ochshorn, P., Marshall, D., Streke, A., & Stackpole, K. (2000). School-based adolescent drug prevention programs: 1998 meta-analysis. *Journal of Primary Prevention*, 30, 275–336.

Tomasello, M. (1995). Joint attention as social cognition. In: C. Moore & P. Dunham (Eds.), *Joint attention: Its origins and role in development*. Hillsdale, NJ: Lawrence Erlbaum.

Tomasello, M. & Carpenter, M. (2007). Shared intentionality. *Developmental Science*, 10, 121–125.

Tømmerås, T. & Ogden, T. (2015). Is there a scale up penalty? Testing attenuation effects in the scaling up of Parent Management Training in Norway. *Administration and Policy in Mental Health and Mental Health Services*. 44, 203–216.

Topping, K. (2012). Framework for improving the impact of school-based social competence programs. In: B. Kelly & D. Perkins (Eds.), (2012). *Handbook of implementation science for psychology in education*. Cambridge: Cambridge University Press.

Tremblay, R., Pagani-Kurtz, L., Mâsse, L., Vitaro, F., & Pihl, R. (1995). A bimodal preventive intervention for disruptive kindergarten boys: Its impact through mid-adolescence. *Journal of Consulting and Clinical Psychology*, 63, 560–568.

Uher, R., Caspi, A., Houts, R., Sugden, K., Williams, B., Poulton, R., & Moffitt, T. (2011). Serotonin transporter gene moderates childhood maltreatment's effects on persistent but not single-episode depression: Replications and implications for resolving inconsistent results. *Journal of Affective Disorders*, 135, 56–65.

Undheim, A. & Sund, A. (2005). School factors and the emergence of depressive symptoms among young Norwegian adolescents. *European Child and Adolescent Psychiatry*, 14, 446–453.

US Public Health Service (2000). *Youth violence: A report of the Surgeon General.* Washington, DC: US Public Health Service.

Van der Stouwe, T., Asscher, J., Stams, G., Deković, M., & van der Laan, P. (2014). The effectiveness of Multisystemic Therapy (MST): A meta-analysis. *Clinical Psychology Review*, 34, 468–481.

Van Yperen, T. & Boendemaker, L. (2008). Interventions. In: R. Loeber, N. Wim Slot, P. van der Laan & M. Hoeve (Eds.), *Tomorrow's criminals. The development of child delinquency and effective interventions.* Surrey: Ashgate.

Wakschlag, L., Henry, D., Tolan, P., Carter, A., Burns, J., & Briggs-Gowan, M. (2012). Putting theory to the test: Modeling a multidimensional, developmentally-based approach to pre-school disruptive behavior. *Journal of the American Academy of Child & Adolescent Psychiatry*, 51(6), 593–604.

Waldron, H., Brody, J., & Hops, H. (2017). Functional family therapy for adolescent substance use disorders. In: J. Weisz & A. Kazdin (Eds.), *Evidence-based psychotherapies for children and adolescents* (3rd ed.). New York, Guilford.

Waldron, H., Slesnick, N., Brody, J., Turner, C., & Peterson, T. (2001). Treatment outcomes for adolescent substance abuse at 4- and 7-month assessments. *Journal of Consulting and Clinical Psychology*, 69, 802–813.

Waldron, H. & Turner, C. (2008). Evidence-based psychosocial treatments for adolescent substance abuse. *Journal of Clinical Child and Adolescent Psychology*, 37, 238–261.

Walker, H., Ramsey, E., & Gresham, F. (Eds.), (2004). *Antisocial behavior in school: Evidence-based practices.* Belmont, CA: Wadsworth/Thomson.

Walsh, C., Reutz, J., & Williams, R. (2015). *Selecting and implementing evidence-based practices: A guide for child and family serving systems.* California: The California Evidence-Based Clearinghouse.

Wampold, B. (2001). *The great psychotherapy debate: Models, methods and findings.* Mahwah, NJ: Erlbaum.

Wampold, B. & Budge, S. (2012). The 2011 Leona Tyler Award address: The relationship – and its relationship to the common and specific factors of psychotherapy. *The Counseling Psychologist*, 40, 601–623.

Wampold, B., Mondin, G., Moody, M., Stich, F., Benson, K., & Ahn, H. (1997). A meta-analysis of outcome studies comparing bona fide psychotherapies: Empirically, "all must have prizes." *Psychological Bulletin*, 122, 203–225.

Wandersman, A., Duffy, J., Flashpoler, P., Noonan, R., Lubell, K., Stillman, L., ... Saul, J. (2008). Bridging the gap between prevention research and practice: The interactive systems framework for dissemination and implementation. *American Journal of Community Pscyhology*, 41, 171–181.

Washington State Institute for Public Policy. (2002). *Washington State's implementation of Functional Family Therapy for juvenile offenders: Preliminary findings* (No 02-08-1201). Olympia, WA: Washington State Institute for Public Policy.

Waters, E. & Sroufe, L. (1983). Social competence as a developmental construct. *Developmental Review*, 3, 79–97.

Waxman, R., Weist, M., & Benson, D. (1999). Toward collaboration in the growing mental health–education interface. *Clinical Psychology Review*, 19, 239–253.

Weare, K. & Nind, M. (2011). Mental health promotion and problem prevention in schools: What does the evidence say? *Health Promotion International*, 26, i29–i69.

Webster-Stratton, C. (1992). *The incredible years: A trouble-shooting guide for parents of children aged 3–8*. Toronto, ON: Umbrella Press.

Webster-Stratton, C. & Lindsay, D. (1999). Social competence and conduct problems in young children: Issues in assessment. *Journal of Clinical Child Psychology*, 28, 25–43.

Webster-Stratton, C. & Reid, M. (2017). The incredible years parents, teachers, and children training series: A multifaceted treatment approach for young children with conduct problems. In: J. Weisz & A. Kazdin (Eds.), *Evidence-based psychotherapies for children and adolescents* (3rd ed.). New York, Guilford.

Weersing, V. & Weisz, J. (2002). Mechanisms of action in youth psychotherapy. *Journal of Child Psychology and Psychiatry*, 43, 3–29.

Weinberg, W., Harper, C., & Brumback, R. (2005). Substance use and abuse: epidemiology, pharmacological considerations, identification and suggestions towards management. In: M. Rutter & E. Taylor (Eds.), *Child and adolescent psychiatry* (4th ed.). Oxford: Blackwell Publishing.

Weissberg, R., Durlak, J., Domitrovich, C., & Gullotta, T. (2015). Social and emotional learning past, present, and future. In: J. Durlak, C. Domitrovich, R. Weissberg, & T. Gullotta (Eds.), *Handbook of social and emotional learning: Research and practice*. New York: Guilford Publications. Retrieved March 16 2017 from www.casel.org/wp-content/uploads/2016/06/Social-and-emotional-learning-Past-present-and-future.pdf

Weissberg, R. & Greenberg, M. (1998). School and community competence-enhancement and prevention programs. In: W. Damons, E. Siegel, & K. Renninger (Eds.), *Handbook of child psychology: Vol 5. Child psychology in practice* (5th ed.). New York: John Wiley.

Weissberg, R., Kumpfer, K., & Seligman, M. (2003). Prevention that works for children and youth. An introduction. *American Psychologist*, 58, 425–432.

Weissman, M., Wickramaratne, P., Nomura, Y., Warner, V., Pilowsky, D., & Verdeli, H. (2006). Offspring of depressed parents: 20 years later. *The American Journal of Psychiatry*, 163, 1001–1008.

Weist, M. (1997). Expanded school mental-health services. In: T. Ollendick & R. Prinz (Eds.), *Advances in clinical child psychology, Vol 19*. New York: Plenum Press.

Weist, M. & Albus, K. (2004). Expanded school mental health. Exploring program details and developing the research base. *Behavior Modification*, 28, 463–471.

Weist, M., Sander, M., Walrath, C., Link, B., Moore, E., Jennings, J., & Carrillo, K. (2005). Developing principles for best practice in school mental health. *Journal of Youth and Adolescence*, 34, 7–13.

Weisz, J., Hawley, K., & Jensen Doss, A. (2004). Empirically tested psychotherapies for youth internalizing and externalizing problems and disorders. *Child and Adolescent Psychiatric Clinics of North America*, 13, 729–815.

Weisz, J., Jensen, A., & McLeod, B. (2005). Milestones and methods in the development and dissemination of child and adolescent psychotherapies: review, commentary, and a new deployment-focused model. In: E. Hibbs & P. Jensen (Eds.), *Psychosocial treatments for child and adolescent disorders: Empirically based strategies for clinical practice* (2nd ed.). Washington, DC: American Psychological Association.

Weisz, J., Southam-Gerow, M., Gordis, E., & Connor-Smith, J. (2003). Primary and secondary control enhancement training for youth depression: applying the deployment-focused model of treatment development and testing. In: A. Kazdin & J. Weisz (Eds.), *Evidence-based psychotherapies for children and adolescents* (pp. 148–164). New York: Guilford Press.

Weisz, J. & Kazdin, A. (Eds.). (1998) (2010) (2017). *Evidence-based psychotherapies for children and adolescents* (1st to 3rd eds.). New York, Guilford.

Weisz, J., Chorpita, B., Palinkas, L., Schoenwald, S., Miranda, J., Bearman, S., … Gibbons, R., The Research Network on Youth Mental Health. (2012). Testing standard and modular designs for psychotherapy treating depression, anxiety, and conduct problems in youth. A randomized effectiveness trial. *Archives of General Psychiatry*, 69, 274–282.

Weisz, J., Weersing, V., & Henggeler, S. (2005). Jousting with straw men: Comment on the Westen, Novotny, and Thompson-Brenner (2004) critique of empirically supported treatments. *Psychological Bulletin*, 131, 418–426.

Welsh, B., Sullivan, C., & Olds, D. (2010). When early crime prevention goes to scale: A new look at the evidence. *Prevention Science*, 11, 115–125.

Wentzel, K. (1991). Relations between social competence and academic achievement in early adolescence. *Child Development*, 62, 1066–1078.

Wergeland, G., Fjermestad, K., Haugland, B., Öst, L., & Heiervang, E. (2011). Effectiveness of manual-based CBT for anxiety disorders in western Norway child mental health clinics. Results presented at the 41st European Association for Behavioral and Cognitive Therapy, Reykjavik, Iceland.

Williams, R., Chang, S., & Addiction Center Adolescent Research Group. (2000). A comprehensive and comparative review of adolescent substance abuse treatment outcome. *Clinical Psychology, Science and Practice*, 7, 138–166.

Wilson, D., Gottfredson, D., & Najaka, S. (2001). School-based prevention of problem behaviors: A meta-analysis. *Journal of Quantitative Criminology*, 17, 247–272.

Wilson, S. & Lipsey, M. (2007). *Effect of school violence prevention programs on aggressive and disruptive behavior: A meta-analysis of outcome evaluations*. Manuscript. Nashville, TN: Center for Evaluation Research and Methodology, Vanderbilt Institute for Public Policy Studies.

Wittchen, H., Jacobi, F., Rehm, J., Gustavsson, A., Svensson, M., Jönsson, B., … Fratiglioni, L. (2011). The size and burden of mental disorders and other disorders of the brain in Europe 2010. *European Neuropsychopharmacology*, 21(9), 655–679.

Wolpert, M., Humphrey, N., Belsky, J., & Deighton, J. (2013). Embedding mental health support in schools: Learning from the targeted mental health in schools (TaMHS) national evaluation. *Emotional and Behavioural Difficulties*, 18(3), 270–283.

Zeiner, P. (1998). Barn og unge med alvorlige atferdsvansker. Hva kan nyere viten fortelle oss og hva slags hjelp trenger de? [Children and Youth with Serious Behavior Problems. What can Contemporary Knowledge Teach Us, and What Kind of Help do They Need?]. Oslo: The Norwegian Research Council.

Zins, J., Weissberg, R., Wang, M., & Walberg, H. (Eds.). (2004). Building academic success on social and emotional learning: What does the research say? New York: Teachers College Press.

Zucker, R. & Harford, T. (1983). National study of the demography of adolescents' drinking practices in 1980. *Journal of Studies on Alcohol*, 44, 974–985.

INDEX

Note: figures are indicated by page numbers in *italics*.

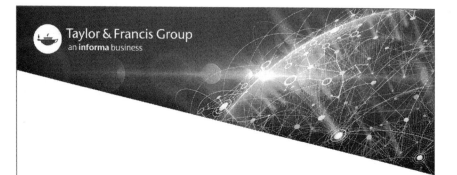